FREUD ON COKE

FREUD ON COKE

DAVID COHEN

Published in 2011 by Cutting Edge Press
116 West Heath Road, NW3 7TU

www.cuttingedgepress.co.uk

© David Cohen and Cutting Edge Press

David Cohen has asserted his moral rights under the 1988 Copyright and
Designs and Patents Act to be identified as the author of this book.

Typeset by Keyboard Services, Luton, Bedfordshire
In 12.5/15 Bembo
Distribution Turnaround
Printed by MPG Biddles Ltd, Rollesby Rd, Kings Lynn

ISBN 978-0-9565445-0-6

Dear John,
You asked me what I consider essential personal qualities in a future
psychoanalyst. The answer is comparatively simple. If you want to be
a real psychoanalyst you have to have a great love of the truth, scientific
truth as well as personal truth, and you have to place this appreciation
of truth higher than any discomfort at meeting unpleasant facts,
whether they belong to the world outside or to your own inner person.

Anna Freud

I hate what the drug does to me. It makes me cry. It makes me crazy.
It makes me think people are out to kill me. I hate what it does but I
love it. I love the looks of it. I love the taste, I love the smell, I love
the feel, I love it more than anything else I have ever loved.

A cocaine user

In memory of William S. Burroughs Junior (not his father), and all other casualties and prisoners of the 'War on Drugs'.

Contents

Acknowledgements

I owe two large debts – the first to my son Reuben Cohen, the second to my colleague Martin Hay. They played a decisive role in suggesting this book and then provided a huge amount of both personal and editorial support. Freud would have had something to say about a son editing his father's book and I would like to thank Reuben for his work. It required delicacy as well as intelligence.

I would also like to thank Jeremy Robson who published my earlier book, *The Escape of Sigmund Freud*. He had every reason to expect I'd offer him the chance of publishing my second book on Freud and was extremely generous when I explained why I could not.

The librarians of various institutions were very helpful – especially those at the MS Collection of the Library of Congress in Washington, at the Wellcome Library in London and at the Institute of Psychoanalysis. The Wellcome's collection of the *Chemist and Druggist* turned out to be something of a treasure trove for illustrations of ads for various cocaine products from the 1880s.

Josh Brown has made useful suggestions and compiled the references very carefully. Vera Lustig checked for all my errors. Beth MacDougall advised on the design. My friend and agent Sonia Land was supportive as she has been with many projects, literary and not just literary. Her colleague Gaia Banks pulled off the coup of selling the Russian rights before I had finished the book, very skilful in today's difficult publishing climate. Ray Buckland typeset over the Christmas holidays. Top QWERTY indeed.

I would also like to thank Tracey who runs a wonderful shop selling illustrations, for digging out a number of advertisements for Vin Mariani.

The mistakes remain, of course, my own.

Prologue

A Tale of Two Addicts

When Billy was four years old, he watched his father shoot his mother, blowing her head off with a handgun. Following his mother's death, Billy was sent to live with his doting and protective grandparents. They lied and told the boy that his father was an explorer, his absence a matter of duty, while he mapped remote parts of South America.

As with all the best lies, there was an element of truth in this, for Billy's father was hiding out in Mexico – though he was eventually acquitted of murder, as he had fired the gun with his wife's consent, and had no intent of harming her. It was a party trick they called their 'William Tell routine'. Billy's father thought himself a crack marksman, and had often shot an apple off her head, while Joan giggled, high on speed. Billy saw his father only three times in the ten years after the shooting.

The French say 'tel père, tel fils'. At the age of thirteen, Billy himself shot a boy through the neck, nearly killing him. Billy's grandparents sent him to a sanatorium for 'psychological rehabilitation'. A year later, Billy went to live with his father in North Africa, but they did not find it easy to be around each other, and daddy was not an ideal parent to a troubled teen-age boy. He drank heavily, paid local boys for sex, and was constantly stoned on hash, heroin and opium, smoking endless cigarettes which burned down till they singed his anaesthetised fingers.

Violence and neglect took their toll. By the time he was fifteen, Billy had a drug problem too, which was hardly surprising, as his father's sperm must have contained a veritable pharmacopeia, and his mother didn't let her pregnancy interfere with her love of amphetamines. Billy was born vulnerable to addiction and became one of the many speed freaks of the 1960s. There was more to him than drugs, though, as Billy was a gifted writer and like many addicts, not without insight into his own condition. In his words: 'I've never know when to quit. I've always wanted to continue beyond X point. That is, I've always been kind of dumb.'

One definition of 'dumb' could be – being unable to change your way of life when your way of life is killing you. If so, Billy was dumb and fixed in his dumbness, but in fact, intelligence has nothing to do with susceptibility to addiction: many addicts are hopeless failures, as are many alcoholics, yet many of both are also high-achievers. It's well-known that Winston Churchill drank from breakfast to nightcap, and experimented with amphetamines: John F. Kennedy was high on speed throughout the Cuban Missile crisis, in addition to the Demerol (known in the UK as pethidine, a powerful synthetic opiate) prescribed for his war wounds. Many famous artists, musicians and writers have been regular drug users – as, indeed, has many a doctor.

Billy never managed to stop using drugs and died of liver failure when he was only 34, despite a liver transplant. By that point, his drug of choice was alcohol. His gun-toting father, who would go on to outlive his son by almost twenty years, did not go to Billy's funeral.

Another drug user, Solomon, also hated funerals. He arrived late for his own father's and gave a pathetic excuse; he could not get a barber to shave him in time. Some years later, Solomon did not attend his mother's funeral, either, though he claimed that he had always loved her.

Solomon was the son of a small businessman with a very poor head for business. Three months before Solomon's birth, his grandfather had died. Solomon's father was devastated as he had loved his father, even revered him. When Solomon was a toddler, his baby brother also died. Solomon had a nanny who he loved, but, when he was about three, the family sacked her for alleged theft. He missed her and then there was a new trauma. The family had to leave their comfortable house and travel to a large city where they could only afford to rent a tenement in a poor working class area. Solomon wrote later that he never lost his fear of poverty.

Solomon was also fond of his uncle, who often brought him presents back from business trips to England, including sticks of Blackpool rock.

When the boy was ten, this uncle was arrested and sentenced to ten years in prison for forgery. Newspapers reported the case. The family was publicly humiliated.

Six years later, Solomon's father lost all his money again, in another failed business. When Solomon grew up, he was himself arrested a number of times for failing to report for mandatory army service. Both Billy and Solomon had traumatic childhoods marked by violence, loss, poverty and displacement. Many children who suffer that kind of early life become addicted to drugs and alcohol.

I heard many similar stories from the heroin addicts I interviewed in 1985, for a documentary film called *Kicking the Habit*, a study of the treatment of addiction at the time. The UK was in the grip of a heroin epidemic, made all the more serious by the spread of Aids through shared needles. The addicts I interviewed had little in common with Billy or Solomon who both, despite their tortured pasts and drug use, were talented writers.

When Billy was 22, he wrote his first novel, *Speed*, which the poet Allen Ginsberg praised as a 'coherent account of an impossibly wobbly subject – inside the Methedrine Universe.' The book tells a frightening tale – of a desperately lost and lonely boy, who wanders from crash-pad to alleyway, jail cells punctuating his injections of methedrine, amphetamine, cocaine. But the book is also warm and humorous, wry in its self-deprecation and peppered with small insights and compassion. Billy's best, and often only, friend was a well-meaning but somewhat deranged Ginsberg, who at one point offered to show Billy pictures of his mother in the morgue. *Speed* is no masterpiece, but a powerful debut, very much of its time, and should be required reading for all those who romanticise the late 1960s drug culture. There was no peace or love in Billy's drug universe.

Billy published a second autobiographical novel, *Kentucky Ham*, also an excellent account of an addict's life and attempts at recovery. Though he was a stylish writer, Billy – William S. Burroughs Junior – never became as famous as his father, William S. Burroughs, author of *Junkie, The Naked Lunch,* and *Cities of the Red Night,* amongst many other experimental novels that some critics compared to the linguistic innovations of James Joyce, but which can equally be dismissed as the scatological opium dreams of a profoundly disturbed personality obsessed with sex and centipedes. Billy Burroughs Jr, speed freak, alcoholic, and son of the man who killed his mother, was warm and human on the page, where his father, though undoubtedly original, was frigid and obscene (with the exception of the moving and uncharacteristically non-experimental novella *Queer*).

Burroughs Senior became a counter-cultural fashion icon, the High Priest of Heroin, and is revered to this day by many junkies, new and old. He swore blind to anyone who'd listen that he wrote the horrific *Naked Lunch* to dissuade young kids from trying drugs: but he was either lying, or kidding himself. Casting himself as Faust for the alienated youth of the late 20th century, Burroughs portrayed addiction as the devil's bargain, a battle for one's soul, a dark aesthetic that appealed to the ever-alienated youth of the late 20th century. Marianne Faithfull has claimed, in interview, that she set out to intentionally become a heroin addict after reading his work. Some tribute!

It is time to end the hide and seek of this prologue. Solomon became even more famous than William S Burroughs. Solomon is the proper form of the Yiddish name 'Shlomo' and was the middle name given to Sigmund Freud, the founder of psychoanalysis and one of the most influential figures of the 20th century. As in Billy's case, Freud's drug use finally killed him. He developed cancer of the jaw in his early sixties and refused to stop smoking cigars. He underwent sixteen operations and had to have a prosthesis inserted in his jaw. He hated the fact that he could not eat without dribbling all over himself, but still could not stop smoking. Freud's daughter nagged him to stop, and his wealthiest friend and patient, Princess Marie Bonaparte, had some nicotine-free cigars specially made for him. Freud thanked the Princess for her concern, told her he hated them and went back to the real stuff.

Billy Burroughs Junior might, had he lived, have become a great writer, and Sigmund Freud certainly was. Whether he was a great scientist – or a scientist at all – is a rather different matter, but even his fiercest critic, the psychologist Hans Eysenck, accepts that Freud was a fine literary stylist.

When assessing Freud and his legacy, we should remember that psychoanalysis, that odd exercise where the patient tells their dreams and opens their soul from the couch, was invented by a man from a deeply traumatic background. A man, indeed, who was to become a habitual user of cocaine – as well as a chain-smoker of the cigars that finally killed him. Freud was eager to conceal his difficult and grief-stricken background and his loyal followers did not ask too many probing questions, so we do not generally think of the young Freud as damaged, vulnerable, and a promising candidate for addiction. Yet the long-suppressed evidence is clear. He was a child from a home never quite broken, but often damaged by bad luck, poor judgement and bereavement, and this childhood left its mark in many ways – tendencies to hypochondria, depression and self-medication. Generations of Freud scholarship have neglected these crucial aspects of his personality.

The founder of psychoanalysis, who often wrote that he identified with Moses, should be assessed not as the sage he and his followers so longed to believe in, but in human terms. He could no more escape his childhood than could poor Billy Burroughs Junior. Freud was neither the flawless prophet nor the deceitful monster that contemporary critics, be they devotees or sworn opponents of analysis, are so keen to portray; he was profoundly damaged and traumatised and did not like to reveal these 'intimacies'.

Freud's own experience with cocaine began on April 30th, 1884, a week before his 28th birthday. It was *Walpurgisnacht*, an ancient pagan festival, the night when, so legend has it, witches rejoice at the arrival of spring, of new sap, new life. Freud's favourite author, Goethe, set a famous scene of his *Faust* on that same night. Mephistopheles appears with cloven hooves and tempts Faust into the arms of a naked young witch, who then turns into the snake-haired Medusa. Freud knew the play well. As a parable, it could be used to represent a drug user's descent into addiction: the radiant temptress, the drug, revealing itself, at last, to be a monster of voracious appetite.

Freud had ordered a gram of cocaine from Merck of Darmstadt, one of several pharmaceutical companies that were then selling the drug quite legally. He measured out 1/20th of a gram of pure cocaine. There is a strange coincidence, here; according to some Goethe scholars, the writer modelled his Mephistopheles on the apothecary Merck himself.

Merck's supply – unlike contemporary cocaine sold on the street – was *pure* – in all likelihood, 98–99% pure cocaine hydrochloride. This is a very different substance from what is generally sold as cocaine today, as police analysis of cocaine seizures in the UK has shown a marked drop in purity in recent years. Sometimes a 'gram' of street cocaine, sold at prices ranging from £30 – £60, will contain no more than 5% of actual cocaine, and increasingly, semi-legal analogues and dental anaesthetics are used to 'cut' or adulterate it – much to the frustration of modern users. Of more serious concern, however, is the now widespread practice of adulterating cocaine with Levamisole – a substance known to suppress the production of white blood cells with potentially fatal consequences. Such 'cutting' is a consequence of the illegality of cocaine – to which, as we shall see, Freud's own work with the substance contributed.

Freud was not sure how he would pay for his first gram. Though he had recently qualified as a doctor, he did not have a proper job and was forced to borrow money constantly. He had been engaged to Martha Bernays for two years, but they could not fix a date for their wedding as he was too poor to rent a decent apartment. He was still living in a student hostel, and resented his poverty. He did not intend for it to last.

Having studied the literature on cocaine, Freud knew the drug was a powerful stimulant which would make his temperature, heart rate and blood pressure rise immediately. He swallowed the cocaine and waited to feel its effects. He was not disappointed, as he wrote:

'A few minutes after taking cocaine, one experiences a sudden exhilaration and feeling of lightness. One feels a certain furriness on the lips and palate, followed by a feeling of warmth in the same areas; if one now drinks cold water, it feels warm on the lips and cold in the throat.'

Sometimes the main effect was a rather pleasant coolness in the mouth and throat. 'The psychic effect' was ... not disturbing for 'the exhilaration and lasting euphoria does not differ in any way from the normal euphoria of a healthy person. The feeling of excitement which accompanies stimulus by alcohol is completely lacking; the characteristic urge for immediate activity which alcohol produces is also absent.'

When he swallowed the 1/20th gram Freud was not seeking a euphoric effect for its own sake, but wanted to gain a clearer understanding of the drug's potential. He was undertaking medical research, hoping to find a clinical use for the drug that would bring him fame and fortune. The results of this first taste were promising, but inconclusive. After that first gram he bought another. And then another, then still more ... almost as if he was acting under some form of compulsion.

A year later, Freud found himself working for Merck's American rivals, Parke-Davis, testing their latest batch of cocaine. He had become a recognised expert on the drug, and Parke-Davis used his endorsement to advertise that their cocaine was the best on the market. We do not know if he was given free supplies in exchange, but he was paid 60 marks. Freud had no idea that cocaine might prove addictive. Indeed, he believed the claims Parke-Davis made; that it could be a *treatment* for morphine addiction.

Freud's experiments with cocaine would exert a powerful influence on the social, cultural, and medical perception of drugs – an influence that is still with us. They helped shape the conventional great divide between good, therapeutic, medicinal drugs, prescribed by good, sensible doctors and evil recreational drugs peddled by demon dealers. Often, in fact, doctors prescribe and dealers peddle the same chemicals – opiates and amphetamines being the most obvious examples. Where drugs are concerned, perception – and politics – are all. Few words in the English language have as many possible, and even contradictory, meanings as the four-letter word: 'drug'. We know that when police and politicians speak of the 'drug problem' they are not referring to the wares peddled by pharmaceutical companies: and, in the USA, that one can no more buy cocaine or cannabis at a 'drugstore' than one can at a UK 'Superdrug' franchise. Yet, we do not question this nuance but generally accept that there is 'good' drug use, therapeutic drug use, under the prescription of a medical professional, and 'bad', immoral drug use, often described as 'recreational' or pleasure-seeking. Freud's experience with cocaine casts doubt on the validity of this distinction and this is no mere matter of semantics.

Viewed dispassionately, global policies intended to regulate drug use, medicinal and otherwise, are clearly both irrational and ineffective. If a journalist takes illicitly purchased amphetamines (speed) to stay up all night and meet a deadline, they are guilty, in the UK, of possession of a Class B drug, and could, theoretically, face up to 5 years in jail. However, if they have been diagnosed with 'Adult Attention Deficit Hyperactivity Disorder' (ADHD) – a controversial diagnosis for which there are no objective tests, and the same drugs have been prescribed to them, they have committed no crime. This is the logic of *Alice in Wonderland* and her famous white rabbit but politicians dare not say it.

Freud's own drug use contributed to the conditions that established this bizarre paradox, enshrining a distinction between therapeutic and recreational drug use that may well be more apparent – and a political illusion, at that – than real. His legacy in this regard has also been neglected by the prolific Freud industry.

Freud's cocaine experience would set a blueprint for experiments, some lethal, that continue to this day, amongst both certain doctors – and a global network of drug users who have an ever-greater selection of legal and illegal highs to choose from; this 'introspective drug-using' tradition has been taken up by scholars, writers, scientists and laymen, who consume chemicals and then write up their experiences of the substance – or substances – concerned. A worldwide community of such introspective drug users has taken shape, in particular, since the launch of Alexander Shulgin's 'research chemicals' – discussed, below, in chapter 13.

For what began on that *Walpurgisnacht* continues to this day, on a far greater scale – greater than is understood by either press or politicians – and has begun, in the era of the internet, to render drug law and official policy all but irrelevant. The true story of Freud on Coke is an important and untold secret history, one that must be reassessed, in order to attain both a clearer picture of the legacy of psychoanalysis and of the confused culture of drugs, in all their forms, which has eluded successive attempts at regulation and control.

JOSHUA HOFFS 1977

The many faces of Freud – an interesting but too symmetrical montage, given the vicissitudes of Freud's career.

Chapter 1

Freud – the Conquistador

In April 1884, few could have imagined that Freud would be in the running for the Nobel Prize for Medicine one day. In later years, though often rumoured to be on the short-list, he was never awarded the prize and this remained a source of bitter disappointment to him. He is one of the most important thinkers to be denied the award – and one of the most prolific.

The Standard Edition of Freud's works runs to 32 volumes. He wrote about dreams, sex, brain anatomy, jokes, Neanderthals, Hamlet, Leonardo da Vinci, the Moses of Michelangelo, the original Moses, Jesus, the deficiencies of US President Woodrow Wilson, parenting, therapy, mistakes, the uncanny, the mind, money, lack of money, the death instinct (*Thanatos*, eternal opposite to the urge to life and sex, *Eros*), Shakespeare, Dostoevsky, Zionism, strange goings on in monasteries, art, plagues, dogs, frogs, Judaism and war. There is, however, no paper on cocaine in the Standard Edition: though Freud wrote four papers on the subject and was, at time of publication, very proud of them.

Freud befriended and tangled with many important men and women of his time, including Albert Einstein, William James, Carl Jung, Thomas Mann, Stefan Zweig, the pioneer sexologist Havelock Ellis, H.G. Wells, Virginia Woolf, Salvador Dali and a certain Father Schmidt who was a confidant of the Pope. Schmidt hated Freud because, he claimed, the man was a devil, an atheist *and* a Jew. Freud's patients included Princess Marie Bonaparte, the great-granddaughter of Napoleon, the poet Hilda Doolittle and the first American ambassador to the Soviet Union, William Bullitt.

We tend to think of Freud as calm and self-possessed, but he was volatile and quarrelled with many of his 'disciples' such as Carl Jung and

1

Wilhelm Reich, author of the classic *The Mass Psychology of Fascism*. Jung thought Freud placed too much emphasis on sex; Reich thought he understated its importance. These battles were not simply about sex, but about authority, as became clear when Freud and Jung sailed to America together in 1909. Freud had been invited to lecture at Clark University in Worcester, Massachusetts, for the 25th anniversary of Clark's founding.

On the ship, Jung told Freud his dreams but Freud refused to reciprocate, saying he had to preserve his authority. Jung shouted and sulked; Freud fainted, as he sometimes did when anxious and threatened. Jung never forgave what he saw as an insult. These analysts were models of maturity indeed. Freud could be utterly outrageous, for example, when he decided, again as a question of 'authority', that only he could analyse his daughter Anna; no other analyst could hear Freud family secrets. Today it would be considered completely unethical – not to mention ludicrous – for a father to analyse one of his own children. Freud sensed he had crossed a boundary, as he insisted on keeping the fact that he had analysed Anna secret for more than 25 years. Jung was no saint either; he bedded at least one of his patients, and, if not a Nazi himself, was no opponent of the Third Reich.

When he took cocaine, as noted in the preface, Freud was emulating many doctors, artists and scientists of the 19th century, by experimenting on himself in order to study his own thoughts, feelings and sensations under the drug's influence. As early as 1799, the great chemist Humphry Davy took nitrous oxide ('laughing gas', or 'hippie crack' to contemporary recreational users) to explore its effects. In Paris, a Hashish Club was started in 1844; its members included Victor Hugo, Balzac, the painter Eugène Delacroix and the poet Charles Baudelaire. William James, the pioneering American psychologist, took nitrous oxide and wrote extensively of his experiences with the gas. Others in 'the introspective drug-taking tradition' include Havelock Ellis, William Halsted, the father of American surgery and Aldous Huxley, author of *Brave New World*. One of the more unlikely of these explorers was the Vice-President of J.P. Morgan Bank from 1943 to 1963, Robert Wasson, whose experiments with hallucinogens did not make him play the stock market recklessly, though he probably did not chomp on magic mushrooms during working hours.

Two of the most important introspective drug explorers of the last 60 years have been chemists. In 1938 Albert Hoffman synthesised LSD while he was working for the pharmaceutical company Sandoz, while, some years on, Alexander Shulgin worked for Dow Pharmaceuticals. Both men had distinguished conventional careers. Hoffman discovered a compound that helped ease labour pains, while Shulgin created one of the most profitable pesticides in history. Their true legacy, though, lies not in these triumphs, but the creation of hallucinogens.

The first psychologists saw introspection as an essential method for their discipline. Introspection, however, did not mean to late Victorians what it tends to mean to us now, thinking about our personal feelings and problems; rather it meant *thinking about thinking* in the hope of discovering the basic atoms of thought. This does not come naturally and the early psychologists had to train themselves to do it. It was a kind of 'cognitive athletics'.

Psychologists were imitating what they believed 'proper scientists' were doing in *their* research. Physicists and chemists studied the atoms of matter, so psychologists had to study the atoms of mind to discover the basic particles of thought. Ambitious psychologists spent hours staring at circles, triangles, contemplating nonsense syllables like VUT or brightly-coloured squares and reporting what they thought or felt. William James, who set up the first psychology lab in America in 1879, carped that these were 'impoverished sensory stimuli' as normal people did not spend much time gazing at triangles or nonsense syllables, but most of his colleagues took little notice, as they imagined studying so-called 'pure' stimuli was more scientific than trying to make sense of the complexities of consciousness.

As it happened, subjects gave rather consistent descriptions of what they felt and saw when they looked at triangles and other stimuli but psychologists could not agree what this meant. Were the basic atoms of mind, thoughts, sensations or images? Could you have thought without images? Could you have images without thought? And where did emotion fit into this picture?

These endless disputes, British and American psychologists argued, proved that introspection was pointless, as it was not possible to be objective about anything so subjective as thinking. The empirical camp insisted that psychology would never progress if it did not study behaviour which could be observed and measured. Unless one of us is drunk, demented or colour-blind, we will both see a red London bus in motion as red, moving and on the street. These methodological disputes changed psychology for fifty years. Introspection disappeared from empirical Anglo-American psychology and 'survived' only in marginal, maverick studies, including studies of drug experiences. The rejection of introspection all but removed thoughts and feelings from psychology, as psychologists focused on simpler matters, such as watching rats find their way around a maze.

Until he began his studies of cocaine, Freud wrote conventional scientific papers on subjects like the brains and sex lives of eels, papers that did not require him to think about his own thinking. Taking cocaine forced him to learn the techniques of self-observation. The consequences were far-reaching. If he had not been confident about his ability to observe himself, he would never have started to study his own dreams and embarked upon his famous self-analysis, on which the 'invention' of psychoanalysis was based.

Freud, however, never admitted that cocaine played a part in his intellectual or emotional development. He attributed his originality and success as a thinker to two factors. First, as a Jew he was doomed to being an outsider and so could be 'the bold oppositionist' who was not shackled by orthodoxies. Second, he could dare so much because his mother's love and the fact that he was her 'indisputable favourite' made him feel like 'a conquistador'.

There is some historical irony to this. When he called himself a conquistador, consciously or unconsciously, Freud was identifying with the Spaniards who sailed across the Atlantic, conquered Mexico and Peru and wrecked two great civilisations in the process. The Spanish explorer Hernan Cortés landed in Mexico in 1519 with a mere 400 soldiers and defeated the Aztec Empire; these men have gone down in history as the 'conquistadors'. Romantic historians stress that the Aztecs believed Cortés was a manifestation of their god Quetzalcoatl, 'the plumed serpent' while the more pragmatic stress that Cortés had guns and horses while the Aztecs only had bows, arrows and llamas. Shortly after landing in Mexico, the conquistadors discovered the uses of coca. Freud thus identified with the first Europeans to sample coca, the leaf from which cocaine is extracted.

I am neither a card-carrying Freudian nor a virulent critic of his work, but the longer I have studied Freud (for over 40 years), the more obvious it has become to me that he was not always wholly honest or accurate when he wrote about himself. He may have compared himself to a conquistador, but he would not have lasted long in Cortés's crew. First, he was a terrible sailor, and became constantly seasick on the crossing to America. Secondly, Freud couldn't ride a horse. Thirdly, and most importantly, he showed few signs of the confidence that he attributed to his mother's great love for him till he was well over forty. Until then, Freud often doubted himself and deferred to both his elders and his peers. Cocaine gave him social confidence and provided easy relief when he felt unwell, as he did regularly, being something of a hypochondriac. He even gave it to his fiancée, Martha Bernays, and his letters to her suggest they may have explored its aphrodisiac properties together. Freud was relatively honest about his need for cigars but far less so about his need for cocaine.

When I studied psychology at Oxford in the late 1960s, Freud was out of favour with empirically-minded British psychologists, who claimed his theories were impossible to prove or disprove. They were just too vague to be verifiable or refutable, as philosophers of science put it. Refutability was the criterion by which one judged whether or not a theory could be deemed 'scientific', and Freud was nimble in avoiding refutation, but that did not impress the empiricists.

However, one of my tutors, Brian Farrell, made me read Freud's *The Project for a Scientific Psychology*, which he wrote while taking a good deal of cocaine. I was baffled rather than inspired by the book, a kind of fantasy about brain anatomy, and how in the not-too-distant future it would be perfectly understood. This in turn would allow psychiatrists to correct any dysfunction with a tailor-made 'magic bullet' of a drug or surgical procedure. Science, Freud was certain, was shortly to conquer the internal frontiers, learn the language of brain function in exact and comprehensive terms, and make the primitive 'talking cures' of psychotherapy redundant.

To historians of psychology, there is a delicious irony here: such blind faith in 'bio-psychiatry' remains the guiding philosophy of many psychiatrists who dismiss Freud as a woolly-minded charlatan-fantasist and psychoanalysis as the enduring, ludicrous fad he spawned. Freud never allowed *The Project* to be published in his lifetime. He was, of course, wildly over-optimistic in thinking science would soon make it possible to understand the brain, but he was far from alone in that faith. A hundred and twenty five years on, we know it's not that easy, and have seen a great many 'magic bullets' miss their targets, yet still the faith endures.

After leaving Oxford I interviewed famous psychologists for the *New Scientist* and the French magazine *Psychologie*, interviews that became my first book, *Psychologists on Psychology*. I was not conducting a survey of Freud's reputation, but inevitably, his name came up, and these interviews showed how many leading psychologists of the last 50 years saw him and analysis. Two were sworn opponents of the man and his system. I met Hans Eysenck, who became both famous and infamous for arguing that the accumulated evidence of standardised tests showed racial differences in IQ scores. Eysenck was immensely courteous in person, but like Freud, he was a bold oppositionist. Students demonstrated against him and called him a fascist, which must have stung; as the grandson of a Jewish woman, Eysenck had been forced to flee the Nazis. Freud wrote beautiful German, Eysenck admitted, but went on to snipe that what was new in Freud's work was not true, and what was new in it was not true.

I had expected B.F. Skinner, the pre-eminent behavioural psychologist from 1930 to 1975, to be as dismissive of Freud as Eysenck had been. When I met him in his house near Harvard – he was dressed in Bermuda shorts – he astonished me by saying:

'Freud made some very important discoveries and also brought attention to discoveries which had been made by other people. We have changed as a result. We no longer believe in whim, accident or caprice. There are reasons why you forget appointments, for instance. I don't think he always gave the right reasons but I accept his determinism. I think his great mistake was to invent the mental apparatus, as he called it, a fantastic creation out of German will psychology.' By this, Skinner meant Freud's rather gothic picture of the subconscious mind as a steaming pit of unacknowledged desires and hidden motivations. Skinner even criticised Eysenck for being 'perhaps a little extreme' in his comments on the failures of analysis.

The day before I met Skinner I talked to Neil Miller who published a book with John Dollard in 1950, in which they attempted to reconcile psychoanalysis and learning theory, then the dominant model of psychology. They thought that testing Freud's ideas against the 'rigour' of learning theory would be useful. Miller told me: 'I don't think we thought it was perfect by any means but we were happy with the general approach.' The book was presented as a modest vindication of some Freudian thinking.

I also interviewed Michel Jouvet, a French neurophysiologist who investigated sleep and dreaming. Jouvet and other researchers had discovered that we dream in a particular stage of sleep, and he did some pioneering work on the brains and dreams of cats. Jouvet was no fan of Freud's but he had embarked on a study of 1400 of his own dreams – a project partly inspired by the book that made Freud's reputation, *On the Interpretation of Dreams*. Jouvet's studies left him thinking Freud was wrong on many points, but that he had, nonetheless, opened up an important area of research. Rather more than Freud seems to have done, Jouvet self-consciously used his understanding of his dreams to change his behaviour.

The strongest advocates of Freud I interviewed were R.D. Laing, whose first book, *The Divided Self*, did more to humanise psychiatric patients than any other single text, and Karl Menninger. R.D. Laing was a quixotic and charismatic character, who suffered the great misfortune of having written his best book first: his subsequent decline into alcoholism, drugs, and writing dreadful poetry was a tragic loss to both himself and to progressive psychiatry. Menninger, sober almost to a fault, played an important part in developing psychoanalysis in America and went to Vienna in 1934 to meet Freud. Freud made him wait for an hour

7

which 'nettled me' – a question of authority again – but Menninger soon got over it. He noticed Freud was in pain and that 'he bore his pain with incredible bravery.' Menninger then wrote:

> 'But what impressed me most about Freud was the inner pain which he was obviously suffering, underlying his gentleness and his sweetness, a kind of inner pain that may have derived in part from the content of his great discoveries because, like the atomic physicists, he may have felt his discoveries transcended comprehension of the effects and their control by the discoverer.'

Menninger was astute in picking up on Freud's inner pain, which plays an important part in the cocaine story. He also gave a plausible account of why psychoanalysis succeeded in America. 'Freud was optimistic about human beings being able to help themselves ... and this struck a responsive chord in a pioneer country where we feel there is nothing which we cannot accomplish if we put our minds to it.'

Of all the psychiatrists I met who had encountered Freud, the most conflicted, by far, was Viktor Frankl. When Frankl was just 18 years old, he sent Freud the draft of a paper and asked for his comments. Freud did not reply and Frankl felt slighted by his silence. Four years later, Frankl saw Freud walking on the street in Vienna, went up to him and asked: 'What did you think of my paper, Herr Professor?' Freud, by then in his late seventies, had no idea who Frankl was. Deeply hurt, Frankl became hostile to analysis, devoted himself to de-throning Freud and devised a different kind of therapy, logotherapy. Psychoanalysis has always provoked both great loyalty and great fury. Conventional Freudians hated Frankl even more than he loathed them.

In his study Frankl had many photographs of himself climbing mountains. I didn't realise then that while Freud lacked many of the qualities of a real conquistador, he was a good mountain walker and once reached the top of the Dachstein, a 9800 foot peak in the Upper Austrian Alps. The most relaxed photographs of Freud are those that show him dressed in *lederhosen* and walking in the mountains or collecting mushrooms, a hobby of his. Frankl's photographs showed he had conquered many more Alps. Even if his theories were not as well-known as Freud's, Frankl had the satisfaction of being a better mountaineer.

Neither Menninger nor Frankl were part of Freud's early Viennese psychoanalytic circle. Melanie Klein, however, was one of the first women analysts and eventually had a series of bitter battles with Anna Freud about the significance of the breast. In the 1970s I met Melanie Klein's daughter, Melitta Schmideberg, a famous therapist herself, and she made me very aware of the personal feuds and schisms endemic to the world of psychoanalysis, feuds that were rarely resolved, however abstract their origins. She and her mother had not been on speaking terms for years. Schmideberg lived in a house stuffed with antiques and had fond memories of Freud, who was especially grateful to her husband Walter, a cavalry officer who supplied the analyst with cigars during the 1914 war. Schmideberg told me that after 40 years, she had come to the conclusion that the best form of therapy was to listen to patients' descriptions of their problems – and, whenever possible, to serve them wholesome soups.

She had concluded that too much theory, be it Freudian, Jungian, Kleinian, Reichian or of any other provenance, was of little help to either patients or therapists. She exuded the wisdom of an old woman who had seen much, but smiled like a happy young girl when she showed me a silver spoon that Freud had given her.

At Oxford I also studied Freud's fellow Viennese, the philosopher Ludwig Wittgenstein. He was something of an eccentric and apparently once brandished an iron poker at the influential philosopher of science Karl Popper, so Freud was lucky to emerge only lightly boiled from Wittgenstein's *Lectures and Conversations*:

'Freud is constantly claiming to be scientific. But what he gives is speculation – something prior even to the formation of an hypothesis.'

But after the condemnation came the praise:

'Wisdom is something I would never expect from Freud. Cleverness, certainly; but not wisdom.'

This book does not attempt to analyse the extent of Freud's wisdom or the value of his contribution to psychology and psychiatry. In *Psychologists on Psychology* I argued psychologists were far more combative than other scientists because their theories about human nature reflected on them as human beings. If I say we are biochemical machines, then I can hardly pretend I am a unique individual, different from all other such machines, and the proud owner of an immortal soul. The never-ending Freud wars show all too clearly how hard psychologists find it to be dispassionate.

It is only fair to warn readers that you are now entering a war zone.

In 1984, Harold Bloom, the celebrated literary critic and philosopher, offered a nuanced defence of Freud in a review of Janet Malcolm's *In the Freud Archives*. Freud always remained aware that the unconscious was his hypothesis or metaphor, Bloom argued, but 'the psychoanalytical profession has literalized Freud's metaphors as part of its anguished quest for the status of science.' Some modern analysts were so inane they compared psychoanalysis to surgery or even fixing a car. Bloom went on to quote an anonymous analyst as saying: 'Analysis isn't intellectual. It isn't moral. It isn't educational. It's an operation. It rearranges things inside the mind the way surgery rearranges things inside the body – even the way an automobile mechanic rearranges things under the hood of the car.' Bloom lambasted such literalism. 'Whatever Freud's metaphors may have sometimes implied, Freud did not confuse the mind with the internal combustion engine.'

Bloom praised Freud for being 'charmingly capable of writing that the theory of the drives was, so to speak, his mythology, nevertheless defended his claims to science by reminding us that the language of physics was also a figurative discourse. This defence allows that psychoanalysis is an interpretation rather than a fact, but Freud's sophisticated literacy has not been bequeathed to the analysts, some of whom indeed are the disease of which they purport to be the cure.'

Freud called America 'a gigantic mistake' and, according to Bloom, he had a good point when it came to many American psychoanalysts.

In a review for the *New York Review of Books*, Sarah Boxer pointed out that by 1990 'there was a relatively small group of people chipping away at Freud's reputation.' Especially vicious was the writer Stanley Fish, who praised one of Freud's patients, the so-called 'Wolf Man', for having had the good sense to observe 'that Freud was a Jewish swindler' who wanted to use him 'from behind' and defecate on his head. Hard scientists do attack each other, of course, but not, for the most part, in quite such childish ways.

In recent years, Boxer argues, the debate has become yet more vitriolic. Contemporary critics 'will happily hack at any fiber of Freud still twitching. They are a single-minded and humorless group.' One such critic, Eric Miller, goes even further and calls Freud 'murderous'. Boxer counters by citing John Forrester who complained that these new critics tried 'to show that psychoanalysis is deeply flawed ... not only because it is a bad and outdated theory, but principally because Freud was untrustworthy, demented, mendacious.' All the things, in short, one looks for in a doctor.

I have offered snippets of this literature to make evident the fury Freud arouses. For all that some of the more moderate critics have identified genuine flaws, inconsistencies and worse in Freud's thinking, he was still right to insist that psychology has to study more than mere behaviour. It cannot simply ignore what we feel and think because our thoughts and feelings make up our psychological reality and are the ways in which we know ourselves. Studying the complex interaction of brain processes, some of which we can now view through neuro-imaging technology, and subjective thought and feeling, requires some introspection. The perfect scientist watching the flows and eddies of chemicals and electricity in my brain at a given moment, would not, however perfect his computer imaging, know what I was feeling. Mind and body can't be explored using the same methods or in the same language. The scientist may see the pattern of neurons that fire when I taste ripe camembert or look at a painting by Hockney but seeing the pattern of my neurochemical and electrochemical activity does not tell that observer much about *my* human, intrinsically subjective, experience.

Curiously, many of the best examples of introspective research today are to be found in first-person studies of cocaine and other drugs, legal, illegal, and all shades in between. Since leaving Dow Chemicals, Alexander Shulgin has not just cooked up over 300 new psychoactive compounds, most of them hallucinogens, but also devised a psychological scale to compare the effects of different concoctions on the mind and body, starting with his own. He has inspired a generation of drug creators who routinely report on the effects of their latest invention, and a generation of followers who write reports on whatever dubious cocktail of drugs they can get their hands on.

The web now pulses with reports of new substances and users' accounts of them. Some of these reports are as well set out as conventional scientific papers. For example, a report on Mephedrone, a psychedelic stimulant drug with similarities to MDMA (ecstasy) and cocaine that made many headlines prior to its banning in April 2010 noted:

> *Positive: Elevated mood; mild euphoria; empathogenic effects; mild to moderate stimulation; increases in motivation, sociability and mental clarity; no notable come-down or hangover; aphrodisiac after comedown. Neutral: Slightly raised heart rate; pupil dilation; chattiness; appetite suppression.*
> *Negative: Difficulty sleeping after primary effects had subsided.*

On the web, of course, most users remain anonymous – which may well intrigue and frustrate future historians, as it is almost certain some of those who are now posting their experiences with illegal drugs online will rise to positions of influence and fame.

President Barack Obama has written that he used marijuana and 'blow' to ease his pain when he struggled to define his racial identity and sense of self. Vice-President Al Gore, son of a distinguished Senator, admitted to using cannabis heavily at Harvard as did John Kerry who ran against George W. Bush in 2004. Bush, the grandson of a famous Senator and son of a President, would not be specific about his own drug use beyond admitting that 'when I was young and stupid, I was young and stupid', perhaps one of his finest sentences. He has admitted heavy drinking in his youth, and refused to confirm or deny claims that he used cocaine and marijuana. Bill Clinton famously didn't inhale as he was more of a cigar man but his contemporary at Oxford, Christopher Hitchens, has claimed that Clinton was partial to the odd hash brownie. David Cameron has simply refused to answer the question about whether he took cocaine and ecstasy at Oxford. He did not challenge a biography, however, that claimed he had smoked cannabis at Eton.

When they reach high office, politicians are usually prudent enough to stop using – or at least, are unlikely to get caught – but the same is not true of show-business celebrities and Wall Street players. In 2007, in the *Investment Dealer's Digest*, Tom Granahan reported on Wall Street stock dealers' use of cocaine, other drugs and alcohol. They are paid enough to snort and imbibe any substance they wish. Granahan noted: 'They have lives which are often responding to the next crisis. They have access to drugs, drug-using friends, and associates, and they feel that drugs are part of the spectrum of entitlement.' If you do the deals, you deserve more than Dom Perignon and if you don't do the deals, you need even more. But there's a price to pay. Dr Alden Cass, president of Catalyst Strategies Group told Granahan: 'I see a lot of patients addicted to prescription medications aimed at improving concentration or focus or numbing some emotions.' Ritalin, Adderall (both stimulants), Vicodin, and Oxycontin (painkillers derived from opium) are the most common, he said. Cary Cooper, a well respected psychologist, spent months observing traders in dealing rooms and was astonished by the level of drug use he saw. Most contemporary research on drug use, however, is conducted in clinics or treatment centres whose clients are not Wall Street wizards. We know far more about users who are badly damaged than about those who may snort and pop pills, or even inject themselves, but still manage to work and have 'normal' family lives.

Class and money also matter. Wall Street 'workers' usually do not get sent to jail for using drugs – and the same is true of actors, models, artists and other celebrities. In September 2005, the *Daily Mirror* carried photos of supermodel Kate Moss that seemed to show her snorting lines of a white powder, presumed to be cocaine, at a recording session. She could not be charged with any crime on the basis of that alone, and her friends sprang to her defence. Stella McCartney, Naomi Campbell, Helena Christensen, the great French actress Catherine Deneuve and Moss's ex-boyfriend Johnny Depp all supported her. The designer Alexander McQueen wore a T-shirt saying 'We love you Kate'. Moss is now working closely with Sir Philip Green, the retail magnate currently advising David Cameron on the parlous state of British public finances.

The more famous the person, the more likely society will turn a blind eye to their drug use, abuse and addiction. The Queen knighted Elton John, Mick Jagger and Paul McCartney though all have admitted drug use. Mick Jagger infamously began an affair with supermodel Carla Bruni when she was seeing his close friend Eric Clapton, who has written of his own addiction to cocaine and alcohol. Ten years after leaving a heartbroken Clapton, Bruni dedicated these lyrics to her new husband, Nicolas Sarkozy, President of France:

'You are my drug
More deadly than Afghan heroin
More dangerous than Colombian white.'

Implying that she was no stranger to Colombian white did not stop Bruni being welcomed by the British Royal Family at Buckingham Palace (Mme Sarkozy has also admitted to 'experimenting with various drugs' in her youth). But then the Palace has had its own experiences with drugs over the years. Cocaine is the high of high society, after all, the champagne of stimulants. Princess Margaret allegedly enjoyed the occasional snort. Princess Diana's last lover, Dodi Fayed, was banned from the set of *Chariots on Fire*, a movie he helped finance, for selling cocaine to the cast and crew. It has been alleged that cocaine was found in Princess Diana's handbag by the Paris transport police after the fatal crash, and the evidence quietly suppressed.

Declaration of Interest

Academic journals now routinely ask authors for a declaration of interest. This is my fourth book on an individual psychologist. In 1979 I published a biography of John B. Watson, the founder of behaviourism and concluded that his theory did not explain his own behaviour well. I then wrote a book about Carl Rogers, the founder of humanist psychotherapy.

Again he was no paragon as, like Watson, he drank too much – Rogers' daughter warned him he stank of vodka – and his wife complained that he thought he was God. My first book on Freud looked at how he managed to leave Austria in 1938 after the Nazi *Anschluss*. Like many Jews, Freud did not see the dangers of staying in Vienna and only agreed to leave after the Gestapo interrogated his daughter Anna. The wisest of men are far from infallible, and brilliant psychologists may not be that brilliant at understanding themselves.

The second part of my declaration of interest concerns my own drug use. I was 15 when I first tried cannabis but as I was never much good at inhaling, I am not sure how much I sucked in. I did try cocaine a couple of times, and found it to be a potent aphrodisiac, and, on one occasion, took a dose of mescaline that made me see central London bathed in flowing mistiness. It was pleasant, though I would be lying if I pretended it led to anything particularly profound. The lamp-posts outside my flat were in soft-focus, but there weren't any angels draped round them.

I had one very unpleasant drug experience, though I am not certain exactly what I'd taken. I became acutely paranoid and saw small policemen crawling out of the toilet to arrest me. I lived behind police flats at the time, so my fantasy referred to something real, in its addled way.

I smoked cannabis a few times a year till my children reached their teens, when I just stopped, without giving it a thought. In the past 20 years I must have smoked three joints and have found cannabis dull, in comparison to cigars. My own drug experience is thus relatively limited: but I have explored addiction as a psychologist and journalist, and witnessed it in friends and family members. Time and again, I have noted how drug experience can seem to change both an individual and affect society – from Freud on coke to the world on Prozac.

This book is part history and part polemic. The first part explores Freud's cocaine use, discusses the four papers he wrote about the drug and examines what the 'cocaine episode' reveals about his work and personality. It highlights three important relationships. Freud prescribed cocaine to one of his teachers, Ernst Fleischl Marxow, in an attempt to cure him of his morphine addiction. The treatment was a dismal failure, but Freud could never fully admit the mistake, or the terrible effect that cocaine had on Fleischl.

Between 1884 and 1887, Freud was friends with a colleague at the University of Vienna, Carl Koller. Soon after first trying cocaine, Freud realised it might be an effective local anaesthetic but he did not pursue that insight seriously. It was to be Koller who carried out the key experiments and showed cocaine could indeed be used to anaesthetise the eye, becoming famous for a discovery that Freud could have made – and, perhaps, should have made.

Crucially, in 1887, Freud met the Berlin ear nose and throat specialist, Wilhelm Fliess, who became his closest friend for 15 years. Fliess believed in the tonic and therapeutic use of cocaine and Freud wrote to him in intimate terms about his ideas, his fears, how much cocaine he had taken, the particular stresses that triggered his drug use and how cocaine affected him. All this influenced *On the Interpretation of Dreams*, the book that made Freud famous. Its success finally gave Freud the confidence he had struggled to achieve for so long. If his mother had not loved him, perhaps he would never have written the book, but, if he had not written the book, his mother's love would never have been enough to make him the titan he became. Once Freud had the confidence that came with success, it became possible for him to stop using cocaine, though nothing he wrote suggested he ever admitted that to himself.

The cocaine episode came back to haunt Freud after Wilhelm Fliess died in 1928. Fliess's widow, Ida asked Freud to buy back the letters he had written to her husband; she knew they contained material which by then would be embarrassing as they detailed both his use of cocaine and mistakes that had been made in treating patients. The saga of buying the letters caused Freud endless anxiety but he managed to persuade Princess Marie Bonaparte to provide the money that was needed. Freud died in London in 1939 thinking those letters would never be read by scholars, let alone published. Marie had other ideas.

Later sections of the book examine the evolution of the introspective drug-using tradition after Freud. By 1920, heroin, morphine and cocaine were illegal and could only be obtained on prescription in Britain, America and most of Europe. Subsequent introspective pioneers became more interested in hallucinogenic compounds such as LSD and mescaline that did not become illegal till much later. By the 1960s, getting stoned was part of the counter-culture, seen by some as an inherently revolutionary act, as exemplified byTimothy Leary's famous advice to America: 'turn on, tune in, drop out.'

A year before Freud's death, Alfred Hoffman, a 28-year-old Swiss chemist who worked for Sandoz, synthesised LSD. The discovery of LSD's remarkable properties made drugs existentially glamorous again, as the hallucinogens seemed to open the mind to new experiences, even to enlightenment, while governments explored their possible uses in war. Hoffman inspired a cascade of research after the end of the 1939–1945 war. Later LSD research did advance our understanding of the brain, though perhaps less so than many early users had hoped, and suggested that the drug has a variety of therapeutic uses. Exploration of these was suppressed for decades, but recent years have seen a renaissance in clinical trials on psychedelics and related compounds, with even the US government now investigating the uses of MDMA in treating post-traumatic stress.

During the 1950s a parallel between the new waves of legal and illegal drugs began to emerge. Just as cocaine was first hailed as a panacea, only to be damned as a curse, the first anti-depressants and anti-psychotics were welcomed as wondrous cures for mental illness, until it became clear they also caused appalling side-effects. This pattern has recurred with each new generation of psychoactive medications, from widely-prescribed compounds such as Prozac and Provigil to black market drugs such as MDMA. This should be no great surprise. The brain is easily the most complicated known structure in the universe; the great psycho-linguist Noam Chomsky once told me that he doubted the human brain could ever understand how the brain worked. We tinker with it by consuming drugs, but we may never know the full reality of what we're tinkering with.

Finally, the book looks at the complex and confused situation today, as commercial drug makers create and market new recreational substances which have been designed to circumvent existing drug laws. Governments are failing to keep up with this rapidly moving target, and many of these new drugs would appear to be considerably more dangerous than those long since proscribed. Any dispassionate observer of the current confused drugs scene knows that the forces of law, order and convention are not doing well against the internet and aficionados of its drug sites. Research into drug use and personality is also making slow progress, as most drug users refuse to be methodical. The overwhelming majority of them go in for poly-drug use, making it impossible to isolate why a particular person takes a particular drug.

Freud did attempt to divine the deeper reasons behind drug use but with decidedly mixed results. One cannot appreciate the importance of Freud's cocaine story without understanding his ideas. The next chapter offers an outline to the essential Freud.

Chapter 2

The Essential Freud

In 1931 Freud's close friend Stefan Zweig, one of Europe's greatest 20th century writers, published *Mental Healers*. The book offered one of the first serious examinations of Freud's work. For Zweig, Freud was a hero. Over fifty years, Freud had seen a procession of the 'complaining, questioning, eager and excited, hysterical and irate; always the sick, the oppressed, the tormented, the mentally disordered,' Zweig wrote.

Psychoanalysis aimed 'to effect disillusionment and to dispel ungrounded fantasies ... It makes no promises at all, offers no consolation and is silent when asked for one or the other.' Zweig praised Freud's honesty which made his work 'amazing in its moral significance.' Zweig said nothing about cocaine, of course.

In 1933 the American psychologist Joseph Jastrow wrote the more critical *The House That Freud Built* and argued that historians may 'well regard the great mass of psychoanalytic literature as one of the strangest anomalies and fantastic vagaries of the early 20th century. And yet if he is tolerant, he may equally find in the same movement one of the truly notable moments in the understanding of the perpetual enigma – the human psyche.' Psychoanalysts were far more willing to listen to patients and their accounts of their suffering than other psychiatrists had ever been, Jastrow pointed out.

This may seem like a minor detail, but within the disciplines of 'mental healing' the notion of *listening to patients* was at the time a radical, even revolutionary development. It did not occur to many 19th century psychiatrists, or 'asylum doctors' as they were called, to ask their patients what was bothering them because, after all, the patients were mad, their thoughts and feelings pathological. Patients were 'demonstrated' like exotic specimens, wheeled into lecture theatres, asked embarrassing

Cocaine, Freud believed, would have cured de Quincey!

questions and sometimes told to perform bizarre tasks so students could ogle their behaviour. To put it in more formal terms, they were reduced, in the medical eye, to objects for the doctors to work on and manipulate. This was, of course, a highly unethical and dehumanising view. Freud changed that by learning to listen. He was the world's first great psychiatric listener.

The first subject he heard was himself – and his dreams.

In the Hebrew Bible, which Freud knew well, despite his atheism, dreams were often prophecies. In the section of Genesis sometimes called the 'Joseph Novella', Joseph, favoured son of Jacob, interprets Pharaoh's dream of seven fat cows and seven lean. This far from cryptic vision foretold that seven years of plenty would give way to seven years of famine, so a wise ruler would build up stores for the hard times ahead. Pharaoh, impressed by this ground-breaking Jewish analyst, put Joseph in charge of Egypt's farm belt (a somewhat unusual promotion, from psychoanalyst/prophet to Minister of Agriculture, but things were different then).

As a devout materialist, Freud did not believe in prophecy but divined in dreams a complex code that could expose the hidden aspects of both past and present. Freud claimed *all* dreams are wish-fulfilments, but as our deepest desires are often violent, erotic or shameful, these wishes are generally concealed in symbolism and narrative that might well be impenetrable to the conscious mind, and so need an analyst's interpretation. Dreams might be 'the road royal to the unconscious', but the unconscious was turbulent, a bubbling swamp where monsters, and monstrous lusts, lurked. Most of us do not want to face the full reality of our darkest, most deviant desires. The poet T.S. Eliot was influenced by Freud and noted that humankind cannot bear too much reality. (Eliot certainly couldn't, and had his first wife committed to a lunatic asylum.)

Know thyself, is the philosopher's advice.

'If I knew myself, I'd run away', was Goethe's response, and he was, of course, Freud's favourite writer. It is something of a paradox that Freud should have so revered a writer who suggested it was best not to know too much about the self. The whole point of psychoanalysis was to attain self-knowledge. To achieve that, Freud wrote, we must search our dreams for their hidden – or latent, in the analytic jargon – meanings. Our deepest hopes, our greatest fears, the best in us, the worst in us, all aspects of the psyche, are secreted in our dreams. We have to know ourselves if we want to be whole and healthy. Dreams, viewed in this light, function as psychological X-rays. If we know how to interpret them, they reveal where we are hurt and how we can be healed. Self-knowledge is power: power, however, that must be mediated by a third party, the analyst, guiding the patient through the murk of their subconscious.

The analyst must first help the patient in remembering their dreams, and then dig out the latent, buried meaning. The surface content – the images and words that linger in a patient's memory – was often sanitised and euphemistic. To find the latent meaning, the analyst had to decode symbolic representations of those desires patients could not admit to themselves. Though warning that the meaning of such symbols was not always fixed, Freud then went on to give examples of what would seem to be fixed symbols. A tunnel was, he claimed, quite clearly a vagina while a chimney was a penis and the box in which a woman kept her jewels signified a womb. A house of many rooms was said to be a brothel. The analyst was a code-breaker. Freud was also fond of telling his patients that they were digging for gold, the gold of truth. He sometimes also spoke of digging for oil and added that, to reach the oil and gold, the analyst had to create a setting in which the patient felt safe enough to confess the most intimate secrets.

Freud qualified as a doctor in 1881 at the age of twenty-five, but did not embark upon the project of analysing his own dreams for another 15 years. When this nocturnal self-analysis began, Freud liked the fact that what he found in his own unconscious would shock many of his contemporaries. There was always something of the naughty boy to the great sage.

Many books have been written about the contradictory sexual attitudes of the Victorians. Sex was considered dirty, women were not supposed to enjoy it and (though this is sometimes claimed to be an apocryphal notion) piano legs were often covered because they might provoke erotic thoughts. Outwardly, Victorian London was a 'moral city' but this was little more than self-serving propaganda: in places, it was a cesspit of vice. William Gladstone, who served as Prime Minister on four separate occasions between 1868 and 1894, was a devout Christian, constantly preaching the importance of ethics. In the evenings, however, he roamed the streets of Piccadilly talking to prostitutes, and some historians have suggested he did more than just attempt to save them from a life of vice. Gladstone recorded these encounters in a secret diary; he felt deeply guilty about them, and usually flagellated himself to atone for his 'sins'.

Freud was the 'bold oppositionist' here. He argued that sex was not just natural but a primal force. Every human being has a libido, or life-giving, pleasure-seeking, instinctual energies. These drives conflicted with the conventions of civilised behaviour or what George Bernard Shaw's marvellous dustman, Alfred Doolittle, dismissed as 'middle class morality'. Freud was not the only doctor of his time to argue we should not be ashamed of sexuality. Havelock Ellis, who wrote *Sexual Inversion* and *Sex in Relation to Society* and the physician, novelist and playwright Arthur Schnitzler both praised sexual freedom in more radical terms than Freud. Schnitzler was an ear nose and throat specialist like Wilhelm Fliess, but is remembered for a series of plays and novels of which the best known is *La Ronde*, a romp with a message in which one lover leads to another lover, partners are swapped and swung in an erotic merry-go-round which circles back, at the play's end, to the first lover. The message, though, was not entirely merry, as most of the play's characters contracted syphilis.

Sexuality did not begin at puberty, Freud argued. One of his most remarkable contributions was his theory of child development, with its three distinct stages – the oral, anal and genital. Each had its orifice. When babies are tiny, they find pleasure through the mouth as their mother breastfeeds them. Around 18 months of age, infants become fascinated by excretion: the anal phase. They then move on to the genital phase of development, becoming Oedipal. Freud had six children of his own and seems to have been an attentive and observant father.

Freud's patients then provided what seemed to be remarkable evidence of a hidden and horrific aspect of middle-class life in Vienna.

In the five years before he wrote *On the Interpretation of Dreams*, patients often told him that their parents had molested them sexually; Freud had apparently stumbled on a shocking secret. In many homes, respectable men and sometimes women were seducing their own children. Around 1905, Freud changed his mind about this, and decided that his patients' claims were false: these memories of abuse, he came to insist, were fantasies. Being Oedipal, small children wished to be touched, kissed and made love to by their mothers and fathers; the children's wishes were unconscious, and so manifested in fantasy, which solidified into false memories.

In 1983, Jeffrey Masson, then the co-director of the Freud Archives, suggested Freud had changed his mind not for scientific reasons, but cynical ones. Freud was afraid, Masson argued, that if he insisted on his scandalous theory of widespread abuse, psychoanalysis would never be accepted – and he would remain an eternal outsider, dismissed as a crank by the medical establishment. No one wanted a science which proved parents abused their children. Masson was sacked from his position at the Archives after publishing his thoughts on the subject, and remains a virulent critic of Freud.

Freud was more self-critical than Masson allowed. He did not seek to conceal this dramatic change in his position, writing: 'these scenes of seduction had never taken place, and they were only fantasies which my patients had made up or I myself perhaps had forced on them.' The last sentence is, of course, telling. Freud was aware he might have inadvertently, planted the suggestion that they had been abused in his patients' minds, his unconscious leading their unconscious on to a wished-for, pre-determined, conclusion. There has been much subsequent evidence that therapists can lead suggestible patients to 'recover' false memories of abuse. Janet Malcolm gave a good account of the scandal Masson provoked over 'seduction theory' in her short book, *In the Freud Archives*.

Freud's ideas on childhood sexuality were influenced by his study of the Greek myth of Oedipus, a study which started when he was very young. At the age of thirteen he won a school prize for translating 33 verses of Sophocles' play *Oedipus Rex*. The play was first staged around

460 BCE and has been performed regularly for 2500 years, which suggests it does reflect some deep truth.

Oedipus arrives in Thebes just after the murder of its ruler, King Laius. The plague is ravaging the city and it will not stop until someone solves the riddle of the Sphinx, the oracles say. The question is:

What walks on four legs, then on two, then on three?

The answer is a human being. A baby crawls on all fours; an adult stands on two legs while in old age, we walk with the third leg of a cane or stick.

Oedipus solves the riddle, the plague disappears and the riddle-solver wins the crown of the late Laius as well as the hand, and bed, of the king's widow, Jocasta. Twelve years later, however, the plague returns and the blind seer, Tiresias reveals that Oedipus himself killed Laius. Jocasta now admits to Oedipus that the oracles predicted her son would kill his father and have children by her, his own mother. When the baby Oedipus was born, Jocasta gave him to a shepherd and ordered him to kill the child so that the curse-prophecy could never be fulfilled. But Jocasta picked the wrong shepherd as he was too merciful to kill a baby and brought Oedipus up as his own child.

The truth then comes out. It is revealed the Oedipus did kill his father Laius, without knowing who he was: and then married his mother Jocasta, again, with no idea of their relationship as mother and son. The play's ending is fearful and blood-splattered. Jocasta hangs herself. Oedipus stabs out his eyes and goes into exile. For Freud, stabbing out the eyes was a symbol of castration, a fitting punishment for the primal sin of sleeping with one's mother.

The story revealed a universal truth, Freud believed. Unconsciously, small boys long to sleep with their mothers and kill their fathers but they know, again, unconsciously, that they should be punished for such thoughts. The Oedipal tragedy spoke the psychological truth. Below the surface, our minds boil with primeval passions which can never be admitted into consciousness. Small girls have the equivalent Electra Complex – they want to sleep with their fathers and kill their mothers.

'When I insist to one of my patients on the frequency of Oedipus dreams in which the dreamer has sexual intercourse with his own mother, he often replies "I have no recollection of having had any such dream",' Freud wrote. The conscious mind may censor and lie but it cannot change the raw truths of the unconscious. 'Disguised dreams of sexual intercourse with the dreamer's mother are many times more frequent than straightforward ones,' Freud argued. This claim was as revolutionary as anything Karl Marx ever said.

Freud sensed he had to find some objective evidence for his claim that toddlers were sexual creatures and, surprisingly, it was not hard to find in the academic psychology of the time. Sanford Bell, a well known American psychologist, had gathered 2500 observations of infants and published the results in *The American Journal of Psychology* in 1902. Bell wrote 'The emotion of sex love ... does not make its appearance for the first time at the period of adolescence as has been thought.'

When he gave his lectures at Clark University, Freud referred to Bell, saying:

'He (Bell) says of the signs by which this amorous condition manifests itself: "The unprejudiced mind, in observing these manifestations in hundreds of children, cannot escape referring them to sex origin. The most exacting mind is satisfied when to these observations are added the confessions of those who have as children experienced the emotion to a marked degree of intensity, and whose memories of childhood are relatively distinct."'

Sceptics 'will be most astonished to hear that among those children who fell in love so early, not a few are of the tender ages of three, four, and five years.' Freud insisted that doctors had 'forgotten their own infantile sexual activity under the pressure of education for civilisation and do not care to be reminded now of the repressed material.' Some children were fascinated by genitals at a very young age and even showed signs of arousal. 'They are said to be degenerate,' Freud said, but that was unfair and misconceived. The children were just human. We are sexual creatures from birth on.

Freud never admitted to having any Oedipal dreams about his

mother but in 1897, he confessed, in a letter to Fliess, that he remembered one dream which showed inappropriate, that is to say sexual, feelings towards his daughter Mathilde, who was nine years old at the time. He was, as we shall see, often using cocaine at this point. Though we have known about this letter for over 25 years, very few Freudians have discussed its implications. There is not a shred of evidence that Freud ever molested his own children or any other child, but this dream clearly influenced him. He knew fathers had sexual fantasies about their daughters because he had had at least one himself. He then proceeded to claim, however, that it was the children who fantasised about their parents. Any attempt to understand Freud has to confront the fact that he was, at times, a master of denial. The great unanswered question is whether he was aware of that aspect of himself.

The power of the Oedipus Complex explained two peculiar facts about human development, Freud argued. Roughly between the age of six and puberty, children stop being so interested in their bodies and go into sexual 'latency'. The 'psychic' (Freud's word) effort it took to resolve the Oedipus Complex explained why we remember so little of our early lives.

By the time boys and girls are three or four, they are sufficiently aware of the rules of family life to 'know' they cannot sleep with and marry their mothers or fathers, so children repress these 'bad' desires. The repression soaks up so much psychic energy, however, that all memories of early childhood are wiped out, which is why we suffer from 'childhood amnesia'. We can't remember *what* we suffered but that doesn't stop us feeling its consequences. This is why so many people – ideally, *all* of us – need analysis to remember accurately, so that we can be free 'to love and to work,' as Freud put it. Biologists now offer a simpler explanation for childhood amnesia; a structure in the brain called the hippocampus plays a crucial part in the retention of memory and takes some years to mature, so our early memory traces are unstable – and fragment away.

Freud often used analogies to make his points dramatically clear. His love of walking in the mountains provided a powerful analogy for describing the role of analysis and its practitioners. The analyst had to play the role of a mountain guide on a particularly difficult slope, but the patient wanted more than a mere guide. The patient thus projected love, hate, need, anger, all kinds of feelings on to the analyst who had to recognise that these emotions were a by-product of therapy and actually impersonal: the patient was just working through conflicts from childhood. Whatever they might think, the patient did not actually love, or hate, their analyst: but were shifting their feelings for their parents on to him. Freud called this projection 'transference'. Unlike parents, the analyst could – indeed had to – stay detached and use his professional skills to guide the patient to the mountain top.

A better image might be that of a maze. The analyst guides you through the maze to the centre where you find the ultimate prize – your true self, the self that is not haunted, maimed, or incomplete, the self that can indeed 'love and work.'

One of the most balanced critiques of analysis is Janet Malcolm's *Psychoanalysis: The Impossible Profession*, in which she stresses the paradox of Freudian therapy: 'The unexamined life may not be worth living but the examined life is impossible to live for more than a few moments at a time... The crowning paradox of psychoanalysis is the near-uselessness of its insights. To 'make the unconscious conscious' – the program of psychoanalytic therapy – is to pour water into a sieve. The moisture that remains on the surface of the mesh is the benefit of analysis.' This poetic but telling image would seem to humble the more extravagant claims for the power of analysis, a humility Freud himself occasionally shared.

Freud also became famous for his simpler claim that no behaviour was truly accidental, the claim B.F. Skinner so admired. In his often amusing books *The Psychopathology of Everyday Life*, and *Jokes and Their Relationship to the Unconscious*, Freud gave examples of conversational 'mistakes', which were not accidents, but revealed something that could not be said, in polite society at least. For example, he told the story of a rather vain man who said he talked with someone tête à bête, not tête à tête. The barb made it clear the speaker didn't rate the other man's intelligence; the man was a 'bête', a beast. In colloquial French, 'bête' also means stupid. This is an example of the 'Freudian slip', a term that long ago entered popular culture.

The First World War changed Freud's ideas, as the slaughter of millions in the trenches made him realise that the libido, the life-giving life-making pleasure principle, was not the only driving force in human behaviour. The libido had a dark mirror image, the 'Nirvana principle', 'Thanatos', or death instinct. Life is just too demanding. We want to stop struggling, escape into sex, drugs and booze. We flirt with, and sometimes commit, suicide. Lemmings are the only other species capable of killing themselves. This was the subject of Freud's *Beyond the Pleasure Principle*.

The 1914–1918 war also led to a strange coincidence. Hitler developed hysterical blindness at the front and was sent to Pasewalk Hospital where psychiatrists usually accused disturbed soldiers of malingering to escape being sent back to the trenches. Corporal Hitler was treated by Edmund Forster, a psychiatrist who was impressed by Freud's ideas and recognised that Hitler was no malingerer, but desperate to carry on fighting. Forster treated him with hypnosis and suggestion, techniques Freud used sometimes, even after he 'discovered' analysis. Forster told Hitler he had a destiny to fulfil, for which he needed the power of vision. At great cost to humanity, the treatment worked and Hitler saw again. The cure gave him confidence and the sense that he was a man of destiny; it also made Hitler aware of the possible uses of psychotherapy. Sixteen years later, when he became Chancellor of Germany, he had Freud's books burned as 'obscene Jewish literature', but he also felt that an Aryan version of analysis might have something to offer. It could produce happier and more efficient Nazis who would indeed 'love and work' so Hitler supported the creation of a Reich Institute for Psychotherapy, which appropriated most of Freud's ideas, without ever acknowledging their Jewish origins.

After the First World War, Freud developed a map of the mind which he sub-divided into the Ego, the Id and the Super-ego. As with the 'Freudian slip', these terms have become part of our culture. The Id has been defined as a wild-eyed sex maniac, a violent body of raw animal desire, the Super-ego as a disapproving moralist who lays down constant prohibitions, while the Ego is the voice of reason desperately trying to mediate between the nymphs and satyrs of the Id and the Inquisitor-Priest of the Super-ego.

His 1909 lectures at Clark University established Freud's psychiatric reputation. After the 1914 war, he became an international celebrity. The American writer Max Eastman came to Vienna to interview him for a book called *Heroes I Have Known*; the others included Charlie Chaplin, the great dancer Isadora Duncan and Leon Trotsky. Trotsky's great grand-daughter would go on to become one of the world's great experts on addiction.

From the 1920s onwards Freud was seen as one of the wisest men on earth.

In 1932, another such anointed sage, Albert Einstein, asked Freud to collaborate on *Why War?*, an exchange of letters which was published by the League of Nations, the forerunner of the United Nations. The two titans hoped they could help prevent future wars by giving the world the benefit of their insights.

The founder of psychoanalysis didn't think it would be easy to curb human aggression or believe that 'in some happy corners of the earth ... there flourish races whose lives go gently by, unknowing of aggression or constraint. I would like further details about these happy folk,' Freud said. Sadly, such joyful and pacific souls weren't to be found on either enchanted tropical islands or in the deepest jungle. Human beings would always, he maintained, be governed in large part by aggression and constraint.

Freud hoped 'a strengthening of the intellect, which tends to master our instinctive life,' would make humans less eager to grab their machine guns and diminish 'the aggressive impulse.' We might then become intelligent and emotionally adjusted enough to avoid wars, or at least, to have rather fewer of them.

Einstein replied on December 3rd, 1932:

'You have made a most gratifying gift to the League of Nations and me with your truly classic reply. You have earned my gratitude and the gratitude of all men for having devoted all your strength to the search for truth and for having shown the rarest courage in professing your convictions all your life.'

Perhaps the most charming proof of Freud's importance in America is that James Thurber, who was one of the star writers for *The New Yorker* magazine in the 1930s and 40s, wrote two hilarious works, *Six-Day Bicycle Riding as a Sex Substitute*, and *Let Your Mind Alone! and Other More or Less Inspirational Pieces*, poking fun at psychoanalysis and its founder. Satirists only mock those who have status. Neither book touched on Freud's experiences with cocaine, however, as by the time Thurber turned his hand to ridiculing analysis, they had been long forgotten and, to some extent, suppressed.

In his last book, *An Outline of Psychoanalysis*, written just before he died, Freud looked back on his life and ideas and argued that the future was bright, returning to the bio-psychiatric faith of his youth. One day, chemicals would provide the best cure for psychological ills, he predicted. Analysis was a temporary measure that would fade away, redundant, when scientists learned enough about the brain to heal any dysfunction with the right dose of the right substance, properly targeted.

Again, there is a curious irony here, for the evangelists of Prozac and related drugs more or less proclaimed, back in the early 1990s, that this moment had arrived: such contemporary bio-psychiatrists generally reject psychoanalysis as mystical, obscurantist drivel. As we shall see, the Prozac-pushers, to put it charitably, were a little premature in claiming our knowledge of the brain and its neurotransmitters had reached that point of near-perfect understanding: and the conviction they share with Freud, of such a thing being possible, remains a matter of faith, and faith alone. Such prophecies are the central tenets of the creed sometimes referred to as 'Scientism' – a blind faith that science can and will uncover all secrets of the universe. As such faith is generally held by harsh critics of conventional religion, they are typically unable to perceive the essentially religious – and unscientific – nature of their own faith. The evolutionary biologist and popular writer Richard Dawkins has become, in effect, the High Priest of this religion-by-another name, or the 'Pope of Scientism'.

It is impossible to make sense of either psychoanalysis or the complex relationship between drugs, psychiatry and culture without understanding Freud's 'cocaine story'. Orthodox Freudians have tried to play it down as a neurotic blip, a youthful aberration he soon cured himself of. Freud did his best to make sure that was the narrative and, as we shall see, destroyed letters that referred to his use of cocaine.

Freud could not, however, burn the papers he published about the drug as they had appeared in learned journals, but he did his best to airbrush them from history. They are not in the Standard Edition of his works and some letters about the episode are still embargoed. There are 19 boxes of papers in the Freud Collection in the Library of Congress which are restricted; some cannot be opened till 2020, some till 2050 and some are closed in perpetuity. The perpetually closed files include notes about patients, and it seems reasonable to assume some concern those to whom Freud prescribed cocaine, with disastrous results. One such patient was the brilliant physician and polymath, Ernst Fleischl.

Three previous books have discussed Freud's involvement with cocaine. The most substantial, Elizabeth Thornton's *Freud and Cocaine* was waspish, far too much so to be reliable. I interviewed her in the 1980s and she was very much the outraged spinster-librarian. Freud was a fraud, pure and simple, in her eyes. His use of cocaine distorted his work and robbed his theories of any value. She said:

> 'This book makes the heretical claim that his central postulate, the unconscious mind, does not exist, that his theories were baseless and aberrational and, greatest impiety of all, that Freud when he formulated them was under the influence of a toxic drug with specific effects on the brain.'

Thornton conveniently forgot that Davy, James, Victor Hugo and many other artists and scientists had used a variety of drugs. In fact, only 51 pages of Thornton's 330 page book deal with cocaine and less than 100 pages deal with Freud though she claimed her book was 'an alternative biography'. Thornton did not even refer to the two earlier books – Eyguesier's *Comment Freud devint Drogman* (How Freud became a drugman) and Von Scheidt's *Freud und Das Kokain* (Freud and Cocaine). The first was flimsy and at times bizarre as the author was a disciple of the well-known French analyst Jacques Lacan who whittled the analytic hour down to a mere ten minutes; 600 seconds with the maestro was enough to cure the most complex of complexes. The best part of the book is Eyguesier's analysis of the famous men and women who took cocaine between 1860 and 1890.

Von Scheidt's very short book offers a fair précis of Freud's papers on cocaine and argues it was far from accidental that the first dream Freud discussed in *On the Interpretation of Dreams* involved cocaine. Neither book has been translated into English.

The year after Freud first took cocaine doctors started to report on its dangers. In his short book *Opium, Morphine and Cocaine*, the Parisian doctor, Jean Brodereau coined a nice word, 'cocomaniaques' – or cocomaniacs. He applied the term both to users and to doctors who prescribed the drug. It was obvious to him by then that cocaine was dangerous.

The Biographies

In 1925, Freud's nephew Edward Bernays told him an American publisher was prepared to pay generously if he would write his life story, but Freud was not tempted. 'What deprives all autobiographies of value is their tissue of lies,' he told his nephew. 'Let's just say parenthetically that your publisher shows American naïveté in imagining that a man, honest until now, could stoop so low for five thousand dollars. The temptation would begin at one hundred times that sum, but even then I would renounce it after half an hour.'

Twelve years later Freud's friend, the socialist writer Arnold Zweig, asked for his permission to write his biography. Freud was again emphatic:

'Anyone who writes a biography is committed to lies, concealments, hypocrisy, flattering and even to hiding his own lack of understanding, for biographical truth does not exist and, if it did, we could not use it.'

He added a quote from his beloved Hamlet: 'Was the prince not right when he asks who would escape whipping were he used after his desserts?'

But most biographers do not give their subjects their just 'desserts'. Many writers idealise their subjects, and so 'forgo the opportunity of penetrating into the most fascinating secrets of human nature'. In the end, however, Freud knew he could not avoid a biography being written, so he made sure it would be the 'official' approved story of his life, told by a man who he, and his daughter Anna, could control.

Freud chose Ernest Jones for the job, a Welsh doctor who was the first Christian to play a major role in psychoanalysis. The fact that he was not Jewish was important because Freud feared that psychoanalysis could be seen as some kind of Jewish sect; a Christian doctor devoted to the 'cause' was very welcome even though Jones came with baggage, having survived a number of scandals in his earlier career. Today, he would have forfeited his licence for seducing a number of his young female patients. Freud knew of those incidents, because Jones turned to him for advice.

Jones would find it hard to be objective, Freud knew, because the Welshman admired him so much. To ward off criticism on this point, Jones pronounced that his own 'hero worshipping propensities had been worked through' before he ever met Freud. This was wishful thinking, and his three volume study *Sigmund Freud: Life and Work* is described by many critics as less a biography than a hagiography.

Jones wrote that little was known about some aspects of Freud's childhood and focused instead on the memories and dreams that Freud chose to tell him. Some were dramatic. As a young boy, Freud admired his father, and was upset when Jacob shouted 'the boy will amount to nothing' after Freud used the chamber pot in his parents' bedroom.

Freud also described an incident in which a gentile deliberately knocked his father's hat off his head but Jacob Freud dared not respond to the insult. He bent down and picked the hat up without protest. A sensible Jew in the Vienna of the day did not provoke a row with a Christian. Freud was disappointed to see such meekness in his father.

Jones did not, however, thread together the traumatic events in Freud's childhood as a more disinterested biographer might well have attempted. Instead, he gushed that the precocious child became the perfect man, and that by the time Freud was 45 years old he 'had attained complete maturity, a consummation of development that few people really achieve.' So mature was Freud, indeed, that he occasionally fainted when under pressure, was neurotic about travelling by train and quarrelled with many of his important followers before dramatically turning his back and excommunicating them from his clique. In 1957, Freud's critic, Hans Eysenck, argued that there was a link between neurotic personality traits and drug-taking. Freud, it seems, fitted the profile of the neurotic drug user all too well.

Jones, however, did not begin to speculate on why Freud was drawn to cocaine. Rather he portrayed his hero as ascetic and disciplined in the manner of a saint. Freud's theories might be daring, even scandalous, Jones said, but he himself was almost a monk. Freud lost interest in the 'passionate side of marriage after he turned forty.' Jones skated over – the verb is apt as Jones was an accomplished figure skater and his most successful book before his biography of Freud was *The Elements of Figure Skating* – the questionable aspects in Freud's career.

The cocaine saga however, had left too many traces to be ignored. Jones devoted one chapter to the 'Cocaine Episode'. In fairness, he was more critical in dealing with this than with any other aspect of Freud's work. He wrote that from 1884 to 1887 Freud 'pressed' cocaine 'on his friends and colleagues; he even gave it to one of his sisters and his fiancée. In short, looked at from the vantage point of our present knowledge, he was rapidly becoming a public menace.' But Jones still managed to turn a tragedy into something of a triumph. He concluded by saying:

'. . . what is interesting about the cocaine episode is the light it throws on Freud's characteristic way of working. His great strength, though sometimes also his weakness, was the quite extraordinary respect he had for the singular fact. This is surely a very rare quality. Unlike many scientists who would dismiss an inconvenient fact which went against orthodox thinking, the single fact would fascinate him and he could not dismiss it from his mind until he had found some explanation of it. However distressing or shocking, the fact had to be faced and studied as when, for example, Freud found in himself previously unknown attitudes to his parents he felt immediately that they were not peculiar to himself and that he had discovered something about human nature in general; Oedipus, Hamlet and the rest soon flashed across his mind.'

Jones ended with a flourish, 'this is the way the mind of genius works.'

Although Freud stopped using cocaine, he never conquered his other chemical dependency: nicotine. His last doctor, Max Schur, wrote a touching book about his patient and described him as a proud, wise, hardworking, caring old man – and an addict. Freud admitted it himself in 1929 when he responded to a survey. Famous men and women were asked about their smoking habits. Freud replied:

'I began smoking at the age of 24, first cigarettes but soon exclusively cigars and am still smoking now (at $72^1/2$) and very reluctant to restrict myself in this pleasure. Between the ages of 30 and 40 I had to give up smoking for a year and a half because of heart trouble which may have been due to the effect of nicotine but was probably a sequel to influenza. Since then I have been faithful to my habit or vice.'

Freud was neither the perfect scientist nor the perfect man. The founder of analysis spent nearly 20 years of his life using cocaine – which may have played a part in his 'heart trouble', too – and for the rest of his life smoked around 20 cigars a day; he was clearly vulnerable to substances. Freudians don't like to advertise their founder's flaws as a flawed human being might produce flawed theories.

It is now over 70 years since Freud's death. His cocaine adventure needs to be told in full, which requires delving not just into his childhood, but events that preceded his birth. Three months before Freud was born on May 6th 1856 in Freiburg, Moravia, his paternal grandfather died. Sigmund Freud was born into a house of mourning.

Chapter 3

A Traumatic Childhood

According to Freud, every aspect of our personality is the result of our childhood experiences. He claimed to have first tried cocaine mainly out of scientific curiosity but his own theory as well as much recent research does not make that a very convincing, let alone full, explanation. It is remarkable that none of Freud's many biographers have asked what happened to Freud as a child to make him susceptible to cocaine – especially as his theories provide useful clues. The analyst did not analyse himself where it hurt most.

By the time he was ten Freud had lived through a number of traumas, as argued in the introduction, but also had what we would now call 'stepfamily issues'. Jacob had two sons by his first marriage, Emanuel and Philipp. After the death of his first wife, Jacob remarried but little is known about his second wife; Rebekah has vanished out of history almost entirely. In 1855, the twice-widowed Jacob married Amalie Nathanson, some 19 years his junior. Sigmund was their first child and he was circumcised on the eighth day of his life, as the Torah commands all Jewish boys must be.

Soon after Sigmund was born, his mother Amalie became pregnant again. She and Jacob adored their second son but he was a sickly baby. Historians of analysis have neglected to ask whether Amalie, scared Julius might die, might have cuddled him far more than his elder brother and so 'rejected' Sigmund. Likewise, the earlier literature has not posed the delicate-indelicate question: did Amalie stop breastfeeding Sigmund so that she would have more milk for Julius?

Julius died when he was only eight months old. This was the second bereavement the family had suffered in a two-year period – first Jacob's father, now his youngest son. Victorian parents were used to children

No sign of the Super-ego.
The Victorian ad-smiths seem to have used all the tricks of the Madison
Avenue trade when selling coca wine.

dying but that did not make the death easy to bear, especially for a teenage mother such as Amalie. Language reflects the horror of losing a child. We call a child who loses his parents an 'orphan' but there is no specific term for parents who lose a child, a grief literally too great for words. In the aftermath of such a loss, being good parents to surviving siblings is very difficult indeed.

Freud had done nothing, of course, to cause his baby brother's death but, forty years later, when he analysed his dreams he 'discovered' he had been jealous and wanted Julius dead so he could have his parents to himself. Julius' death became an event of major significance for Freud's map of his own unconscious. His 'evil' wish had come true which explained, Freud said, some of his neurotic reactions, especially his irritating habit of fainting at odd times. Any triumph he enjoyed recalled his 'triumph' over Julius, so Freud fainted to avoid feeling guilty because his unconscious 'believed' he had killed his brother by just wishing the baby dead. Such primitive beliefs, in analysis, are seen as overpowering the rational mind.

There may have been a very different trauma in the family, as well as Julius's death, according to the German historian, Marianne Krull. In her book *Freud and His Father*, she suggests Amalie, Freud's mother, had an affair with Philipp Freud, Sigmund's 20-year-old half-brother and her stepson. According to Krull, the first secret Freud stumbled on was his mother in bed with Philipp. Her evidence for this sensational claim is not very solid as she relies mainly on an image that appeared to Freud in a dream; a mother-figure being carried by a bird-headed creature that resembled the part-animal humanoids of ancient Egyptian myth. In German the word for a bird, '*vogel*' is very similar to the word for intercourse, '*vogeln*' not the kind of 'evidence' for her bold claim that would be much use in court.

There are two suggestive hard facts though, which may support Krull's thesis. In *Freud and the Christian Unconscious*, Vitz points out that this stepfamily drama may explain why the family left Freiburg. Most of Freud's biographers attribute the move to economic pressures, but Vitz has delved into local archives and found that the town was prospering at the time. It wasn't economics but fear of adultery that made Jacob take his family away. He found out, or began to suspect, his young wife was having an affair with his 20-year-old son so Jacob decided to take Amalie far away from Philipp. It is clear that after leaving Freiburg for Manchester, Philipp never saw his father again. Philipp's brother Emanuel, on the other hand, often visited the family in Vienna. Of course, none of this constitutes proof of an affair, but Amalie and Philipp would not have been the first stepmother and stepson to at least flirt.

In Freiburg the Freuds were able to employ a nanny, Resi Wittek, who was a devout Catholic and took Freud to church. In *On the Interpretation of Dreams*, Freud makes a surprising revelation: 'Today's dream has, under the strongest disguise, produced the following: she was my teacher in sexual matters and complained because I was clumsy and unable to do anything.' Freud never explained what he meant by saying she had been his teacher in sexual matters – or even considered whether it had been a wish-fulfilling fantasy of his own. When Freud's sister Anna was about 30 months old the nanny was sacked, but for more prosaic stated reasons. The devoted Catholic, the family claimed, had stolen from them.

The local archives, Krull and Vitz both argue, show no evidence of any police or legal action against the nanny. They suggest Resi Wittek had to be stopped from gossiping about any relationship between Philipp and Amalie, and accusing her of theft was simply a clever pretext for her sacking. If she did start gossiping, no one would believe her, as such tittle-tattle would be seen as a dishonest woman's ploy for revenge on the Freuds. All that can be said with any certainty is that the family accused her of theft, and ended her employment. The rest is speculation.

In 1859 Sigmund's half-brothers Philipp and Emanuel left Freiburg for Manchester. In the space of 18 months the family had seen one son die, a nanny sacked in dramatic, if finally mysterious, circumstances and two children from the father's earlier marriage move to a different country. The baby Freud suffered a classic case of separation anxiety which may well have been made more acute by the fact that his parents were so absorbed in grief. The link between separation anxiety and addiction has been examined by, among others, Loas *et al.* (2000). They studied a control group of 784 healthy subjects and 708 subjects who presented with a variety of addictive disorders. They found a strong link between dependent personality disorder (DPD) and separation anxiety. The roots of Freud's use of cocaine and cigars lay in his traumatic childhood. Separation anxiety was not his only problem, though.

Freud argued that all babies first find their satisfaction orally. Long before he started smoking, Freud was apt to chew leaves and grasses: chewing gives oral satisfaction, just like smoking. Smokers know well the pleasure nicotine produces in the mouth and lips. Freud had great oral needs and given Julius' sickness, his own theory points to an obvious cause; he did not get enough time, milk or suck at his mother's breast. Classic analytic theory would suggest that this makes a child especially susceptible to frustration. Many drug users admit they find it hard to cope with frustration, which makes them crave the instant gratification of their next dose.

To analysts, cigars and cigarettes are 'nipple substitutes' and a man who can't do without them is fixated at the oral, the most infantile, level of development. A letter of Freud's suggests he had some strange ideas about oral fixation as he wrote that he missed his daughter Anna in a way that could be compared to missing a good cigar. As a cigar is a rather obvious phallic symbol as well as a nipple substitute, this was a truly odd statement for a father to make, and may have been the underlying motive for Freud's somewhat self-contradictory admission that 'sometimes a cigar is only a cigar.'

Psychologists today speak of significant 'life events'. By the time he was four Freud had suffered six traumatic life events – the deaths of his grandfather and little brother, the loss of his beloved nanny, who he would later identify as his 'teacher in sexual matters', the family's move to Vienna and the emigration of his two half-brothers. Then his father lost most of his money, leaving the family in dire straits. Freud only ever wrote about two of these traumas, the death of Julius and poverty, which haunted him. In his own words: 'Something I remember from my boyhood is that when wild horses on the pampas have once been lassoed they retain a certain anxiousness for life. I once knew helpless poverty and have a constant fear of it.'

When they arrived in Vienna, the impoverished Freuds could only rent a very modest apartment in a tenement block near the city's famous Carmelite Church. The block was in Vienna's Jewish district, Leopoldstadt, a working-class area that functioned as a ghetto for most of the city's 7000 Jews.

Over time, the family recovered. After Julius died, Jacob and Amalie had four daughters; their only other son, Alexander, was born when Freud was eleven years old and already much-admired for his intelligence, so he did not have to wish his new brother dead, subconsciously or otherwise. Freud in fact suggested that his brother should be called Alexander after the great conqueror and his parents did as he asked. Alexander always looked up to Freud, who in turn always loved his younger brother.

At first, Freud was educated at home, almost certainly because his family was too poor to send him to school. His sister Anna complained he was given a room of his own so he could study, while the other children were crammed into one room.

The next traumatic incident in Freud's childhood was more public. In the Freud papers at the Library of Congress, I stumbled on an envelope marked 'Top Secret: only to be opened by Kurt Eissler', who founded the Freud Archives in 1951. Inside was a microfilm of three pages from a Vienna newspaper published in 1865. The paper could, in fact, be read by anyone who bothered to go to the Austrian National Library in Vienna but it contained a story that Freudians wanted to suppress.

After Freud's two half-brothers, Emanuel and Philipp, emigrated to Manchester they had business dealings with uncle Josef, Jacob's brother. The three family members then became involved in a major criminal conspiracy. In June 1865 Vienna's *Neue Freie Presse* reported the police were tracking ring of counterfeiters, forging Russian roubles. The Austrians had sent a sample 50-rouble note to St Petersburg and the Russian Ambassador informed them that he had 'the honour' of confirming the note was a forgery.

On June 20th, one Simon Weiss invited Josef Freud to the Hotel Victoria in Vienna and introduced him to a 'client'. Josef then went home to fetch more of the notes. While he was gone, Weiss and the police prepared a trap. A number of policemen disguised themselves as waiters.

When Josef returned to the hotel, he counted out a hundred

50-rouble notes. At this point, the policemen stopped serving strudels and tea and arrested him. They went to his apartment where they found 259 further rouble notes as well as two incriminating letters from Emanuel and Philipp. The first said that 'there is as much money as there is sand by the sea' and that 'if we are wise fortune will not fail to smile.' The second letter asked if Josef could find a bank for the 'merchandise where the turnover would be larger, faster and more profitable.'

Josef was sentenced to 10 years in prison for forgery. When his uncle was convicted, Freud had just started attending the Gymnasium or secondary school in the Sperlgasse, close to where he lived. Vienna was a deeply anti-Semitic place, and for a Jewish boy to be the nephew of a man accused of forgery could not have been easy, but Freud never wrote about the subject. He was not frank about his uncle's inglorious criminal career, merely writing that Josef had 'allowed himself to become involved in a transaction of a kind that is severely punished by law and he was in fact punished for it.' Emanuel and Philipp became moderately successful businessmen in Manchester. They had what now seems a dramatic telegraphic address: Freud Manchester.

In *Questions for Freud* Rand and Torok suggest the scandal of uncle Josef's trial made Freud wary of outlining his theories in detail because committing too many specifics to paper would allow his ideas to be tested and, therefore, potentially proved false or 'forgeries'. It was wiser to keep it all a bit vague and muddled. This was not, of course, a conscious decision Freud made, the authors argue; his unconscious fears made him imprecise and thus irrefutable: precisely why most of my Oxford psychology teachers dismissed his ideas.

Ernest Jones proclaimed that Freud was always a seeker after truth, but Rand and Torok suggest that was only so 'as long as what he finds will obey his control.' Freud had to be sure he would not be exposed as a peddler of false ideas or forgeries as his uncle had been. It is an interesting argument, if one as 'unverifiable' as any of Freud's own.

The uncle Josef drama might have taught the young Freud that it was dangerous to take risks, but caution was alien to his personality. Once he had mastered his lack of confidence, Freud became the conquistador, very willing to take risks, good or bad, risks with himself and great risks with his patients.

One other great psychologist who seems to have had as traumatic a childhood as Freud was John B. Watson, the founder of behaviourism. Watson's father was a drunk who ran away from home when the boy was ten. Watson drank and smoked heavily throughout his life. He was also rather neurotic and could only sleep with a light on. Watson managed his career badly, an affair with his graduate student/assistant Rosalie Rayner leading to his sacking from Johns Hopkins University when he was 39. Unlike Freud, however, Watson never lacked professional self-confidence, partly because he achieved success at a very early age with a pioneering study on learning in rats.

Freud never wrote about the legacy of the tragedies I have outlined but the traumas made it likely he would suffer from anxiety, depression and a lack of confidence. It is hardly surprising therefore that he needed something to give him a boost in young adulthood – and that 'something' was cocaine.

As one of my aims is to put Freud's history with cocaine in context, the next chapter looks at the history of the drug and its source, the coca leaf, a history Freud knew in outline when he took his first 1/20th of a gram.

Chapter 4

Chew for Perfection

Human beings have been chewing and brewing coca leaves for at least 7000 years in Central and South America. They were not known in Europe until Cortés landed in Mexico with his brave and greedy band of 400 men. The governor of Cuba had chosen him to establish a small colony in Mexico; neither he nor Cortés had any idea that they were pitting an army of four hundred against the great Aztec Empire. But the conquistadors had an advantage – the Aztecs were despised by the tribes that they had enslaved, and Cortés formed alliances with several tribal leaders.

Ritual cruelty was part of Aztec culture and religion. Vaillant, in his dramatic *History of the Aztecs* (1944) describes how priests would seize a slave 'by either arm forcing him backward while two others pulled his legs under him until his body curved belly upward over the altar. A fifth priest ploughed his flint knife in a long sweep from the breastbone to the base of the stomach and reaching into the aperture with a dexterous twist tore out the heart. This he burned while it was still throbbing.' The tribes had every reason to turn against the Aztecs.

Days after he landed, Cortés captured a young Aztec princess who became his interpreter and lover. Lola introduced him to the coca leaf, widely used in Aztec culture as both stimulant and aphrodisiac. With Lola's help, Cortés reached Tenochtitlan, now Mexico City, in November 1519 and was graciously received by Montezuma, the Aztec Emperor. The Emperor had the misfortune to believe Cortés was a god. Cortés repaid the trust by having the Emperor imprisoned and murdered in circumstances that historians still debate.

In a letter to Charles V, the Holy Roman Emperor, Cortés described the wonders of Tenochtitlan which included 'a herb street, where may

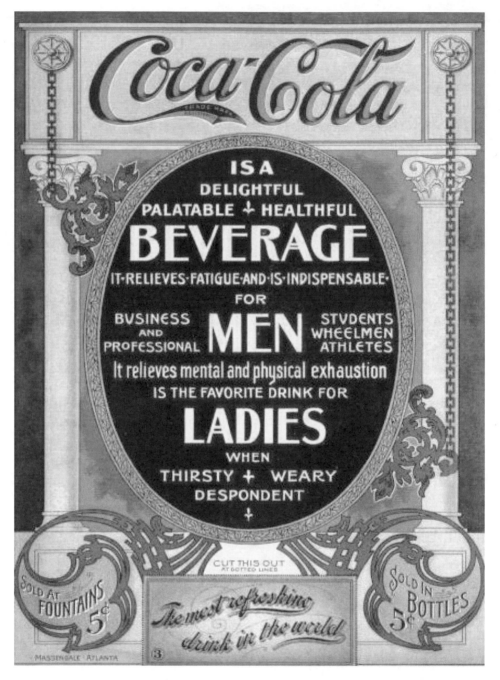

Coca-Cola's early days. An advertisement from when it still contained cocaine.

be obtained all sorts of roots and medicinal herbs that the country affords. There are apothecaries' shops, where prepared medicines, liquids, ointments, and plasters are sold.' Coca leaves were stocked by such outlets in many forms. When chewed, the leaf was mixed with a small quantity of *ilucta* (a substance made from the ashes of burned quinoa plants), both softening the flavour and activating the alkaloids within.

The Church initially banned the use of coca leaves, but the Spanish soon saw coca had many advantages. Natives would work harder and longer, as well as eat less, if allowed to chew the leaves. Ever practical, the Church compromised. The natives could munch on their beloved leaves as long as the Church was allowed to charge a tithe of one tenth of the value of any crop.

The coca leaf, however, was hardly the greatest treasure the New World offered the Old. Spanish galleons brought gold and silver from the mines of Latin America. Coca could not rival the impact chocolate, tobacco and the potato made on life in Europe. One sharp Spanish bishop noticed in 1676 that chewing the leaf alleviated toothache, but his observation – and its implications – were ignored at the time.

The end of the 18th century saw the first methodical study of how a drug could affect perception and emotion. That drug was not coca but nitrous oxide, 'laughing gas', which was first synthesised by Joseph Priestley in 1772. The famous engineer James Watt invented a machine to produce 'Factitious Airs' (i. e. nitrous oxide) and a crude 'breathing apparatus' to inhale the gas. Watt worked with a well-known doctor, Thomas Beddoes, who suggested tuberculosis could be treated by breathing these 'Factitious Airs'. An enthusiastic Beddoes set up the Pneumatic Institution for Relieving Diseases by Medical Airs in 1798 and hired a practical and very clever young man to build a larger version of Watt's machine – Humphry Davy, who became one of the most significant chemists of the 19th century. Davy turned 21 on December 17th 1799 and five days later, he experimented on himself, breathing in enough gas '... as to produce excitement equal in duration and superior in intensity to that occasioned by high intoxication from opium or alcohol.'

On Boxing Day, Davy put himself in an 'air tight breathing box of the capacity of about nine and one-half cubic feet, in the presence of Dr Kingslake.' Kingslake could always pull him out and put an end to the experiment if it became too dangerous. Twenty quarts of nitrous oxide were pumped into the box.

After four minutes Davy 'began to feel a slight glow in the cheeks and a generally diffused warmth over the chest, though the temperature of the box was not quite 50 degrees.' Twenty-five minutes later 'the animal heat was 100 degrees, pulse 124'. In thirty minutes twenty quarts more of gas were introduced and Davy felt 'a sense of exhilaration similar to that produced by a small dose of wine.' After an hour, his pulse had slowed to 99 and he asked for a further 20 quarts of air to be pumped into the box.

'I had now a great disposition to laugh, luminous points seemed frequently to pass before my eyes, my hearing was certainly more acute, and I felt a pleasant lightness and power of exertion in my muscles ... rest was painful.'

Davy now came out of the box and Kingslake clamped an air bag over his face. As he breathed in pure nitrous oxide, the effects grew stronger. Davy wrote:

'I felt a sense of tangible extension highly pleasurable in every limb; my visible impressions were dazzling and apparently magnified, I heard distinctly every sound in the room, and was perfectly aware of my situation. By degrees, as the pleasurable sensations increased, I lost all connection with external things; trains of vivid visible images rapidly passed through my mind and were connected with words in such a manner as to produce perceptions perfectly novel. I existed in a world of newly connected and newly modified ideas. I theorized; I imagined that I made discoveries.'

He wanted to tell the world about what he had discovered and 'exclaimed to Dr Kingslake, "Nothing exists but thoughts! The universe is composed of impressions, ideas, pleasures, and pains."'

Davy's account of his experiences set a pattern for future introspective drug research. He was also sharp enough to realise the potential of nitrous oxide and wrote:

'As nitrous oxide in its extensive operation appears capable of destroying physical pain, it may probably be used with advantage during surgical operations in which no great effusion of blood takes place.'

Davy did not, however, pursue this hunch, which delayed the discovery of a useful anaesthetic for 44 years. Despite Davy's account of his experiment and his growing fame, no one followed it up, partly because another drug had become so fashionable. Opium had captured the romantic imagination, as Alethea Hayter would sub-title her definitive work on the subject, *Opium and The Romantic Imagination*.

Opium was well-known in the ancient world. Egyptian physicians prescribed it for sick children and it is referred to in both the Hebrew Bible and Virgil's *Aeneid*. Arab physicians also used the substance and the Crusaders brought it back with them to Europe. In 1522, the great doctor Paracelsus referred to an opium-based elixir which he called *laudanum* (generally tiny fragments of opium resin floating in alcohol) from the Latin word *laudare* meaning 'to praise.' It was a potent painkiller, but Paracelsus, wisely, warned that it should be used sparingly. As laudanum became popular, this warning was all too often ignored. Thomas de Quincey certainly did not pay attention to such calls for temperance.

De Quincey was a friend of the poets Wordsworth and Shelley; he had fled his overbearing family and survived years of destitution before encountering opium as an Oxford student. In *Confessions of an English Opium Eater* (1821), de Quincey praised:

'Oh! just, subtle, and mighty opium! that to the hearts of poor and rich alike, for the wounds that will never heal, and for 'the pangs that tempt the spirit to rebel,' bringest an assuaging balm; eloquent opium! that with thy potent rhetoric stealest away the purposes of wrath; and to the guilty man, for one night givest

49

back the hopes of his youth, and hands washed pure of blood...'

Opium soon became the fashionable drug of the day. Poets loved it. Shelley drank laudanum to calm his nervous headaches, Keats used it as a painkiller and Byron took it in a form called Kendal Black Drop to calm himself. Even Jane Austen's prim mother recommended it for travel sickness.

The romantic view of opium marked a change in our understanding of the self, Hayter argued. The drug was seen as the key to a new freedom, freedom to explore the misty realms of pipedreams and the shadows that inhabit them, to experience new forms of perception and sensation as well as the freedom to numb all pains, physical and emotional. Genius as we now understand it is very much a Romantic concept. The genius is portrayed as a great artist, touched by some divine spark of inspiration, who embarks on an inner journey to find themselves. Opium was the first popular drug to open what Aldous Huxley would call 'the doors of perception'.

But opium also had its political and commercial side: the addictive nature of opium itself (the latex extracted from inside poppy pods, which then hardens into a resin) made it an ideal consumer product. The alkaloid morphine was extracted from opium in 1804 and companies like Merck quickly offered it for sale in pure form. Opium has two active components – morphine and codeine, the latter being far weaker, though some 10% of any codeine ingested is metabolised by the body into morphine. The outside of the opium poppy pod contains other active chemicals, including thebaine, from which the highly lucrative *opioids* – the term used to describe those drugs with opiate-like effects which are not derived directly from opium proper – are made. These include hydrocodone and oxycodone, major sellers in the USA.

The political effects of the 19th century opium trade are with us still. The Chinese insisted on the return of Hong Kong to their sovereignty in part because they had been humiliated in the 19th century opium wars. Opium was big business, and in 1840, the British demanded compensation from the Chinese when The Emperor wanted to bring an end to the opium trade. He had the bizarre idea of getting his subjects to stop smoking the stuff, which did not endear him to Queen Victoria's ministers, who fumed that wily Orientals were trying to rob the Empire of its inalienable right to exploit the natives. The navy was sent in and routed the Chinese.

The Chinese, in defeat, had to sign what they dubbed 'the first Unequal Treaty', which gave the British a free hand to do as they wished and continue making huge profits from opium. When the Chinese had the temerity to object again, there was a second Opium War and a second 'Unequal Treaty' when the Chinese again lost to the British, who like the Conquistadors against the Aztecs, came armed with superior technology.

Other introspective experiments centred on hashish, which had also been used, medicinally and otherwise, since time immemorial. In 1844 a Parisian psychiatrist, Dr Jacques-Joseph Moreau, founded the Hashish Club. When he took hashish he experienced euphoria, hallucinations and incoherence. Moreau, at least, had the wit to realise it was not sensible to experiment on oneself with a drug which induced hallucinations. So he set up a club where the finest minds in Paris could enjoy the 'intellectual intoxication' of hashish.

Members of the Hashish Club included the author of *The Three Musketeers*, Alexandre Dumas, the author of *Les Misérables*, Victor Hugo, the poet Charles Baudelaire and the painter Eugène Delacroix. The group met between 1844 and 1849 and usually dressed in Arab clothes. They drank strong coffee, laced with hashish, which Moreau called 'dawamesk', its Arabic name.

In his essay 'Le Club des Hachichins', Moreau's friend, the writer Théophile Gautier, described entering the room where Moreau stood by a buffet and handed out portions of hashish. Then, being French, they had a five-course meal of oysters, hash, filet mignon, camembert, more hash, cognac, and more hash. By the meal's conclusion, Gautier wrote, the others seemed 'somewhat strange. Their pupils became big as a screech owl's; their noses stretched into elongated probosces; their mouths expanded like bell bottoms. Faces were shaded in supernatural light.' But the experiences fascinated him.

The poet Baudelaire gave the best introspective account of the effects of hashish:

'At first, a certain absurd, irresistible hilarity overcomes you. The most ordinary words, the simplest ideas assume a new and bizarre aspect. This mirth is intolerable to you; but it is useless to resist. The demon has invaded you . . . (People) started to improvise an endless string of puns and wholly improbable idea relationships fit . . . but after a few minutes, the relation between ideas becomes so vague, and the thread of your thoughts grows so tenuous, that only your cohorts . . . can understand you.

'Next your senses become extraordinarily keen and acute. Your sight is infinite. Your ear can discern the slightest perceptible sound, even through the shrillest of noises. The slightest ambiguities, the most inexplicable transpositions of ideas take place. In sounds there is colour; in colours there is a music. . . You are sitting and smoking; you believe that you are sitting in your pipe, and that your pipe is smoking you; you are exhaling yourself in bluish clouds. This fantasy goes on for an eternity. But then you look at the clock and discover the eternity turns out to have been only a minute.'

The hashish smoker then entered the third phase of 'complete happiness. There is nothing whirling and tumultuous about it. It is a calm and placid beatitude. Every philosophical problem is resolved . . . Every contradiction is reconciled. Man has surpassed the gods.'

The Hashish Club stopped meeting in 1850, just as coca finally began to make a profound impression in Europe. In 1857 the German botanist Johan von Tschudi went to Latin America and observed a 'cholo of Hurain' called Hatan Huamang who he'd employed to perform manual tasks, especially digging. Hatan was a heroic digger as long as he was chewing, von Tschudi saw: 'During the five days and night he was in my service, he never tasted any food and took only two hours sleep each night'. The coca leaves even allowed Hatan to keep up on foot when von Tschudi rode a mule on a long journey. 'The village priest assured me that this man was 62 years old and had never known a day's sickness in his life.'

Von Tschudi added that in April 1859, a native was sent to walk the 249 miles from La Paz to Tacna and deliver the mail. He made it chewing coca leaves all the time.

Charles Darwin made his name when he sailed on the *Beagle*. It took the Holy Roman Emperor 24 years to order a similar naval expedition but in 1858 he finally sent a frigate, the *Novara*, round the world. The ship's botanist gathered coca leaves and sent them to be analysed by Albert Niemann (1834–1861), a young chemist at Göttingen University. Niemann worked out a process for purifying the active chemical component from the leaves and named it 'cocaine'. In his doctoral dissertation *On a New Organic Base in the Coca Leaves*, Niemann wrote of its 'colourless transparent prisms... Its solutions have an alkaline reaction, a bitter taste, promote the flow of saliva and leave a peculiar numbness, followed by a sense of cold when applied to the tongue.'

The 'peculiar numbness' was something that Niemann did not explore further as he died in mysterious circumstances at the age of only 26. The brilliant young chemist was also working on an early form of mustard gas. He was fascinated by toxic substances – and paid the price, it seems.

After that there was a flurry of enthusiasm for the drug. The Italian neurologist and author of medically-themed fiction, Paolo Mantegazza, wrote lyrically:

'...I sneered at the poor mortals condemned to live in this valley of tears while I, carried on the wings of two leaves of coca, went flying through the spaces of 77,438 words, each more splendid than the one before... An hour later, I was sufficiently calm to write these words in a steady hand: God is unjust because He made man incapable of sustaining the effect of coca all life long. I would rather have a life span of ten years with coca than one of 10 000 000 (and here I have inserted a line of zeros) centuries without coca.'

53

Victorian businessmen seized the opportunity. Coca wines, cordials, ointments, lotions and potions were peddled as energetically as any snake oil. They were proposed as cures for constipation, blisters, insomnia, impotence and probably warts, too. Travellers took cocaine before crossing the English Channel as protection against seasickness. The journal *Chemist and Druggist* carried many reports of its wonders.

After reading Mantegazza's work on coca, the Corsican chemist Angelo Mariani concocted the first coca-wine, Vin Mariani, which became hugely popular. Mariani made effective use of celebrity testimonials; Thomas Edison, Émile Zola, Queen Victoria and three Popes all praised his product. Pope Leo XIII even presented Mariani with a gold medal 'in recognition of benefits received from the use of Mariani's tonic'. It obviously made His Holiness feel closer to God.

A rival brew, Metcalf's Coca Wine, was advertised to public speakers and singers because it 'strengthened the vocal chords'. Sex was a good selling point even in supposedly prim Victorian days as Metcalf added that, 'to the elderly it is a dependable aphrodisiac superior to any other drug.'

Cocaine was sold not just as an aphrodisiac and tonic, but touted by some as offering a path to spiritual enlightenment. By the late 1860s the Victorians were keen on spiritualism and contacting 'the other side'. The French writer Judith Gautier explored cocaine's alleged 'spiritual side' with the following perfect drivel:

I had only to taste a drop of your wine magical
To become an Inca priestess fantastical
And recite the verses liturgical
Coca yhamuspa sachamanta
Cutichin hinti guagtaste
Yathun socoyock hui
Napipa huinnaimincama

Coca wines and cordials were sold openly and legally, for by 1860 the sale of just one drug was restricted in Britain – arsenic. After a spate of murders, the Arsenic Act forced chemists to record every sale of the substance and the identity of all its buyers. The British domestic murderer was not going to be inhibited by bureaucracy and started to use other drugs to kill off unwanted spouses. In May 1868, when it was discovered prussic acid and strychnine were effective murder weapons, the Pharmaceutical Society introduced a bill in the House of Lords that would allow the sale of such powerful drugs only on prescription. The bill was defeated because it limited traditional British freedom but as a concession, twenty drugs were added to the Arsenic Act and their sales controlled. Neither cocaine nor any opiate was numbered amongst these twenty.

Cocaine also became the first widely-used performance-enhancing drug in sport. The first recorded athletic coca leaf chewers were members of the Toronto Lacrosse Club. A Canadian doctor noted that the members of the club, all men, 'were of sturdy build' and that at the end of a stifling hot day – he recorded the temperature as 110 F – they were still enthusiastically flinging the lacrosse ball all over the field. Their opponents, who had not chewed cocaine, however, were 'thoroughly exhausted' and could hardly be 'roused to take part in concluding the game' while the Toronto Chewers 'were as elastic and as apparently free from fatigue as at the commencement of play.'

There was also a vogue for what we would now call 'extreme sports' such as super marathons. Runners tried to run over 100 miles in 24 hours. One champion 'pedestrian', as they were called, was Edward Weston (1839–1899) who wrote for the *New York Herald*. In one race, Weston kept walking for 22 out of 24 hours and managed 17 hours without stopping. He then paused for two hours before hitting the road again. By way of sustenance, Weston drank tea, coffee, egg yolks and Liebig's Extract of Meat, a bouillon which is still available today but which then was laced with a soupçon of coca. To keep his spirits up Weston also chewed coca leaves.

Some races lasted a whole week. An American doctor, Edward Palmer, described a race in which six women kept running for seven days. On day six, he noticed a 17-year-old runner, L.C., was on the verge of collapse. He gave her a bracing glass of Fraser's Wine of Coca. L.C. then shrugged off her sprained ankle and finished 350 miles in just under seven days.

The first systematic studies of the effects of cocaine on athletic performance were performed in Edinburgh. Sir Robert Christison, the president of the Scottish Medical Association, experimented on students around 1875. His subjects, who had taken very little strenuous exercise for five months, walked for 16 miles and came back exhausted. They were starving, but Christison persuaded them to take 'an infusion of two drachms of cuca' – he spelled coca *cuca* as a number of authors did – in place of food. Thereafter: 'all sense of fatigue soon vanished, and they proceeded to promenade Princes Street for an hour; which they did with ease and pleasure.' They got home where they finally ate well, slept well 'and next morning – awoke quite refreshed and active.'   .

Christison then tested coca on himself. His report is a model of meticulous introspective research and self-observation, taken to the extreme of analysing his own urine and stools every two hours. He walked fifteen miles in four stages, with intervals of half an hour, at a four-mile pace, ending with a stage of six miles. He ended the walk 'as effectually tired out as I remember ever to have been in my life, even after thirty miles at a stretch forty or fifty years before.' Four days later he repeated the ordeal but with one essential difference, 'during the last forty-five minutes of the second rest I chewed thoroughly eighty grains of my best specimen of cuca, reserving forty grains more for use during the last stage.'

The coca worked its magic once again. Christison was surprised 'to find that all sense of weariness had entirely fled, and that I could proceed not only with ease, but even with elasticity.' He walked six miles in 90 minutes and found 'it easy when done to get up a four-and-a-half mile pace, and to ascend quickly two steps at a time to my dressing-room, two floors upstairs: in short, had no sense of fatigue or other uneasiness whatsoever. During the last stage, I perspired as profusely as during the two previous walks.' His pulse fell to a normal 72 two hours later 'the excitement of the circulation being thus much less, and its subsidence more rapid, than after the same amount of exercise without cuca.' He found his 'urine-solids' were normal, so he had a hearty dinner and slept soundly. He woke up 'free from all sense of fatigue, and from all other uneasiness.' He also discovered he could read more easily than he had done for years and decided to keep what remained of his cuca, or coca, for a trial he would conduct during his autumn holidays.

On September 15th, Christison climbed to the top of Ben Vorlich which rises 3224 feet above the sea. The last 700 feet, he wrote, 'were very steep.' He got to the top without feeling tired and repeated the climb eight days later. Climbing 3224 feet is not that remarkable a feat in itself, for a strapping young mountaineer: but Christison was 78 years old when he reached the top of the mountain.

The far more celebrated pioneer of introspective research in psychology, William James, did not take cocaine but nitrous oxide. James was more spiritually inclined than Davy and found that 'the keynote of the experience is the tremendously exciting sense of an intense metaphysical illumination. Truth lies open to the view in depth beneath depth of almost blinding evidence. The mind sees all the logical relations of being with an apparent subtlety and instantaneity to which its normal consciousness offers no parallel.'

James is worth quoting at some length:

'The centre and periphery of things seem to come together. The ego and its objects, the *meum and the tuum*, are one. Now this, only a thousand-fold enhanced, was the effect upon me of the gas.'

James felt a sense of 'a higher unity in which it is based; that all contradictions, so-called, are of a common kind; that unbroken continuity is of the essence of being; and that we are literally in the midst of an infinite'. As with Baudelaire on hashish, all differences and distinctions seemed to disappear. James found he had written:

'... sheet after sheet of phrases ... during the intoxication, which to the sober reader seem meaningless drivel, but which at the moment of transcribing were fused in the fire of infinite rationality. God and devil, good and evil, life and death, I and thous, sober and drunk, matter and form, black and white, quantity and quality, shiver of ecstasy and shudder of horror, vomiting and swallowing, inspiration and expiration, fate and reason, great and small, extent and intent, joke and earnest, tragic and comic, and fifty other contrasts figure in these pages in the same monotonous way. The mind saw how each term belonged to its contrast through a knife-edge moment of transition which it effected, and which, perennial and eternal, was the nunc stans' or the now it stands of life.'

James offered examples of a few jumbled sentences that seemed very profound under the influence. They were:

'What's mistake but a kind of take?
What's nausea but a kind of -usea?
Sober, drunk, -unk, astonishment.
Everything can become the subject of criticism –
How criticise without something to criticise?
Agreement – disagreement!!
Emotion – motion!!!!
By God, how that hurts! By God, how it doesn't hurt!
Reconciliation of two extremes.
By George, nothing but othing!
That sounds like nonsense, but it is pure onsense!
Thought deeper than speech ... !
Medical school; divinity school, school! SCHOOL!
Oh my God, oh God; oh God!'

The most coherent sentence was: 'There are no differences but differences of degree between different degrees of difference and no difference.' Then, James found himself gripped by a 'sense of a dreadful and ineluctable fate.' He found the change 'from rapture to horror is, perhaps, the strongest emotion I have ever experienced.'

Extensive 'objective' studies were conducted in parallel with these introspective exercises. Five years after Christison had climbed Ben Vorlich, the German physiologist, Theodore Aschenbrandt applied for a post as surgeon to the Bavarian army. The infantry would be his experimental animals. In 1883 he gave tired soldiers cocaine while they were on manoeuvres. Napoleon would have been delighted by the results.

The coked-up infantryman was a superior fighting machine. He had endless energy, hardly noticed pain and could carry on fighting far longer than normal. Aschenbrandt reported on 6 cases in the *Archiv für die Gesammte Therapie*, a leading medical journal. Case LT, for example, was that of a volunteer who collapsed from exhaustion on the second day of a march. The weather was hot, the boots unbearable, the motivation poor.

Aschenbrandt gave LT one tablespoon of water with 20 drops of a cocaine solution and five minutes later, the soldier 'stood up of his own accord and travelled the distance to H, several kilometres, easily and cheerfully and with a pack on his back.' It was an impressive performance.

This was a turning point in both the history of cocaine and Freud's life. The young doctor who was often in trouble for not reporting for army duties read this article; intrigued by Aschenbrandt's results, he ordered his first gram of cocaine.

When Freud ordered the gram, he knew nothing of the man to whom we owe Coca-Cola. The father of all colas, John Pemberton, was badly wounded in the American civil war and suffered constant stomach pains thereafter. He turned to morphine, but did not like its effect, so when coca wines and cordials were advertised as a cure-all, he tried them, and found them far more to his taste. It seems that Pemberton disliked the narcotic and sedating effects of opiates but enjoyed cocaine's euphoric stimulation.

Freud hoped cocaine would bring him fame and fortune. Pemberton had much the same ambition. In 1885 he launched 'Pemberton's French Wine Coca', which he advertised as an 'intellectual beverage' and 'invigorator of the brain'. He faced a problem, though: the alcoholic content of the brew. The rise of the Temperance movement in America made it harder to sell a drink containing alcohol, so he created a 'temperance' cola. This new concoction tasted too bitter, so he added sugar, resulting in a vile sickly-sweet taste. Pemberton poured in some citric acid and finally made a palatable drink.

But Pemberton was still not satisfied, so he converted a large part of his house into a chemical laboratory which had, according to his nephew an 'enormous filter made of matched flooring, wide at the top and narrowing to the base'. This was built through the floor of a second-storey room and filled with Chattahoochee River-washed sand. The ingredients for Coca-Cola were poured into the top of this filter and 'treacled through the several wagon loads of washed sand into a metal trough.'

Pemberton sent samples of every new cola to the soda fountain at the local pharmacy and told his nephews to report people's comments. One day, two businessmen visited, hoping to persuade him to invest in a new colour printing machine. They ended up instead investing themselves in the 'Pemberton Chemical Company'. His assistant, Frank Robinson put the names of the two most important ingredients in the drink together and called it: Coca-Cola (the cola or kola nut being a source of caffeine).

Robinson convinced Pemberton to pay for advertising, designed the classic lettering for Coca-Cola and insisted on extravagances such as giving out free drink coupons and putting advertisements on streetcars. The drink began to sell extremely well. Pemberton did not have long to enjoy his triumph as he became very ill but he remained obsessed with perfecting the Coca-Cola formula. His last variation was to add – it sounds disgusting – celery extract.

While Pemberton was putting the final touches on his cola, an American doctor, W.H. Bentley, made sensational claims for cocaine. In the *Therapeutic Gazette*, he announced he had cured six alcoholics and opium addicts by giving them cocaine. In 1880 a Dr Peckham reported two cures with cocaine, the first a case of tuberculosis and the second of a five-year-old boy with swollen joints.

The year after, G.H. Gray wrote also in the *Therapeutic Gazette* of two cases in which cocaine had been given to opium addicts. In the first case, a 25-year-old man became 'the happiest man in the state' once he took cocaine. In the second, a 34-year-old woman who suffered from emaciation and depression was given three to six drachms of cocaine daily and her condition improved. These accounts persuaded many doctors cocaine might have serious therapeutic possibilities. Freud would be one of them.

Chapter 5

The Clever Student

By the time that he was ten, Freud had suffered an unusual number of family traumas. It is tempting to argue that his formidable intelligence allowed him to cope with the resulting pain and chaos, but there is less evidence of that than one might expect. Psychologists have not examined the question of how intelligence affects personality as much as they perhaps should have done. The best recent study was by Naomi Breslau, who in 2006 studied 718 children who were then aged 17. She researched their histories and compared how many traumatic factors they had faced by the time they were six years old, their IQ scores and their performance later on widely accepted measures of post-traumatic stress syndrome. IQ scores of 115 (which is well above average) or higher did seem to protect children somewhat from the worst consequences of trauma.

Breslau argued that the low incidence of post-traumatic stress disorder among more intelligent children could be linked to better strategies for coping with difficult life events. It is 'the way that people explain to themselves what happened to them, how it fits in with their lives, whether it is their fault or not their fault, whether they can get over it and perform some task,' Breslau added. 'There is no question that there are cognitive aspects with the disorder.' A study of 105 Vietnam veterans also found that intelligent soldiers were less susceptible to post-traumatic stress. The evidence, however, is inconclusive and Joan Freeman, who has made a number of studies of gifted children, suggests their very gifts mean they need subtle and sensitive handling by their parents.

In 1867, Freud passed what may have been the most important examination of his life, winning him admission to the 'Gymnasium' in the Sperlgasse, near his home. The Gymnasium was one of a small

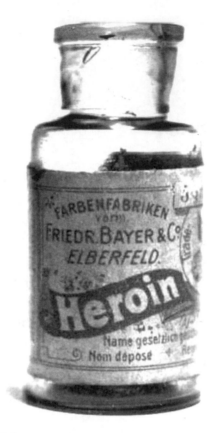

Am. J. Ph.]   7   [December, 1901

BAYER Pharmaceutical Products
HEROIN—HYDROCHLORIDE

is pre-eminently adapted for the manufacture
of cough elixirs, cough balsams, cough drops,
cough lozenges, and cough medicines of any
kind.   Price in 1 oz. packages, $4.85 per
ounce; less in larger quantities. The efficient dose being very small (1-48 to 1-24 gr.),
it is

The Cheapest Specific for the Relief of Coughs

(In bronchitis, phthisis, whooping cough, etc., etc.)

WRITE FOR LITERATURE TO

FARBENFABRIKEN OF ELBERFELD COMPANY

SELLING AGENTS

P. O. Box 2160   40 Stone Street, NEW YORK

Like cocaine, heroin was openly on sale in 1901.

number of elite schools set up by the Kaiser to prepare the cleverest boys in his Empire for university.

We know a good deal about Freud's schooldays, thanks to Hugo Knopfmacher, whose father was in the same class as Freud. Hugo's unpublished essay on Freud at school is revealing because it shows it was a turbulent time for him, again, something Freud never discussed in any of his writings.

At school Freud became involved in a scandal. He was called as a witness when the school wanted to expel two pupils for visiting 'coffeehouses of ill repute and seeing prostitutes'. If Freud was called as a witness, he must have known what the older boys were doing, which suggests he at least accompanied them to the coffeehouses. It is the earliest indication of his taste for taking risks.

Near the end of his school days Freud was given a very flattering assessment of his abilities as a writer when one of his professors told him that he had an outstanding literary style. Freud wrote to his friend Emil Fluss:

'I was suitably impressed by this amazing fact and do not hesitate to disseminate the happy event, the first of its kind, as widely as possible– to you, for instance, who until now have probably remained unaware that you have been exchanging letters with a German stylist ... preserve them [the letters] – have them bound – take good care of them – one never knows.'

One critic has suggested this letter shows the extent of Freud's vanity. There is another possible reading, however. Freud was surprised by 'this happy event, the first of its kind' because no one outside his family had previously told him he might have exceptional talents. It was not so strange that he went on to weave a teenage fantasy of fame from such praise.

By that point, he needed to find cause for faith in himself and his future. In 1873, his father, Jacob Freud lost nearly all his savings when the stock market crashed. The old man had a marked talent for bankruptcy. Ernest Jones never looked at the psychological consequences of that failure, which was the second time the family had faced economic calamity, yet they are not hard to imagine. Freud knew one could lose everything yet again, in an instant.

By 1873, Jacob was sixty while his wife was 38 years old. The business failure became far less of a figure of authority in his own family. The result of that became clear in a story Freud's sister Anna told in her memoirs, which did not see publication until the 1990s.

When she was 16 years old, an 'uncle' from Odessa on the Black Sea came to visit. (Amalie, Freud's mother, had lived in Odessa for a few years; the city had a large Jewish population.) The uncle fell in love with Anna and took her to see *William Tell* at the opera. Amalie had to accompany them as chaperone, while the uncle showered Anna with sweets and sweet-talk. He then proposed marriage. Her would–be husband can't really have been an uncle proper as that would have made the proposed marriage incestuous, but he was clearly some kind of distant relative.

Anna spent a sleepless night picturing her future as a rich wife in Odessa. In the morning, she went to talk to her mother, who was excited by the idea but insisted she discuss the proposal, not with her husband but with Sigmund, Anna's brother, who had not yet turned 18.

'Sigmund was less than delighted,' Anna recalled, 'and explained to mother and me what was involved when a man of 59 [as this uncle was] wanted to marry a girl of 16.' The cradle-snatching 'uncle' was sent back to Odessa on his own. Oedipus killed his father and slept with his mother. Freud did neither, but he assumed, at a young age, the authority that should have belonged to his father. Within the family home, Freud had more than enough self-confidence to act as patriarch. But in the wider world, he was very different.

A year after he had dispatched the 'uncle' back to Odessa, Freud went to the University of Vienna. Freud was now in a setting where his intelligence mattered more than anything else. He dreamed first of becoming a lawyer. We can trace much of his development in his student days through letters he wrote to his friend Eduard Silberstein, the first of many confidants-by-correspondence, on whom Freud seems to have been somewhat dependent. In the context of Freud's later cravings, one letter in particular is of interest. Long before he used either cocaine or cigars, Freud had another habit suggestive of an oral fixation. He often took long walks and was in the habit of eating and chewing grasses and even the bark of trees. He wrote to his friend Silberstein that he was a 'seasoned eater of leaves and branches'.

Most of the letters between the two teenagers display a cerebral love of the absurd and nonsense-games. They wrote to each other in Spanish, the language, as it happens, of the Conquistadors, pretending they were dogs, who were, for some reason, in a hospital at the University of Seville. Freud was called 'Cipion' and Silberstein 'Berganza'. Freud signed himself off as 'p.e.e.h.d.s peerp en el hospital de Seville', or 'dog at the hospital of Seville'. In these canine personas, the boys revelled in their humour, the more silly and erudite the better.

In one letter Freud notes that the English writer Carlyle 'makes fun of us brooding Germans'. Carlyle invented a certain Professor Diogenes Teufelsdrocke (which can be translated as 'Diogenes Devil Shit') who gloried in the title of 'Professor Of Things in General at the University of Weissnichtwo' (which can be translated as the University of I've No Idea Where). At this celebrated academy, Freud wrote, Diogenes was writing an utterly essential thesis on the philosophy of clothes (a reference to Carlyle's *Sartor Resartus*, a satirical book that compared intellectual and sartorial fashions, mercilessly attacking Hegel's philosophical idealism).

In another letter Freud made extravagant fun of the link between religion and food, saying 'religion consumed in moderation stimulates the digestion but taken in excess, it harms it.' Freud blamed Passover 'for having a constipating effect due to unleavened bread and hard-boiled eggs.' Yom Kippur, the Jewish Day of Atonement, was 'lugubrious' but not because God is angry or exhausted at listening to so many pleas for forgiveness, but because Jews have to eat plum jam and plum jam helps, as ads today put it coyly, 'with digestive transport.' Freud noted 'the evacuation it stimulates'. Christian clergy were fat because they never had any religious obligation to scoff plum jam. Freud never lost his love of such scatological humour. Twenty years later, he wrote whimsically of papers in the exact science of 'Drek-studien', as he put it, which translates literally as 'shit-ology'.

The letters between Freud and Silberstein are also full of gossip about their acquaintances, which is of biographical interest, as two of the men who were to be of considerable importance in Freud's life; Josef Herzig and Ignaz Rosannes, were amongst their circle. Herzig and Freud bought a skeleton together and scribbled their names on it, behaviour rather typical of medical students.

Such high-jinks are also typical of extroverted personalities. Extroverts love risk and seeking new sensations. Risk-takers, Hans Eysenck argued, score much higher than average on the personality trait known as extroversion; though he was a sworn opponent of psychoanalysis in all its forms, Eysenck always acknowledged that the concepts of the introvert and extrovert were taken from Jung, Freud's disciple-turned-apostate. There was a biological reason for this, Eysenck argued; extroverts have lower cortical arousal and so need far more stimulation to keep their brains working at a comfortable speed. This makes them seek novelty and new sensations. The extrovert's cortex finds regularity and predictability unpleasant and stifling. New experiences might lead to unpredictable consequences but, as such, provide stimulation. Extroverts are often just as anxious about taking risks as anyone else, but the reward of experiencing something new more than compensates for that. Freud not only had the traumatic childhood experiences common to many addicts, but he was a lover of novelty and discovery.

These extroverted, risk-loving, sensation-seeking aspects of Freud's personality were kept under control in the classroom, as he worked under a stern teacher he greatly admired, Ernst Brücke. In 1847, Brücke and two other gifted young scientists, Helmholtz and du Bois Reymond formed the Berlin Physicalist Society. They outlined their aims in a letter:

> '... no other forces than the common physical-chemical ones are active within the organism. In those cases which cannot at the time be explained by these forces one has either to find the specific way or form of their Action by means of the physical-mathematical method, or to assume new forces equal in dignity to the chemical-physical forces inherent in matter, reducible to the forces of attraction and repulsion.'

The new scientific physiology would not resort to mystical or metaphysical explanations. In 1855, Brücke became professor of physiology in Vienna. He made a lasting impression on Freud, as he admitted in the short autobiography he wrote in 1925. (Freud for once did not object when he was asked to contribute to a series in which famous doctors outlined their careers).

In Brücke's laboratory, Freud said, he 'found rest and satisfaction ... Brücke gave me a problem to work out in the histology of the nervous system; I succeeded in solving it to his satisfaction and in carrying the work further on my own account'. But his mentor was exacting; once he was due to start work early in the morning but: 'It came to Brücke's ears that I sometimes reached the students' laboratory late. One morning he turned up punctually at the hour of opening and awaited my arrival. His words were brief and to the point. But what he said was not important; what overwhelmed me were the terrible blue eyes with which he gazed at me and before which I perished...' (*On the Interpretation of Dreams,* page 422.)

Extroverts are usually more productive if they have to function in a well-defined structure. Brücke's laboratory provided one for Freud who published three promising scientific papers under his tutelage. After a few years with Brücke, Freud had become a world-class expert on the eel.

In his first paper, Freud showed that some cells in the eel's spinal cord evolve to form the posterior root ganglions in their brains. His second paper described the structure of a lobe-shaped organ, which is essential to the eel's sex life. His third paper described the medulla oblongata and how its nerve tracts connected with the cerebellum, a structure in the oldest part of the brain that helps animals maintain their sense of balance. His work might have been serious but Freud was always quipping and noted to Hugo's father, William Knopfmacher, his school friend: 'During these holidays I have moved into another laboratory, where I am preparing myself for my real profession.' He defined this as the 'flaying of animals or torturing of human beings, and I find myself more and more in favour of the former.'

Perhaps the greatest risk Freud took involved direct defiance of the authorities – and has been mostly ignored by his biographers. Like all young Austrian men of the period, he had to serve time in the army, but did not take his military duties seriously. Eight times he failed to turn up for service and, eventually, he was arrested for being absent without leave. It could have ruined his career. Freud never explained why he was so reckless in this regard, which presented real dangers, especially to a young Jew. Such recklessness would also affect his relationship with one of his teachers.

At the university, Freud attended classes in philosophy taught by Franz Brentano, whose work is still read today, and seminars in Higher Mathematics for Medical Students and Physiology, given by Ernst Fleischl. The latter would become the most tragic victim of Freud's Cocaine Episode, though his drug problems pre-dated his acquaintance with Freud.

Fleischl, twelve years Freud's senior, was the nephew of a famous physiologist. After graduating in 1870, Fleischl went to work for a professor of pathology, Carl von Rokitansky, and became his chief assistant. Photographs show Fleischl as an intense young man with staring eyes and the inevitable thick beard; he also favoured bow ties.

Then Fleischl suffered a terrible accident. While performing an autopsy, his thumb became so badly infected that it had to be amputated. But complications followed the operation, resulting in the growth of nerves around the amputation site that caused Fleischl continuous and unbearable pain – and there were few options available to ease it. The best, of course, was the archetypal opiate, morphine. Fleischl knew its dangers but was in desperate need of pain relief and, inevitably, he became addicted to regular injections of the drug. For all the progress we have seen in medicine since Fleischl's day, the opiates are still by far the most effective painkillers.

Following his accident, Fleischl returned to Vienna and was employed as one of Brücke's chief assistants. Lacking one thumb, Fleischl could not perform autopsies and concentrated on studying the electrical activity of the brain, a field which saw great advances in the 1870s as physiologists electrically stimulated human cortical tissue for the first time. He invented new equipment that made more accurate measurements of changes in the brain possible and proved that particular stimuli evoked small electrical changes in the cortex. Despite his pain, Fleischl's productivity was quite astonishing. He described the connections of the optic nerve and worked on the structure of the eye, also developing a haemotometer to measure the amount of haemoglobin in the blood. For light relief, he spent his evenings learning Sanskrit.

Luck plays a part in the lives of many scientists. In 1879, when Freud was still a medical student, one of the world's most famous hypnotists came to play the Ringtheater in Vienna. The Dane Carl Hansen (1833–1897) did not consider himself a mere entertainer and those who went to see his act included the philosopher Brentano, Josef Breuer and Wilhelm Wundt, who came all the way from Leipzig where he had just set up his psychology laboratory to rival William James'. Freud went to see the show with Josef Breuer.

To magnetise a subject, Hansen would make him stare for a while at a glittering piece of glass, stroke his cheeks and close his eyes and mouth. Then 'he would command him to do the most ridiculous acts,' according to Gauld's *A History of Hypnotism*. Hansen would make his hypnotised subject assume cataleptic postures, telling them to lie down and be 'a human plank'. The subject would then be unable to move or speak, until instructed to arise and sing, or to engage in 'preposterous pantomimes'. The routines often included eating a raw potato, believing it to be a pear and drinking imaginary champagne. The bubbles were unreal, and they imbibed no alcohol, but the hypnotised subjects still behaved as though drunk.

Hansen attracted huge audiences and made a great impression on the public, but the Vienna police were troubled by his displays, and consulted experts at the university. As a result, Hansen was forbidden to continue performing in the city. But Freud had seen the power of hypnosis and suggestion and it left a lasting impression.

On May 6th 1880 Freud celebrated his 24th birthday in less than ideal circumstances. He had been arrested again for avoiding military duty. He managed to talk his way out of facing formal charges of desertion and returned to work at the university. By now Freud's letters to Silberstein show that Freud knew his physiology teacher Fleischl well. And Fleischl became something of a hero to him.

Fleischl was promoted to a full professorship in 1880 at the age of only 34. Like many medicinal opiate addicts, his drug use does not seem to have impeded his professional advancement. In one of his letters to Silberstein, Freud wrote that Fleischl was an admirable man. That was true enough, but Freud was less than objective on the subject. He did not tell Silberstein that the admirable man had started to lend him money.

One of the most quoted lines from Freud's beloved Hamlet is the advice Polonius gives to his son Laertes:

'Neither a borrower nor a lender be.'

Freud ignored Polonius' advice for something like twenty years, borrowing money from his father, from his future sister-in-law, from Fleischl, from Breuer, from a certain Baron Sp and probably from commercial money-lenders. Freud complained constantly of his poverty but that did not stop him spending freely on books, French lessons and restaurants; he hardly ever ate at home. He was not frugal, even when impoverished as an adult – perhaps this relative profligacy was a form of 'rebellion' against his fear of poverty or perhaps, simple denial of the fact that he *was* poor.

On June 6th 1880, Fleischl was one of the official examiners Freud faced in tests on botany, biology and chemistry. Freud's performance in these exams was rated excellent. This was a vital step before Freud could qualify as a doctor. As in his childhood, Freud was in the midst of traumas – poverty, problems with the law, and now a crucial examination he had to pass. He was frustrated and anxious. It was at this point that he started to smoke.

In his answers to the smoking survey, which has lain hidden in the Arentz Collection of the New York Public Library since 1929, Freud said 'I believe I owe to the cigar a great intensification of my capacity to work and a facilitation of self-control.' Tobacco was an indispensable prop as he worked; he wrote and smoked, he thought and smoked. He was unwell if he did not get his daily nicotine which is, after all, a stimulant. Many writers have joined Freud in using nicotine this way: the popular and prolific novelist Stephen King has said his daily word count dropped by 50% after he quit smoking.

When Freud finally qualified as a doctor in 1881, it did not change his life immediately. In his autobiographical study, he wrote that he felt no special calling for the profession and that he wanted to pursue his research on brain anatomy which had given him 'satisfaction', but he was not Brücke's only exceptional student. There were only two paid research posts in the laboratory, so Brücke advised Freud to switch to clinical medicine. His father's 'improvidence' did not give Freud many options. In the next few years Freud had to take a variety of jobs, many of them part-time. On July 31st he started to work at the Vienna General Hospital as an assistant surgeon under Theodor Billroth but stayed in the position for only two months. In October 1882 he went to work in the department of Dermatology, where he continued until early 1884, then moving to the department of Nervous Diseases.

We know less than we might wish about this period in Freud's life, as his letters to Silberstein petered out around this time. From 1879 to 1882 Freud did not have a trusted correspondent, and it was often in his letters that he revealed himself most fully. But he was to find a far more intimate companion, in correspondence and otherwise, in April 1882.

Freud came to his parents' apartment one evening to find his sisters had a guest, a 22-year-old woman, Martha Bernays. Martha's brother was courting his sister Anna. Freud's friend Ignaz Schönberg was courting Martha's sister Minna. It was a close group of friends. When Freud first caught sight of Martha, she was peeling an apple. She was petite, attractive, intelligent and rather reserved.

Freud fell in love with her and pursued her with a kind of demonic energy. For once Freud did not lack confidence, especially when Martha responded to him quickly. A few days after they met, she squeezed his hand under a table. Two months later, against the wishes of her rather snobbish family, they were engaged.

On the face of it, Emmeline Bernays, Martha's mother, had some reason to be snobbish about the Freuds. Freud's father was a failed businessman. True, Freud was a doctor but he had few prospects and

71

virtually no patients. Working at the Vienna Hospital, he discovered he had no great talent for surgery. Martha's family, on the other hand, was distinguished. Her uncle Jacob Bernays had been one of the leading Biblical scholars of the mid 19th century. Her grandfather, Isaac Bernays, had been Chief Rabbi of Hamburg, and a friend of the great writer Heinrich Heine.

But appearances were deceptive. There were a number of scandals in the Bernays family too. Like uncle Josef, Martha's father, Berman Bernays, was not a man to trust with one's money. He was a merchant and also worked in advertising but in 1866 he was convicted of embezzlement and spent at least a year in jail. When Sigmund met Martha, the forger's nephew fell in love with the embezzler's daughter. Berman Bernays died in 1879, before the young couple met, but his widow had a selective memory and pretended her husband had been a paragon of prudence; she was appalled when Martha fell in love with a man who could not offer her financial security.

Freud was desperate to impress Martha's mother and set out to make new friends, connections and more money. He courted Josef Breuer, with whom he had gone to see the hypnotist Hansen. At the age of 38, Breuer was a successful doctor with a large private practice. He was Jewish but, again, secularised and modern in outlook. While working with Breuer, Freud became involved for the first time with the regular use of morphine. The case of Anna O is the first, and still one of the most controversial, in the history of psychoanalysis.

Anna O was 21 years old when Breuer first met her in 1880. Her real name was Bertha Pappenheim and she turned out to be a friend of Martha Bernays. Anna had spent a great deal of time nursing her father through serious illness. She clearly found this trying as she began to present a veritable smorgasbord of symptoms; she had difficulties speaking, sometimes even becoming mute, at other times talking only in English, rather than her native German. She suffered from facial neuralgia and sometimes from temporary paralysis, and was prescribed morphine, something neither Breuer nor Freud were wholly frank about in writing of her case. Anna O was a morphine addict from the time her proto-psychoanalytic treatment began and it could be argued that every symptom she manifested was a consequence of this addiction and intoxication.

When her father died in 1881 Anna's symptoms became more distressing, if slightly less peculiar, given Victorian fashions in hysterical behaviour. She refused to eat, lost all feeling in her hands and feet, developed some paralysis, and went into involuntary spasms. She suffered visual hallucinations and dramatic mood swings and made several suicide attempts. But neither Breuer nor any other doctor could find any physical causes for her symptoms.

Anna was no helpless damsel in distress, and she was formidably intelligent. In the evenings, she would sink into states of what Breuer called 'spontaneous hypnosis'; Anna herself called these episodes 'clouds.' In these trance-like states, she could explain her day-time fantasies, and felt better once she had done so. Anna sometimes spoke of these episodes as 'chimney sweeping' and, according to some, referred to this as 'the talking cure.' Anna has, in fact, some claim to have invented aspects of psychoanalysis 15 years before Freud formalised them in his writings, and to an extent she pioneered his introspective methods, by examining her own fantasies. The analyst can be seen as a chimney sweeper who removes the dirt and soot clogging the mind or, to use a German word that Freud was fond of, the *drek*.

These story-telling, chimney-sweeping episodes are strongly reminiscent of the behaviour of the morphine-addicted mother character in Eugene O'Neill's autobiographical play *Long Day's Journey into Night*, and may have had their roots in opiate intoxication. The role played by the drug in this 'first psychoanalytic case study' was understood by neither Freud nor Breuer, it seems: Anna's 'hysterical symptoms' may in fact have been no more than pipedreams.

At times, during her 'chimney sweeping' episodes, Anna would remember an emotional event that turned out to be charged with significance. Soon after she had refused to drink water, for example, she recalled seeing a woman drink from a glass after a dog had just lapped from it. It disgusted her to recollect this, but having done so, she went on to have a drink of water. Her symptom – refusing to drink –

seemed to have disappeared as soon as she remembered the event that had triggered it.

In this way, Anna flushed out symptom after symptom, but she could not do it alone. Whenever she was in one of her hypnotic states, she had to feel Breuer's hands before she said anything. Only Breuer's hands would trigger this effect. Freud wrote that Breuer recognised Anna had fallen in love with him. Even worse, the doctor was falling in love with his patient. Anna was soon telling everyone that she was pregnant with Breuer's child – a wholly hysterical pregnancy. This was the first recorded case of 'transference', that strange process by which the patient falls in love with the analyst, and of 'counter-transference', the equally strange process in which the analyst reciprocates.

Ernest Jones realised this was an important moment for the development of psychoanalysis, as it was Anna's hysterical pregnancy that first alerted Freud to the dangers of transference. Breuer 'fled the house in a cold sweat' when he realised Anna had fallen in love with him. The next day he and his wife left for Venice, according to Jones, but yet again 'Freud's wizard' did not get the story quite right. They in fact went to Gmunden in Austria.

Breuer was never entirely honest about the treatment Anna received. In July 1882, before running off, Breuer took Anna to the Bellevue clinic at Kreuzlingen. Breuer, terrified by her love for him, forgot hypnosis and the subtleties of the talking cure. Instead he ordered Anna to be sedated with high doses of morphine and rushed away. At the age of 26 and with no patients of his own, Freud was in no position to object. He did, however, give a fuller account in a letter to Stefan Zweig years later:

'I was in a position to guess what really happened with Br's [*Br stands for Breuer*] patient long after we parted company when I recalled a communication from Br dating from the time before our joint work and relating to another context, and which he never repeated. That evening, after all her symptoms were overcome, he was again called to her, and found her confused and writhing with abdominal cramps. When asked what was the matter she responded, "Now the child I have from Dr Br.

is coming". At that moment he had in his hand the key which would open the way to the Mothers, but he dropped it.'

By the time Freud wrote to Zweig, he was determined to ensure that Breuer would not be seen as the 'real creator' of psychoanalysis. Many have since called Anna O/Bertha Pappenheim 'the mother of psychoanalysis'. Freud's own reference to 'the Mothers' was a mythological flourish, invoking the Furies of Ancient Greece, and the mother of Cupid's child, a human woman, by the name of 'Psyche'.

Freud went on to criticise Breuer: 'With all his intellectual talents he was devoid of anything Faustian. He took flight in conventional horror and passed on the patient to a colleague. She struggled for months in a sanatorium to regain her health. I was so sure of my reconstruction that I published it somewhere.'

Four months after Freud and Martha met, Martha's mother moved to Wandsbek near Hamburg, taking Martha with her, in a deliberate attempt to keep the young couple apart. On July 16th Freud went to see Martha in her new home and they celebrated her 21st birthday together. It is very likely they discussed Anna's treatment. After their engagement, Freud and Martha wrote to each other constantly. Their letters give a vivid impression of the young Freud; he is ambitious, passionate, driven, but also anxious and insecure. On August 18th, he wrote to her: 'Without you I would let my arms droop for sheer lack of desire to live'.

The Bernays family would find it hard to object to Freud too strenuously as on October 14th, Eli Bernays, Martha's brother and Anna Freud, Sigmund's eldest sister, married. Typically, Freud could not afford to go to the wedding. Two weeks later he wrote to Martha that her friend Anna was doing well in the clinic. In her reply Martha was unusually critical and said 'it has often been on the tip of my tongue to ask you why Breuer gave up Bertha.' Freud replied enigmatically that he and Breuer 'were intimate personal and very familiar, and he (Breuer) told me many things' – some of them which he could not reveal till he and Martha were married.

Anna O was, like a number of the early analytic patients, a substantial, gifted personality. She managed to wean herself off morphine by the end of 1882 and studied nursing. As Bertha Pappenheim, she became one of the founders of modern social work in Europe, establishing a network of orphanages for girls rescued from prostitution, and also published a number of books for children. She is regarded as a pioneering feminist socialist, and an eloquent opponent of early Zionism. It is worth remembering that modern surgery, psychoanalysis and social work were all partly invented by morphine and cocaine addicts.

In December Freud gave Martha a plain garnet engagement ring. It was, the later Freud would have insisted, no accident that a few weeks later, Freud broke the ring Martha had given him in return.

For the next three years the question of when they could afford to get married obsessed him. Freud visited Wandsbek only four times and spent at most forty days with his fiancée over the next four years. Like many Victorian couples, their love involved endless letter writing.

It's intriguing to compare Freud's letters to Martha with his hero Charles Darwin's letters to his fiancée Emma in the late 1830s. Both men discussed their ideas with their betrotheds, but there were many differences between the two couples. When Emma and Darwin discussed where they would live, money was not a problem; the question was whether to rent a house in fashionable Kensington or equally fashionable Bloomsbury. Emma was also far more confident than Martha and, as a fervent Christian, questioned the religious implications of Darwin's ideas. By contrast, the only time Martha seems to have asked Freud a critical question was when she queried Breuer's treatment of Bertha/Anna O. Freud may have lacked self-confidence, but he did not lack self-awareness in all respects; he needed a wife who would not challenge him, and seems to have known it.

A number of dramas increased Freud's sense of insecurity at the time. His father was often unwell, and then on September 12th 1883, his friend Nathan Weiss hanged himself in a public bath.

In his autobiography, Freud stressed that as a Jew he expected to feel 'alien' in Vienna, He was also working in an academic world where the young had to defer to their seniors. But these factors don't entirely explain a certain tendency to submissiveness evident in Freud's relations with his medical colleagues. For all his intelligence, until he turned 45,

Freud seems to have been the dominant partner in only one professional relationship – that with Carl Koller, a fellow student at the university. It seems plausible that the many traumas and bereavements in Freud's life may have conditioned this clever young man to be so deferential. Jones never discussed this because he made little attempt to link the problems of Freud's childhood and youth with his subsequent career.

After the first romantic haze of their early correspondence, Freud also wrote to Martha about his work, the poor conditions at the Vienna Hospital and even of a new method to stain nerve fibres. Again, he was working as a conventional scientist. He used gold chloride to stain nerve fibres. The trick was first to harden the tissue in bichromate of potash and the process, Freud wrote, 'is finished by placing the specimen in alcohol; thin sections are cut by means of a microtome and washed in distilled water.' (Martha was assumed to understand all this). After three to five hours, the fibres 'show in a pink, deep purple, blue or even black colour, and are brought distinctly into view.' Freud had made the invisible visible.

Fleischl arranged for Freud's findings to be published in *Brain*, one of the world's leading neurology journals. If Freud had continued with his anatomical work, Jones argued he might easily have been the first man to describe the neuron theory of the central nervous system.

When Heinrich Waldeyer published his groundbreaking mono-graph in which he first coined the term 'neuron,' however, he ignored Freud's research. Ernest Jones wrote: 'It was not the only time that Freud narrowly missed world fame in early life through not daring to pursue his thoughts to their logical – and not far-off – conclusion.'

Publishing interesting papers had not led to what Freud desperately wanted, security – a proper job at the university and a decent salary. He seems to have needed endless reassurance from Martha. On February 14th, 1884, for example, he wailed in a letter: 'Do you realise it is two whole days since I heard from you and I am beginning to worry!'

He was waiting for something to turn up – and it did. Cocaine would be his salvation. He was all too ready to convince himself of its potential. He told Martha about it in a letter dated Saturday April 21st 1884 nine days before he first took cocaine. He wrote:

'I am also toying with a project and a hope which I will tell you about; perhaps nothing will come of this, either ... I have been reading about cocaine, the effective ingredient of coca leaves, which some Indian tribes chew in order to make themselves resistant to privation and fatigue.'

Freud added:

'I have now ordered some of it and for obvious reasons am going to try it out on cases of heart disease, then on nervous exhaustion, particularly in the awful condition following withdrawal of morphine (as in the case of Dr Fleischl). There may be any number of people experimenting on it already; perhaps it won't work. But I am certainly going to try it and, as you know, if one tries something often enough and goes on wanting it, one day it may succeed.' (13, pp. 107–108)

Freud went into very specific detail, telling Martha:

'My object has a specific name – it is called neuralgia or face ache. The question is whether I shall succeed in curing it ... I am so excited about it, for if it works I shall be sure for some time to come of attracting the attention so essential for getting on in the world. Everything we hope for would be there and Fleischl might even perhaps benefit from it. And even if it wasn't completely sensational something is bound to come from it.'

When Freud ordered his first gram from Merck, the company had become a key player in the increasingly lucrative cocaine business. Merck had established a plantation in Peru which sent 58,000 leaves to Europe in 1881 and more than ten times that amount just two years later. Exports rose to a dizzying 18,396,000 leaves by 1885. Merck even established coca leaf plantations in Java. To make sure Britain didn't fall behind, William Gladstone, Britain's Prime Minister, decided to import coca leaves into India; they were first grown in the botanical gardens in Calcutta. Cuttings were then sent to Ceylon so that tea planters could have a second crop. Like opium, cocaine was capital – even imperial – stuff.

And so we return to the night of 30th April 1884, *Walpurgisnacht*, when Freud first took cocaine. He swallowed the 1/20th of a gram and recorded: 'long intensive mental or physical work is performed without any fatigue ... This result is enjoyed without any of the unpleasant after-effects that follow exhilaration brought about by alcohol.'

Freud was feeling his way into a study utterly different from his work on eels or gold staining. He had started to introspect and did so in a modern way, looking at his own feelings and reactions, rather than the 'impoverished stimuli', in the words of William James, of triangles and nonsense syllables. He went on to gush, of the cocaine experience:

'One senses an increase of self-control and feels more vigorous and more capable of work; on the other hand, if one works, one misses that heightening of the mental powers which alcohol, tea, or coffee induce. One is simply normal, and soon finds it difficult to believe that one is under the influence of any drug at all.'

Crucially, Freud noted that 'absolutely no craving for the further use of cocaine appears after the first, or even after repeated taking of the drug; one feels rather a certain curious aversion to it.' Years later he told Ernest Jones he could detect no signs of craving for it in himself, however often he took it. Jones added that Freud 'was telling the strict truth: as we know now, it needs a special disposition to develop a drug addiction, and fortunately Freud did not possess that'. Jones did not specify what this special disposition was and totally ignored the question of whether Freud was addicted to cigars – or, indeed, whether the frequency of his cocaine use might undermine the 'strict truth' about Freud's lack of cravings.

Indeed, one curious aspect of Freud's cocaine use is this insistence upon an absence of cravings – where modern users often find cocaine to be, of all common recreational drugs, the substance most prone to cause violent, irresistible cravings the instant it starts to wear off. Self-deception may have played a part here, but there is also a key difference between Freud and modern cocaine users. Freud did not snort powdered cocaine or smoke cocaine base (crack), but took the drug orally. This, in contemporary drug parlance, provides less of a 'hit' – the drug, taken orally, is metabolised at a far slower rate than when snorted ('insufflated', in the jargon of pharmacology), and its effects last considerably longer than through the nasal route. Oral doses of cocaine hydrochloride produce a long-lasting effect more akin to the subtle but powerful stimulation of the coca leaf than the comparatively dramatic euphoria resulting from insufflation or injection of cocaine: the effects of which are far shorter in duration, and far more likely to result in cravings and addiction.

Freud's own oral preferences may thus have led him to underestimate the drug's dangers. Fleischl, however, certainly did have the 'special disposition' for addiction to cocaine as well as to morphine. The polymath who had often lent Freud money was to become a victim of Freud's enthusiasm for the drug, in quite spectacular fashion.

Chapter 6

Denial and the Damage Done

Freud's emotional life between 1882 and 1886 was dramatic and unstable. He pursued Martha, wrestled with poverty, had to cope with the suicide of a friend, Nathan Weiss, and tried to help the teacher he so admired and called his ideal – Ernst Fleischl. When he first wrote to Martha about Fleischl, he gave a very flattering portrait. 'He is a most distinguished man for whom both nature and upbringing have done their best,' Freud wrote. Fleischl was 'trained in all physical exercises, with the stamp of genius in his energetic features; handsome with fine feelings, gifted with all the talents. He has always been *my ideal* and I could not rest till we became friends and I could experience a pure joy in his ability and reputation.' (My italics)

From the start, Freud was not wholly honest with Martha as he was already worried by Fleischl's poor health and morphine use. Fleischl himself complained that he often felt weak. On November 5th 1882 he told Rudolf Eitelberger, the first full professor of the History of Art at the University of Vienna: 'I can say nothing else other than it goes really badly with me and I can't at the moment see when it will be better.'

Morphine clearly contributed to Fleischl's confusion and at times he seems to have been paranoid. Instead of publishing his findings on the physiology of the eye, he put the manuscript in a safe deposit at his bank and left instructions that it was only to be opened in 1883. No one has been able to provide a sensible explanation for this behaviour, so it seems likely that his drug use played its part.

Fleischl may have been gifted with 'all the talents' in Freud's eyes, but he had problems forming relationships with women: or at least, committing to them. Freud told Martha that Fleischl: 'has been engaged for ten to twelve years to someone of his own age who was very patient.

Freud, in his mid-thirties, at his most imposing.

She was willing to wait for him,' Freud told Martha. If the true reason for this prolonged indecision was that Fleischl had homosexual inclinations, Freud never suggested as much, but one of his letters to Martha included a most peculiar fantasy.

In his letter, Freud explained to Martha, whimsically, how the distinguished and wealthy Fleischl would make her very happy. She would take the place of his ever-patient fiancée and Fleischl would cease procrastinating and marry her – Martha – at once. Fleischl, Freud's ideal, would replace him as Martha's lover. This was a very odd game to play with his fiancée, and a rather unkind one, at that. A glib agony uncle might say Freud was testing the boundaries of Martha's love, but this teasing could well have been hurtful for Martha, despite the back-handed compliment that it implied. Freud then snapped back to reality, asserting that his own claim to Martha was superior and that she remained 'his own.'

In reality, Fleischl was finding it harder and harder to manage. In August 1883 Brücke wrote that Fleischl, 'the poor boy' was in a wretched state. Although he continued working, his morphine intake seems to have increased around this time, suggesting that the pain was growing worse: or perhaps that Fleischl's tolerance to the drug had become so great that he needed massive or 'heroic' doses, as they are, somewhat oddly, dubbed by pharmacologists, to feel any pain relief at all.

In October 1883 Freud visited Fleischl and spent three hours with him. He wrote to Martha of this visit: 'I asked him quite disconsolately where all this was going to lead to.' Fleischl replied that his parents saw him as a 'great savant' and that he would try to keep working for as long as they lived, but he felt he was doomed. As soon as his parents died, he would find it 'impossible to hold out for long.' This was one of the most intimate conversations with Fleischl that Freud ever reported.

It suggests that suicide was much on Fleischl's mind, and Freud made a striking – and bizarre – prediction. Fleischl's life, he said, would end in tragedy, which 'will move me the way that the destruction of a holy and famous temple would have touched an ancient Greek.' As with the 'Martha and Fleischl love story' flight of fancy, identifying Fleischl with a 'temple' makes it clear that Freud's perception of his 'ideal' man was distorted by many levels of fantasy and hero-worship. Freud perceived him in quite unreal terms, not as a sick and troubled man, with a serious addiction, but as a tragic, mythological figure, destined to face a catastrophic end. As we shall see, this may have been a self-fulfilling prophecy.

On October 28th 1883, before the experiments with cocaine started, Freud told Martha 'you are partly right about Fleischl because he has not been a friend to me in the way Breuer has been.' Fleischl did not usually let Freud into his confidence – the admission of his suicidal thoughts was an exception – and there was always 'an aura of unapproachability around him'.

Three of the letters Fleischl wrote to Freud were found by Jeffrey Masson when he was delving in the Freud archives. They are polite but impersonal, thanking Freud for off-prints and suggesting changes in a paper Freud had submitted to a Berlin journal. Freud was hurt that Fleischl would not allow a more intimate friendship to develop between them. By November Fleischl's condition had not improved. Four months later, in February 1884, he was again talking of suicide.

Nevertheless, Fleischl was well enough to visit his brother in Rome. In April 1884 he returned to Vienna. It was at the end of that month that Freud first took cocaine. Nine days after he had done so, he persuaded Fleischl to try the drug, in the hope it would prove effective in controlling his pain, and allow him to abandon his morphine habit, or at least, drastically reduce his intake of the drug.

Freud started Fleischl's cocaine 'treatment' on May 7th 1884, the day after his own 28th birthday. So Ernst Fleischl became one of the first patients in Europe to be prescribed cocaine as a way of weaning him off morphine. Two days later Freud was writing to Martha happily: 'Triumph. Rejoice for me. Through cocaine we achieved something beautiful.' Freud also wrote to Minna, his future sister-in-law, that he had had some success with a 'Mittel', German for a thing or medicine.

For three days Fleischl took cocaine and managed to stay off morphine. He found himself 'vortrefflich', the German word for 'excellent'. Fleischl told Freud that he thought he could abstain from morphine and then 'we would both be lucky people.' Fleischl would be cured and the cure would make Freud's reputation.

Freud boasted to Martha that cocaine had been a great success. Withdrawal from opiates usually leads to appalling symptoms including diarrhoea, sweating, unbearable depression, and a feverish craving for morphine. After he stopped taking morphine but was taking cocaine Fleischl, however, did not experience these symptoms, Freud wrote.

But we cannot be certain that Freud was correct: he did not constantly monitor Fleischl during those three days, and had only Fleischl's word that he had ceased his use of morphine. It seems possible, if not probable, that Fleischl was lying. Addicts are often dishonest about the extent of their drug intake, and subsequent research has made it clear stimulants do not ease opiate withdrawal. And Fleischl had plenty of reason to lie. If he did, indeed, continue his morphine use along with his newfound cocaine, then he must quickly have stumbled upon what many drug users deem the 'ultimate high', the 'speedball', as combinations of opiates and stimulants (usually heroin or morphine and amphetamines or cocaine) are known.

Though sometimes administered medicinally to terminal patients, as in Britain's 'Brompton cocktail', such cocktails are notoriously dangerous, as they put great strain on the heart and respiratory system. They remain one of the most common causes of drug deaths, accounting for, amongst others, the final breaths of musicians Brent Mydland of the Grateful Dead, Red Hot Chili Peppers founding member Hillel Slovak, Little Feat frontman Lowell George, artist Jean-Michel Basquiat, and actors John Belushi and River Phoenix. Some users find opiates and cocaine so complementary that heroin and cocaine are sometimes referred to, in American street parlance, as 'boy' and 'girl' respectively. Some American street-level dealers provide a small amount of cocaine, free, with every bag of heroin they sell. The motive for such generosity is far from philanthropic: customers addicted to both drugs come back for more all the sooner.

The combined effects of cocaine's stimulation and the narcotic analgesia of opiates seem to produce a euphoria greater than the sum of its parts: other users alternate the use of stimulants and opiates, relying on heroin or pharmaceutical painkillers to 'bring them down' from the anxious after-effects of cocaine and crack use. The specific cocktail of

85

the synthetic opiate Oxycontin and cocaine is so often lethal that it has been dubbed the 'California heart-stopper.' These cocktails are all the more dangerous when they are made up of street drugs – typically heroin and cocaine – of unknown purity. This, of course, was not an issue for Fleischl, who had access to unlimited quantities of pharmaceutical-grade morphine and cocaine.

Cocaine may have allowed Fleischl a very brief respite from his constant morphine injections, but it cannot have taken him long to discover the speedball effect, and the claim that cocaine alleviated all morphine withdrawal symptoms in such a heavy and long-term addict is simply not credible, in light of modern knowledge. Perhaps the high regard in which he held Fleischl prevented Freud from questioning his honesty. The truth died with Fleischl, but it seems that the great sage may well have been out-witted by a drug-seeking junkie, who told him what he wanted to hear.

Blind to that possibility, Freud became more and more enthusiastic about cocaine and tried the drug on another, unidentified patient. Taking cocaine had immediately cured the patient of gastric pain. This success led Freud to tell Martha: 'If it goes well I will write an essay on it and I expect it will win its place in therapeutics, by the side of morphium and superior to it, I have other hopes and intentions about it.'

After he had taken the 1/20th of gram, Freud had 19 doses left and, though again insisting he experienced no cravings, began to use the drug regularly. He did not hide from Martha that 'I take very small doses of it regularly against depression.' But he did not dwell on that 'tonic' use of cocaine, or the causes of his depression, and moved on to the less than romantic theme of his indigestion. Cocaine helped him, and others, with that too. 'I hope it will be able to abolish the most intractable vomiting, even when this is due to severe pain; in short it is only now that I feel I am a doctor, since I have helped one patient and hope to help more.'

It is the first time Freud expressed any pleasure in treating people. He was also frank in admitting to Martha that cocaine might help alleviate the poverty he found humiliating. 'If things go on in this way we need have no concern about being able to come together and to stay in Vienna.' In fact, Freud was prescribing cocaine for Fleischl, who in turn lent him more money. This relationship bears a more than passing resemblance to that of dealer and customer in the contemporary drug world.

Over the next few months, Freud again did not tell Martha the whole truth about Fleischl's response to the cocaine treatment and may have been unable to face that truth himself. The reality has taken decades to establish. The Dutch writer Han Israels argued that the secrecy of the Sigmund Freud Archives had stopped researchers reading crucial letters. Israels stumbled across transcripts of nearly 300 of them and, as he read through the correspondence, a rather unedifying story unfolded. It is no accident that the German translation of Israels's book has the melodramatic title *Freud and His Lies*.

The treatment seemed promising at first. By May 12th, three days after Freud had told Martha to rejoice, he had to admit: 'With Fleischl things are so sad that I cannot enjoy the cocaine successes at all.' The choice of words is interesting. If Fleischl was not getting better, just what cocaine successes were there? Cocaine, which Fleischl took 'continually', did not prevent him from suffering extreme pain and having 'attacks' that left him nearly unconscious. By this point, he was no longer certain he could trust his patient. Freud added: 'Whether in one of these attacks he took morphia, I do not know, he denies it, but a morphinist ... cannot be believed.' It was one of the few times during that month when Freud seems to have been sensibly sceptical.

A few days after May 12th, Freud visited Fleischl with two colleagues. They found their friend lying on the floor 'almost senseless with pain'. By May 20th, it was all too obvious that cocaine had cured neither Fleischl's pain nor the withdrawal symptoms from morphine. One of Fleischl's acquaintances was Theodor Billroth, one of the best-known surgeons in Europe and a doctor Freud had worked for. Billroth now tried a new operation on Fleischl's thumb and effectively put an end to the cocaine experiment. Billroth told Fleischl 'to take considerable amounts of morphia ... and he was given he does not know how many injections' (letter of 23rd May).

Despite the fact that Freud knew every detail, he said triumphantly that 'after ten days he [Fleischl] was able to dispense with the coca treatment altogether.'

The following timetable makes clear the hopes and disappointments.

7th May – Freud gives Fleischl cocaine for the first time.

9th May – the cocaine seems to be working. Fleischl claims to be abstaining from morphine use.

12th May – Freud admits to Martha it is impossible to enjoy the cocaine 'successes'.

20th May – Billroth operates on Fleischl's thumb.

23rd May – Fleischl reacts badly to Billroth's procedure and is told to take more morphine.

Yet Freud continued to claim Fleischl's treatment as a success. Three days after Billroth operated, he wrote to Martha: 'Until then he [Fleischl] had managed excellently with the cocaine. So the cocaine has stood the test very well.'

In the next month Freud visited Fleischl a number of times and saw that he was in a distressing condition. Freud should have been under no illusions about the failure of the 'cocaine treatment' by this point, but instead of confronting that reality, he wrote his essay in effusive praise of the drug. Sympathetic critics argue Freud was blind; unkind critics say that he was lying. There is, however, another possibility – in a sense, that he was both. Freudians may be displeased to discover that Freud's behaviour is probably best explained by someone else's theory.

Cognitive dissonance, the discomfort that stems from holding beliefs which are clearly contradictory, is a crucial concept in social psychology. The theory of cognitive dissonance claims that when caught between cherished, contradictory beliefs, people are strongly motivated to resolve the contradiction, and do so by indulging in whatever justification, rationalisation, denial and blame is necessary to contort the facts to support their beliefs.

A famous early study of cognitive dissonance was conducted by Leon Festinger and recorded in the book *When Prophecy Fails*. Festinger and his colleagues infiltrated a small apocalyptic cult, whose members believed they were a chosen group, about to be rescued by aliens from the imminent end of the world. When midnight struck on the appointed day, and there was a conspicuous absence of alien landings or planetary catastrophe, the group did not question their beliefs. The truth was more exciting; their prayers had won divine sympathy, and saved the planet from destruction. The cult actually gained members in the aftermath of the apocalypse that wasn't. The facts changed, in the group's eyes, to suit their preferred reality.

Freud seems to have fallen prey to such dissonance in observing his patient. When it became obvious Fleischl had become addicted to cocaine as well as morphine, Freud denied the truth and blamed the patient; 'Since I have given him the cocaine, he has been able to suppress the faints and he could better control himself, but he took it in such enormous quantities ... that in the end he suffered from chronic intoxication' (June 26th 1885).

In a desperate, almost hysterical campaign of dissonance and denial, Freud tried to find evidence to support his claims of 'triumph' with cocaine. He started to write articles which praised the drug uncritically, and sought to persuade his peers that the drug was effective.

The Dutch author Han Israels was outraged that this 'complete indifference to reality is staggering and it inevitably reminds us of what Freud himself later described as the "omnipotence of thoughts". Clearly Freud was so convinced of the correctness of his theory that he was ready to modify the facts when they didn't conform.' Israels added: 'No wonder Freud became the theorist of fantasy, wish-fulfillment and primary narcissism: he himself had a remarkable propensity to hallucinate his theories, to dream up clinical data.' Israels gives Freud no quarter. The more dispassionate view is that Freud was just in the grip of cognitive dissonance; he was human, indeed, as Nietzsche might have put it, all too human, given his troubled history. He had invested a great deal of time, effort, and hopes for the future in his cocaine experiments, and simply could not bear to face their failure.

In the midst of the cocaine fiasco, the indefatigable Freud published a paper that has been largely ignored by historians of analysis. Yet it was quite significant. After he became famous, Freud often said that his case histories read more like novels than scientific papers, a comment Eysenck pounced upon in his critique of psychoanalysis, as indicating they were, in essence, fictions. Freud's paper on a young tailor's apprentice was his first case history, a genre at which he would excel. The apprentice had scurvy and had probably suffered a cerebral haemorrhage:

'I hope I have found the material for my first small clinical publication. ... I went to see him (the tailor) again before luncheon and found a number of interesting symptoms from which could be deduced the locality of the haemorrhage (always our chief concern in brain disorders). So I sat beside him all the afternoon and observed the interesting and most variable development of the illness till seven o'clock, when symmetrical paralysis appeared, with the result that until his death at 8 pm, nothing escaped my notice.'

Freud told Martha he wanted to show the link between the lesions in the tailor's brain and his symptoms, but there was a problem. The young man was not his patient, so Freud needed the consent of his superior to publish his findings. He wasn't sure he would receive this approval and told Martha 'I hope he won't refuse; I intend to keep at him.' The comment shows how insecure and lowly Freud's position was.

Über Coca

There were no such problems with the cocaine paper. Freud worked at it feverishly but he had another difficulty – gaining access to all the research that had already been published. Fleischl helped by giving him an introduction to the library of The Society of Physicians which had the latest report of the American Surgeon General on cocaine. On June 5th Freud reckoned he needed another fortnight to complete the paper. It was just five weeks since he had first taken cocaine.

On June 18th, Freud finished his essay, which ran to some 10,000 words; the 'Song of Praise' to cocaine was published in the July 1884 issue of the *Centralblatt für die Gesammte Therapie*.

This essay had 'a tone that never recurred in Freud's writings, a remarkable combination of objectivity with a personal warmth as if he were in love with the content itself,' Jones wrote. 'Freud used expressions uncommon in a scientific paper such as "the most gorgeous excitement" that animals display after an injection of cocaine, and administering an "offering" of it rather than a "dose"; he heatedly rebuffed the "slander" that had been published about this precious drug. This artistic presentation must have contributed much to the interest the essay aroused in Viennese and other medical circles.'

In places, *Über Coca* resembled a more conventional paper — including a routine review of the existing literature, reports of the effects of cocaine in humans and animals, and a description of its appetite-suppressing properties, citing the example of a Bolivian famine, in which many people survived on a diet of coca leaves. But as Jones noted, Freud's attitude towards cocaine was far from scientific: not only did he describe the 'gorgeous offering' of cocaine in sacramental language, but:

> '...He even gave an account of the religious observances connected with its use, and mentioned the mythical saga of how Manco Capac, the Royal Son of the Sun-God, had sent it as 'a gift from the gods to satisfy the hungry, fortify the weary, and make the unfortunate forget their sorrows.'

Jones wanted to convince his readers that, when Freud wrote about cocaine, he was in some bizarre and unfamiliar state. *Über Coca* does not entirely support that reading. After his competent but routine review of earlier research, Freud went on to repeat that cocaine induces '...exhilaration and lasting euphoria, which in no way differs from the normal euphoria of the healthy person.' The cocaine user felt stronger and in control. 'In other words, you are simply normal, and it is soon hard to believe you are under the influence of any drug.'

It seems to have escaped Freud's notice that 'normal euphoria' is a paradoxical term: for euphoria is a rare and extreme experience. Drug users have for generations noted that it is difficult to describe the effects of cocaine, beyond the use of such vague words as 'stimulation' — but the subjective experience of cocaine's stimulant effect is very different from that of, say, caffeine or amphetamines. First-time recreational users are often unable to perceive the drug's effect on them at all: the 'normal' euphoria induced by cocaine is subtle, compared to the amphetamines or effects of psychedelics. This subtlety can blind the user to just how profound the drug's effects on body and brain can be.

Freud noted the effect of 'a moderate dose of coca fades away so gradually that, in normal circumstances, it is difficult to define its duration. If one works intensively while under the influence of coca, after from three to five hours there is a decline in the feeling of well-being, and a further dose of coca is necessary in order to ward off fatigue.' If one did not perform heavy muscular work then the effects lasted longer. Freud insisted cocaine did not lead to any kind of weariness, let alone depression. 'I should be inclined to think that after moderate doses (0.05– 0.10g) a part at least of the coca effect lasts for over twenty-four hours. In my own case, at any rate, I have noticed that even on the day after taking coca my condition compares favorably with the norm. I should be inclined to explain the possibility of a lasting gain in strength, such as has often been claimed for coca by the totality of such effects.'

Freud would test that hypothesis in the only proper scientific experiment he ever carried out on human subjects. For now he noted that he breathed more slowly, felt tired and sleepy and yawned a lot when the euphoria faded.

Often, those who took cocaine experienced an intense feeling of heat in the head. Freud sometimes felt this himself, though cocaine produced dizziness in only two cases he knew of. 'On the whole the toxic effects of coca are of short duration, and much less intense than those produced by effective doses of quinine or salicylate of soda; they seem to become even weaker after repeated use of cocaine.'

The effect on the stomach was startling. Cocaine led to 'a repeated cooling eructation. This is often accompanied by a rumbling which must originate from high up in the intestine; two of the people I observed, who said they were able to recognise movements of their stomachs, declared emphatically that they had repeatedly detected such movements.' Freud then commented on his own eating habits:

'I have experienced personally how the painful symptoms attendant upon large meals – viz, a feeling of pressure and fullness in the stomach, discomfort and a disinclination to work – disappear with eructation following small doses of cocaine (0.025–0.05 grams). Time and again I have brought such relief to my colleagues; and twice I observed how the nausea resulting from gastronomic excesses responded in a short time to the effects of cocaine, and gave way to a normal desire to eat and a feeling of bodily well-being. I have also learned to spare myself stomach troubles by adding a small amount of cocaine to salicylate of soda.'

Cocaine would help thus digestion and nervous stomach disorders. Freud had trouble with his bowels for much of his life and nicknamed them 'Konrad'. His Konrad had a fretful existence and seemed to be soothed by cocaine which, of course, encouraged Freud to use it frequently.

Freud found surprising individual differences in responses to cocaine. 'I have found not a few who remained unaffected by 5cg, which for me and others is an effective dose,' he said, perhaps attesting to the 'subtle' aspect of the drug's effects. He made it clear that his own experience with the drug was extensive. 'I have tested this effect of coca, which wards off hunger, sleep, and fatigue and steels one to intellectual effort, some dozen times on myself.'

'Coca, if used protractedly but in moderation, is not detrimental to the body,' Freud argued. The animals that von Anrep at the University of Würzburg had given moderate doses of cocaine for 30 days did not suffer any detrimental effects. The drug, he claimed, was not addictive. 'It seems to me noteworthy – and I discovered this in myself and in other observers who were capable of judging such things – that a first dose or even repeated doses of coca produce no compulsive desire to use the stimulant further; on the contrary, one feels a certain unmotivated aversion to the substance... Absolutely no craving for the further use of cocaine appears after the first, or even after repeated taking of the drug...' Cocaine was more powerful and a 'far less harmful stimulant than alcohol, and its widespread utilisation is hindered at present only by its high cost.'

Again, Freud did not address the paradox of how this 'aversion to the substance' could co-exist with its protracted use. 'It's not addictive: I take it all the time' would appear to have been his cognitively dissonant 'reasoning' here. The modern reader must bear in mind just how little was understood about drugs at the time: the reference to alcohol as a stimulant is particularly telling. Alcohol in fact *depresses* the respiratory system in the same manner as a tranquiliser – it is not a stimulant at all.

The most controversial recommendation of *Über Coca*, of course, was the claim that cocaine could be used 'in the treatment of morphine and alcohol addiction'. At this point, Freud cited 16 reports of morphine addicts being cured by cocaine. Palmer, who had given cocaine to L.C., one of the woman runners in the super-marathon, suggested morphine should be withdrawn gradually and replaced with cocaine. A Dr Pollak was treating a 33-year-old woman who had become addicted to the morphine prescribed for her migraines; cocaine helped her, too.

Freud also advocated the use of cocaine as a local anaesthetic, writing: 'especially in connection with affections of the mucous membrane.' He cited Fauvel who 'strongly recommends cocaine for treating diseases of the pharynx and the vocal cords. Freud added that 'the anaesthetising properties of cocaine should make it suitable for a good many further applications'.

If Freud had followed that suggestion up methodically, it would have transformed his career, for he had touched upon the one true therapeutic property that cocaine does possess, as a local anaesthetic. (It is now rarely used for this purpose, as non-euphoric alternatives with no abuse potential have since been synthesised, such as lidocaine, which is, ironically, now often used to 'cut' and bulk up street cocaine, as it produces the same sensation of numbness.) Freud concluded that:

'On the whole, it must be said that the value of cocaine in psychiatric practice remains to be demonstrated, and it will probably be worthwhile to make a thorough trial as soon as the currently exorbitant price of the drug becomes more reasonable.'

He added:

'The treatment of morphine addiction with coca does not, therefore, result merely in the exchange of one kind of addiction for another – it does not turn the morphine addict into a coquero; the use of coca is only temporary. Moreover, I do not think that it is the general toughening effect of coca which enables the system weakened by morphine to withstand, at the cost of only insignificant symptoms, the withdrawal of morphine. I am rather inclined to assume that coca has a directly antagonistic effect on morphine.'

Given Fleischl's real condition, this was unadulterated cognitive dissonance. The wonders of coca did not end there, however.

'The natives of South America, represented the goddess of love with coca leaves in her hand, and did not doubt the stimulative effect of coca on the genitalia. Mantegazza confirms that the coqueros sustain a high degree of potency right into old age; he even reports cases of the restoration of potency and the disappearance of functional weaknesses following the use of coca although he does not believe that coca would produce such an effect in all individuals. Marvaud emphatically supports the view that coca has a stimulative effect.'

Freud had put this to the test:

'Among the persons to whom I have given coca, three reported violent sexual excitement which they unhesitatingly attributed to the coca. A young writer, who was enabled by treatment with coca to resume his work after a longish illness, gave up using the drug because of the undesirable secondary effects which it had on him.'

Freud respected the writer's confidentiality, sadly, and never identified him, or the undesirable secondary effects.

Freud, however, was no objective scientist when it came to the erotic potential of coca. He was engaged to a respectable Jewish virgin and advised her to try cocaine – also forewarning her:

'Woe to you, my Princess, when I come. I will kiss you quite red and feed you till you are plump. And if you are forward you shall see who is the stronger, a gentle little girl who doesn't eat enough or a big wild man who has cocaine in his body. In my last severe depression I took coca again and a small dose lifted me to the heights in a wonderful fashion.'

Perhaps the eager, frustrated Freud hoped cocaine would lift Martha to the 'heights' when they next met. Would it work as an aphrodisiac on the gentle little girl? Would the wild man manage to control his wildness? Freud, of course, never told us: it is unclear whether he and Martha enjoyed the libidinous stimulation of cocaine together.

Finally Freud highlighted seven potential uses for the potion-elixir. It might prove valuable:

1. as a mental stimulant
2. as a possible treatment for digestive disorders
3. as an appetite stimulant in case of wasting diseases
4. as a treatment for morphine and alcohol addiction
5. as a treatment for asthma
6. as an aphrodisiac
7. as a local anaesthetic

Seven days after *Über Coca* appeared, Freud wrote to Martha that it had actually cost him money to write and publish the essay because the deadline had forced him to cancel an appointment with one of his few paying patients.

'Coca wasn't finished till last night; the first half has already been corrected today ... the few gulden I have earned by it I had to subtract from my pupil, whom I sent away yesterday and today.'

He also sent her a little to try herself. Martha thanked him, saying that although she didn't think she needed it, she would take some as he suggested. She reported back to her fiancé that she found it helpful in moments of emotional strain. From time to time, Behling says in her biography, Martha 'enhanced her sense of well-being with an invigorating pinch of cocaine'.

Freud might have longed to excite Martha with cocaine, but he could no longer deny the reality that Fleischl was deteriorating. On July 12th, Freud admitted Fleischl was taking cocaine 'regularly'. Over the summer, Fleischl did not improve at all and by the autumn, his friends were extremely concerned by his condition.

By 1884, the Parke-Davis Company provided coca and cocaine in many forms, including cigarettes. The company also offered consumers a handy cocaine kit, including a hypodermic syringe. Hypodermic needles became widely available in the 1880s, and morphine addicts soon discovered their uses. Parke-Davis was proud to sell the best method of taking a drug that 'can supply the place of food, make the coward brave, the silent eloquent and ... render the sufferer insensitive to pain.'

Not to be outdone by their American rivals, Merck wrote to Fleischl and sought his endorsement for their cocaine. Freud told Martha on October 5th: 'Interesting ... that he [Fleischl] has received a request from the big manufacturer Merck in Darmstadt, whose attention has been drawn by his large coca consumption, and who wanted to know what he knew about the value and effects of the substance.'

We don't just have to rely on Freud for this information. Many of Merck's records survived World War Two and the firm has made them available to historians. Hirschmüller has found that the file of letters between Freud and Merck was lost, but he was able to establish some basic facts by studying the company's order books for 1883 to 1886. An order dated April 24th came from Haubner's pharmacy in Vienna, the pharmacy that Freud used. On May 31st there was an order for a much greater quantity of cocaine from the Physiological Institute where Fleischl still worked. Hirschmüller suggests that this order – 10 grams at the very low price of 5 marks a gram – came directly from Fleischl.

Fleischl behaved as one might expect an addict to do, under the circumstances, injecting himself with 'enormous doses' of cocaine –1 gram per day. Again, the reader must remember that it was *pure* cocaine that entered Fleischl's veins.

By the middle of October 1884 Freud was in correspondence with Merck. He must have known that Fleischl was misleading the company into believing their cut-price cocaine was being used for scientific experiments, rather than his own personal consumption. Freud did not confront him about this dubious behaviour. Freud did not tell Merck the truth, but then he could hardly alienate Fleischl, when he both revered him as his teacher and was borrowing money from him, especially as he hoped to borrow more.

Merck now asked Freud if he would investigate ecgonine, another substance derived from the coca leaf, which is both a metabolite and precursor of cocaine. Freud gladly accepted. For Merck it was hugely useful to collaborate with members of Vienna's respected Physiological Institute. On October 21st, they sent Freud 100 grams of ecgonine.

Though the evidence against cocaine's safety and therapeutic utility was accumulating fast, Freud still told a colleague, Leopold Königstein, that the drug had great potential. He made Königstein promise to carry out some tests on the substance, while he went to visit Martha, who he had not seen for nearly two years. He would visit her with some cocaine in his pocket and forget his scientific ambitions. In his absence, cocaine would make another man world famous, for a discovery Freud had already made but overlooked. Again Freud would be the nearly man.

Chapter 7

Cocaine by the Seine

By his late twenties, Freud had studied eels, worked in several different branches of medicine and missed at least one opportunity to make his name as a doctor through cocaine research. One of his friends, Carl Koller, would turn out to be luckier and more methodical in his study of the drug. The Koller episode is of note because this was the first professional relationship in which Freud was the dominant partner. Since this book is in places highly critical of Freud, it should, in fairness, be noted that holding this 'alpha status' in his relationship with Koller made Freud rather generous.

Koller was a year younger than Freud and a fellow Jew. They knew each other well enough for Freud to have asked him to review the first draft of *Über Coca*. A few months after the paper's publication, Koller agreed to take some cocaine and describe its effects on him for Freud. Koller gave a sober account:

> 'We would take the alkaloid internally by mouth and after the proper lapse of time for its getting into the circulation we would conduct experiments on our muscular strength, fatigue and the like measured by the dynamometer.'

It never occurred to Freud that while he was away in Hamburg, 'feeding his plump Princess', Koller would start to work systematically on cocaine. First, Koller gave some to a colleague, Dr Engel, who confirmed that it numbed his tongue. To which Koller replied, 'Yes that has been noticed by everyone who has eaten it.' He wrote that 'in that moment it flashed upon me that I had in my pocket the local anaesthetic that I had searched for some years previously.'

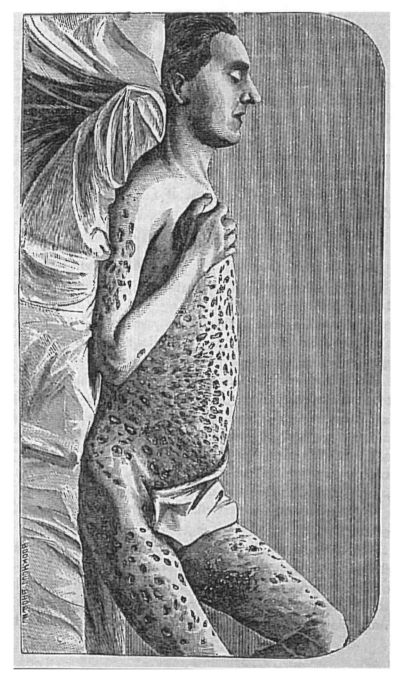

A Victorian image of a patient scarred by subcutaneous injections, such as Fleischl received.

This 'flash' had far-reaching, even revolutionary, implications for surgery – especially operations upon the eye. In most surgery, it does not matter if the patient is unconscious, but eye surgeons often found it necessary to test the reactions of patient to light, or have them adjust the angle of their head on the operating table: thus 'knock-out' anaesthetics such as ether were of no use, as the patient had to remain conscious. This made operations on the eye particularly dangerous and difficult, as patients underwent them in great pain, and would sometimes go into shock. There were no other effective local anaesthetics at the time, and it is difficult to imagine the pain involved in eye operations without anaesthesia. Koller had struck upon the one legitimate medical use of cocaine.

Koller's assistant Dr Gärtner recalled that Koller then said to him

'I hope, indeed I expect, that this powder will anaesthetise the eye.'

'We'll find out about that right away,' Gärtner said excitedly.

Koller dissolved a few grams of cocaine in distilled water, plucked a large and lively frog out of the aquarium and put a drop of cocaine solution into its eye.

After about a minute, Gärtner said, 'came the great historic moment. I do not hesitate to designate it as such. The frog let his cornea be touched and even injured without a trace of reflex action or the slightest attempt to protect itself.' Such reflex actions, of course, contributed to the difficulty of eye surgery because the patient's head might jerk suddenly to protect the eyes, without anaesthesia. Koller and Gärtner then carried out a simple control experiment by trying to touch the frog's other eye. The frog responded normally, jerked and turned away.

Koller then performed the same experiment on a rabbit, a dog and a guinea pig and confirmed his results. Cocaine was an excellent local anaesthetic indeed.

Next Koller and Gärtner tested the effect on themselves. Neither man flinched when his eye was touched. On September 11th, 1884, Koller performed the first operation using cocaine as a local anaesthetic on a patient suffering from glaucoma. The procedure was a historic success.

Only months before, Freud had himself suggested that cocaine might be a good local anaesthetic: but he had not thought to explore this notion systematically. Indeed, on holiday with Martha in Wandsbek, Freud was unaware of Koller's breakthrough.

Koller immediately wrote up a short account of his work and wanted to present it to an ophthalmologic congress in Heidelberg in mid-September. But Koller could not afford to make the trip, a small fact which demonstrates the importance of Fleischl's loans to Freud, who made only a little more than Koller. Unable to raise the fare to attend a major scientific congress a mere 364 miles away, Koller had to ask a stranger, Dr Josef Brettauer, to read his paper for him in Heidelberg.

The paper made a huge impact, Brettauer told Koller, as the audience realised this was a critical advance. A month later, Koller read his own paper to the Viennese Medical Society, and a week later it was published. News of the breakthrough crossed the Atlantic fast. A New York eye surgeon, Dr Henry D. Noyes, who had been at Heidelberg, sent a summary to *The New York Medical Record*. *The Lancet* reported Koller's discovery on December 6th.

Between September 1884 and late 1885, 60 papers reporting the use of cocaine as a local anaesthetic appeared in Britain, the United States and Canada. The American 'father of surgery', William Halsted, surmised that what worked for the eye might work for the teeth, and tested the idea, blocking the inferior dental nerve in a medical student with a small amount of cocaine. There was a flurry of enthusiastic papers in dental journals, and dentists started to use cocaine frequently.

Jones may have been starry-eyed in praising Freud's 'superhuman' maturity, but at least in his relations with Koller, Freud truly was generous and mature, showing no trace of jealousy. There is no record of any disappointment on his part at Koller's success with research Freud had suggested himself and then failed to conduct. Failure did, however, finally spur Freud into action. On his return to Vienna, he carried out a series of experiments with his old friend, Josef Herzig (with whom he had bought the skeleton, eight years earlier). On November 9th, they used a dynamometer to measure how much muscular force they could apply when on or off cocaine. The dynamometer is a device for measuring force, typically the power produced by an engine. On

November 26th, 27th and 28th Freud carried out three similar experiments.

As this is the only experimental study Freud ever performed on a human being, it should be described in detail. The experiment began at 8 am on November 9th. Using the dynamometer Freud found the average pressure exerted by Herzig was enough to lift 63.6 kilos. At 10.22 am Herzig was allowed some breakfast and a cup of coffee. Eleven minutes later he was no stronger than before, and then took 0.10 grams of cocaine. Twelve minutes later Herzig's arm was 20% stronger than prior to the drug's administration, as the average pressure he could exert was now enough to lift 75.3 kilos. On one occasion Herzig got as high as 82.

Herzig's arm only became weaker some two hours later, but after they had eaten lunch, he could again exert pressures to lift 75.3 kilos, and continued to feel euphoric. This euphoria lasted till 3.35 pm by which time the strength of the arm had dwindled back to normal.

The next day the experiment produced similar results, though it started in the evening; Herzig took the cocaine at 8.30 pm, when he was feeling tired after a day's work, and reported a buoyant feeling rather than full-blown euphoria. Freud carried out both an objective and an introspective experiment. He measured Herzig's performance and also made him describe what he was feeling. Herzig both felt different and performed differently on each of the three days. The experiment persuaded Freud cocaine had many possible uses beyond those Koller had discovered. A month later, Freud used it to relieve facial pain in a patient he never named, but who may have been Anna O/Bertha Pappenheim.

Far from resenting Koller, Freud suggested they address each other as '*du*' rather than by the more formal '*sie*'. Their friendship would soon be tested dramatically.

On January 4th 1885 there was a violent clash in the emergency clinic at the university hospital between Koller and another doctor, Freidrich Zinner. Koller was the senior man on duty and had to treat a patient with an injured finger. A rubber bandage had been put on the wound but it was so tight the patient was in danger of developing gangrene. Koller started to cut off the bandage; Zinner objected. Koller ignored him and removed it fully. Though he was Koller's junior, Zinner shouted 'Saujud' – an anti-Semitic insult that translates as 'cheeky' or 'uppity' Jew. Literally, it means 'pig-Jew'.

Jacob Freud might have allowed some gentile to knock his hat into the gutter, but Koller was both now internationally famous and made of sterner stuff. Witnesses saw Koller give Zinner 'a resounding box on the ear . . . (that) was the answer to this insult.' Zinner reeled back. He had been struck by a Jew. No Christian could let a Jew hit him in the deeply anti-Semitic climate of Freud's Vienna, so Zinner demanded a duel.

Duelling was in fashion at the time, especially amongst right-wing, anti-Semitic groups such as the militaristic Burschenschaft Germania, of which Zinner may have been a member. Only men were allowed to join and such fraternities revelled, somewhat romantically, in a cult of the duel. They were a rite of passage, a mark of honour and it didn't take much to provoke a challenge. The famous economist Joseph Schumpeter, for example, had to fight a duel because he had not returned some university library books in time.

Zinner sent Koller his seconds. The etiquette dictated that Koller, who had been challenged, could choose the weapons. Koller opted to fight with foils. The duel would last until one man could no longer defend himself. It took place the next day at the cavalry barracks at Josefstadt. The duellists took off their coats and fought in shirt-sleeves.

Koller was the better fencer. He caught Zinner a blow on the head, then one on the right upper arm, forcing Zinner to admit defeat. The District Attorney questioned both men the next day: while fashionable, duelling was frowned upon by the authorities. Koller refused to say anything while Zinner explained he had to challenge the Jew, because if he did not fight for his honour, he would have had to resign his commission as a doctor in the Army Reserve.

Freud was on Koller's side, not because he approved of his colleague's behaviour, but out of Jewish solidarity. The day after the duel, Freud told Martha: 'You must realise in what conditions we have to live here.' Freud said to Koller he had discussed the drama with Breuer and his wife, who were also outraged, and added that Koller should remember that he had helped many people as a doctor.

The university authorities saw the situation very differently. Anti-Semitism was inscribed in their regulations, and Jews were still not allowed to hold senior positions. Jacob Bernays, Martha's uncle, was one of the great Biblical scholars of the mid 19th century, but never became a professor because he refused to convert to Christianity. Zinner, a Christian, was never going to be forced out of the university for duelling – Koller's victory with the foil, however, ruined his prospects of a permanent position, despite the success of his work on cocaine.

On July 7th Freud told Koller it was clear that the attitude of the hospital was the result of anti-Semitism. 'No Jew can be an assistant, no Jew can become a senior doctor, the Jews can do nothing and understand nothing,' Freud added to Martha.

A week later, writing to Koller, Freud was more critical of his friend and told him that he got 'too easily into bad situations.' Koller did not object to Freud's judgement – he had, after all, punched Zinner first – and the two men corresponded very amicably for two years. I have pointed out above that for once, Freud was the older, stable and dominant party in a professional relationship but I cannot claim to have discovered why that was the case with Koller. On September 28th 1886, for example, he told Koller 'I still feel the confidence that you will come out successful in the struggles of life,' but he warned him not to think of going to America. Koller ignored Freud and left for New York, where he became a very successful eye specialist. Such emigrations were commonplace enough, amongst European Jewish professionals.

Seventy years after the duel, Ernst Freud, Sigmund's son, and Hortense Becker, Koller's daughter, exchanged letters. Ernst admitted that his father's attitude to Koller had changed considerably but Hortense said this had nothing to do with cocaine. In 1895 there was trouble between Koller and one of Freud's relatives in New York, almost certainly his sister Anna Bernays, and though no details of this 'trouble' have survived, it seems to have turned Freud against Koller.

Freud often quarrelled with his associates and found it very hard to make peace with a friend or colleague after such a falling out. Thirty-one years later, in 1926, Koller came to Vienna and wanted to see Freud, but

Freud told him they could not meet as he was out of town. The two men never reconciled.

In his autobiographical sketch, published in 1925, Freud did not blame Koller for his own failure to study cocaine as a local anaesthetic. Instead, with a distinct lack of chivalry, he found the plump Princess responsible for his oversight. Freud wrote:

'I may here go back a little and explain how it was the fault of my fiancée that I was not already famous at an early age. A side interest, though it was a deep one, had led me in 1884 to obtain from Merck some of what was then the little-known alkaloid cocaine and to study its physiological action. While I was in the middle of this work, an opportunity arose for making a journey to visit my fiancée, from whom I had been parted for two years. I hastily wound up my investigations of cocaine and contented myself in my book on the subject with prophesying that further uses for it would soon be found... When I returned from my holiday I found that not he [Königstein], but another of my friends, Carl Koller, whom I had also spoken to about cocaine, had made the decisive experiments upon animals' eyes.'

Freud added: 'Koller is rightly regarded as the discoverer of local anaesthesia by cocaine, which has become so important in minor surgery; but I bore my fiancée no grudge for her interruption of my work.' So little grudge, indeed, that it was 'the fault of my fiancée that I was not already famous at an early age' and he remembered the details of her 'interruption' of his research forty years on, forgetting how eager he had been to see her. He had put love before work, and, many years later, lacked the grace to admit as much – or his simple failure to follow through his own ideas.

In his dealings with Fleischl, Freud was also far from mature. After six months on cocaine, Fleischl was unable to work and suffering violent mood swings. He developed what we now would recognise as a toxic psychosis, resulting from chronic stimulant intoxication. (This side-effect is more commonly associated with amphetamines than cocaine, but protracted use of any powerful stimulant will eventually result in psychosis in many users.) Fleischl's psychotic symptoms appear to have been horrific: in one case, he hallucinated white snakes creeping over his skin. Freud became pessimistic and told Martha that Fleischl would live for six months at most.

Yet Freud did not stop prescribing cocaine, suggesting that he had not made the connection between the drug and Fleischl's symptoms. Indeed, he agreed to give Fleischl injections of cocaine in January 1885. There was no medical logic behind that decision, but there were two obvious reasons for it. If he refused to give Fleischl cocaine, Fleischl might in turn have declined to lend him cash. Additionally, Freud may well have convinced himself, against all evidence, that the injections might help Fleischl – denial again. The next paper Freud wrote was certainly defiant.

In *Nachtrage Über Coca* (published by Verlag Von Moritz Perles), Freud complained that many well-established doctors had 'unjustified fears with regard to the internal use of cocaine.' He countered that he had used subcutaneous injections successfully in cases of long standing sciatica and added that 'for humans the toxic dose is very high, and there seems to be no lethal dose.'

With hindsight we now know this to be false as experimental work has found the LD50 of cocaine – the dose at which 50% of users will die – to be 95.1 mg of cocaine per kilo of bodyweight in mice. For obvious ethical reasons, it is impossible to establish the exact lethal dose in humans through medical research, but cocaine's toxicity is sufficient to have resulted in many a heart attack and stroke.

In February, Freud admitted to Martha that Fleischl's use of cocaine had left him in a worse psychological state than morphine alone. But he was not ready to abandon his belief in the drug, and may, judging from his inconsistency, have been struggling to face – or not – the facts. When Freud gave lectures on March 3rd and March 5th 1885 entitled 'On General Effect of Cocaine' at the Physiological Club and the Psychiatric Union, he was not at all pessimistic about Fleischl, as he said the patient 'had suffered severe symptoms as a result of abstinence in the course of a previous cure. This time his condition was tolerable; in particular, there was no sign of depression or nausea as long as the effects of coca lasted;

chills and diarrhoea were now the only permanent symptoms of his abstinence. The patient was not bedridden, and could function normally. During the first days of the cure he consumed 3dg of cocaïnum muriaticum daily, and after ten days he was able to dispense with the coca treatment altogether.'

But Freud was not telling the truth; Fleischl was consuming far higher doses of cocaine than Freud admitted, and it is unclear whether or not his morphine use was also ongoing. On March 10th Freud wrote to Martha that he had not felt so well 'during these bad days' and he was ashamed to be so short of money. He had to visit Fleischl and ask for another loan. It was urgent. By the end of the week he would be out of money. 'I give you my solemn promise that I will marry you even if I don't get the 1,500 marks,' he told Martha, rather desperately.

Fleischl was so debilitated he found it hard to write, but he seems to have obliged with a loan again. Two days later Freud wrote to Martha 'I never felt so fresh in my life.'

On March 16th, Freud told Martha that Fleischl slept for 52 hours – it seems possible that this was 'rebound sleep' after a period of prolonged wakefulness under the influence of cocaine – but at least he was making beautiful things. Fleischl may have been hallucinating but he could still draw. Freud was in a crisis. He had failed to help Fleischl, found his constant need to borrow money humiliating, and was beginning to experience mood swings, which may have been *caused by* his own cocaine consumption. Freud's elation had turned into depression yet again by March 21st, when, after seeing Fleischl, he told Martha 'I can't stand it much longer.'

Freud was facing other pressures that added to his sense of desperation. He had become protective of his father, who was in danger of losing his sight. On Easter day, Freud took Jacob to see Koller and a day later, on April 6th, Koller operated on the old man using cocaine to anaesthetise his eyes. Freud watched and was relieved the operation was a success. Two weeks later, he himself contracted a mild case of smallpox.

May 7th 1885 was the first anniversary of Fleischl's treatment – and it had clearly been a catastrophic failure. Freud, however, remained in deep denial of this fact. Not surprisingly, increasing use of cocaine and probably morphine only made Fleischl worse. He couldn't sleep, hallucinated and suffered from violent tremors. He told anyone who would listen that his pains were unendurable. Freud told Martha on May 12th that he had been to visit Fleischl three times 'but each time he was asleep.'

A few days later Freud had lunch in Fleischl's room and ate tartare sauce which induced a headache but the familiar remedy was at hand. 'I took some cocaine, watched the migraine vanish at once'. It is not clear whether Freud took the cocaine with Fleischl, or did so later, when he was back in his rooms.

Two years earlier, Freud had told Martha he feared Fleischl would collapse like some ancient Greek temple. Freud was now sitting among the ruins, as the temple's roof caved in. There was, at least, better financial news: Freud had an American patient but he was 'good only for only forty florins a month.'

On June 4th Freud and Breuer were so alarmed by Fleischl's condition that they stayed with him overnight. Fleischl was now suffering from delirium tremens – the syndrome of tremors, hallucinations and convulsions associated with withdrawal from chronic alcoholism, as well as stimulant abuse. The night marked some kind of turning point because, after that vigil, Freud finally admitted to Martha the damage cocaine had done to Fleischl and warned her against taking too much of the stuff herself.

Freud had lunch with Fleischl again at the end of June and was annoyed he had to stay till 4 pm. On June 26th the two men went to a lakeside resort, St Gilgen. The idea was that the fresh air would help Fleischl, but this quaint treatment was hardly equal to the severity of his condition, and does not appear to have worked. Freud told Martha that Fleischl had spent 1,800 marks, or $428, in three months on cocaine, taking a gram a day – a voracious rate of consumption. In modern British terms, a gram of pure cocaine would be 'cut' many times: as noted above, the cocaine content of powder seized and analysed by the police has dropped significantly in recent years. A gram of pure cocaine, on the streets of London, would probably be heavily diluted and sold as ten grams, at a price of £40 each. And few modern users consume ten grams a day, least of all intravenously.

Back in Vienna, Freud went to see Fleischl again on July 5th and was once more too worried by his condition to leave him alone. Fleischl was asleep again and Freud stayed in his room, writing a letter to Martha. He promised he would come to see her soon but as usual he did not have the money. This time, he borrowed money from Breuer to pay for the trip and service his debts.

Freud had to put these problems out of his mind as he was preparing for what he called 'an Oral Exam with 7 or 8 Great Ones'. This time Fleischl was in no state to be one of the examiners. Freud passed with excellent marks on June 13th. His success led to a crucial development in his career.

A week after the Oral Examination, the Vienna Faculty voted 19 to 3 to give Freud a grant to go to Paris, after Brücke made a glowing speech in his favour. The money would pay for him to spend four months studying under the great neurologist of the day, the so-called 'Napoleon of neurosis', as Jean-Martin Charcot was known. In the three months before leaving for Paris, despite the striking evidence of Fleischl's decline, Freud continued to write in praise of cocaine.

In fairness, Freud was not the only doctor of the time to do so. William A. Hammond, one of America's most prominent neurologists, told audiences that cocaine was no more habit-forming than tea or coffee. He also boasted of the 'cocaine wine' he had perfected with the help of a New York druggist: they put in two grams of cocaine for every pint of wine.

Yet evidence of the dangers of cocaine was beginning to accumulate in the journals. In July, Erlenmeyer launched the first of a series of attacks. He had treated eight patients with cocaine and warned, presciently, that the drug was the 'third scourge of mankind', after alcohol and opium. Obersteiner told the Copenhagen Medical Conference that there were serious risks in using cocaine to treat neurotic and psychotic patients, as it produced severe mental disturbances similar to those seen in delirium tremens.

Though he had stopped denying the truth to Martha, in public, Freud ignored these criticisms again and published an upbeat account of the drug a month later, '*Über die Allgemeinwirkung des Cocaïnes*', 'On the Working of Cocaine' in the *Medicinisch-chirurgisches Centralblatt of* August

1885. It was in this paper that Freud committed to writing what Han Israels was right to condemn as a lie:

'I myself have had occasion to observe a case of rapid withdrawal from morphine under cocaine treatment here, and I saw that a person who had presented the most severe manifestations of collapse at the time of an earlier withdrawal now remained able, with the aid of cocaine, to work and to stay out of bed, and was reminded of his abstinence only by his shivering, diarrhoea, and occasionally recurring craving for morphine. He took about 0.40g of cocaine per day, and by the end of 20 days the morphine abstinence was overcome.'

Freud also had no evidence for his next claim. 'No cocaine habituation set in; on the contrary, an increasing antipathy to the use of cocaine was unmistakably evident. On the basis of my experiences with the effects of cocaine, I have no hesitation in recommending the administration of cocaine for such withdrawal cures in subcutaneous injections of 0.03–0.05g per dose, without any fear of increasing the dose.'

Ernest Jones tried to play down some of the chaotic aspects of Freud's behaviour as the kind of credulity that was 'part of the receptivity and open-mindedness that accompanies genius.' Jones, in effect, denied Freud's own denial.

Fleischl's appalling condition was not the only problem Freud faced in the three months before he left to study under Charcot. On August 18th he was asked to report to the police because he had not turned up for army service. Again, he talked his way out of it.

Freud then did something astonishing. On August 28th he admitted it to Martha:

'I have just carried out one resolution which one group of people, as yet unborn and fated to misfortune, will feel acutely. Since you can't guess whom I mean I will tell you: they are my biographers. I have destroyed all my diaries of the past fourteen years, with letters, scientific notes and the manuscripts of my

111

publications. Only family letters were spared. Yours, my dear one, were never in danger. All my old friendships and associations passed again before my eyes and mutely met their doom; all my thoughts and feelings about the world in general, and in particular how it concerned me, have been declared unworthy of survival. They must now be thought all over again. And I had jotted down a great deal. But the stuff simply enveloped me, as the sand does the Sphinx, and soon only my nostrils would show above the mass of paper. I cannot leave here and cannot die before ridding myself of the disturbing thought of who might come by the old papers. Besides, everything that fell before the decisive break in my life, before our coming together and my choice of calling.'

At the age of 17, Freud had told his friend Emil Fluss to keep his letters after a teacher praised his literary style. Twelve years later Freud had not achieved enough to suggest anyone would ever bother to write his biography. It might seem vain to destroy evidence writers might need in the future, should he, in time, turn out to merit a biography. The real reason for this destruction of documents, I would argue, had more to do with failure and, of course, denial than 'envelopment by the Sphinx'. Freud was broke; his father was ill and Fleischl was barely surviving. Having seen Martha for just a few weeks in two years, Freud was almost certainly sexually and emotionally frustrated. Cocaine had made not him, but Koller, famous, while Freud's colleagues were criticising his advocacy of the drug for more general use.

Freud destroyed his letters and manuscripts for a very human reason: he could not face the failures they documented in such detail. We destroy what we can't bear to remember. It's an ultimate flourish of denial.

In 1900 Freud recorded his dream of the outside toilet in which he urinated on a cesspit, washing the faeces down a hill. He recalled the passage where Garguanta pisses on the people of Paris from the top of Notre Dame. In destroying his papers, Freud was purifying his own past – and not for the last time. But the destruction was a decisive act that seemed to give Freud energy and hope. On August 29th he asked Martha if they should get married in a month's time. On September 3rd, using the money Breuer had loaned him, Freud went to see her in Wandsbek where he stayed until October 11th.

As so much of the information we have about Freud's life comes from his letters, we have no idea of what happened when he and Martha were together. We do know, however, that his prospects improved. He somehow escaped any punishment for failing to attend to his military duties and the Ministry for Public Instructions ratified his appointment as 'Privatdocent', or 'private lecturer', a post-doctoral status that is the rough equivalent of an Associate Professorship at an American university. Freud was on track for a successful academic career.

On October 11th Freud left Martha and travelled to Paris by train. It took him two days to reach the city, where Freud again turned to cocaine. He seems to have had no other way of coping with the pressures of working with Charcot at the Salpêtrière, a privileged, but stressful role.

The Pitié-Salpêtrière hospital was founded in the 1660s by Louis XIV to house the poor and mentally ill as well as many prostitutes. It covered huge grounds on the left bank of the Seine, less than a kilometre from the Bastille. By the 1880s the hospital was famous for displaying its more dramatic patients, like a certain Blanche who was called the 'Queen of Hysterics'. She was often paraded for students in a manner that recalls a carnival freak-show. In the 1960s, R.D. Laing criticised similar displays of patients by the psychiatrist Emile Kraeplin, who first described the symptoms of schizophrenia. Such performances showed that psychiatrists of the day were far too willing to 'objectify' their patients.

On November 24th 1885, a month after he arrived in Paris, Freud wrote to Martha, 'Charcot, who is one of the greatest of physicians and a man whose common sense borders on genius, is simply wrecking all my aims and opinions. I sometimes come out of his lectures as from out of Notre Dame, with an entirely new idea about perfection... Whether the seed will ever bear fruit, I don't know; but what I do know is that no other human being has ever affected me in the same way.'

Charcot was 62 years old and perhaps the greatest showman/shaman of 19th century medicine. He had been the director of the Salpêtrière since 1872 and was world famous as a pioneer in neurology and psychiatry. Charcot argued against the received wisdom that hysterics, nearly all of whom were women, were malingering, feigning their symptoms to obtain attention. Hysteria was not 'hysterical', he maintained, but a real illness with consistent symptoms.

It was not just Charcot's ideas that impressed Freud. His house was a palace; Freud was lyrical about the drawing room, telling Martha:

'It is as big as the whole of our future apartment, a room worthy of the magic castle in which he lives... The other section has cases containing Indian and Chinese antiques. The walls are covered with tapestries and pictures; the walls themselves are painted terracotta. The little I saw of the other rooms on Sunday contained the same wealth of pictures, tapestries, carpets – and curios – in other words a museum.'

Consciously or otherwise, Freud imitated his teacher when he could afford it in later life, and the apartment at 19 Berggasse would impress visitors with its collection of figurines and antiquities. By the end of his life he had collected over 3000 of them. A painting of Charcot 'demonstrating' patients hung in Freud's study – and is now in London's Freud museum.

In Paris, Freud studied in a distinguished group. Charcot's pupils and assistants included Giles de la Tourette, who would go on to discover Tourette's syndrome and, in a remarkable case of negative transference, to be shot by one of his own patients, and Alfred Binet, who created the first intelligence tests in partnership with Theodore Simon. William Osler, one of the most influential American doctors of the early 20th century, visited in 1889 and was deeply impressed by the Salpêtrière. Charcot counted as friends the writers Émile Zola and Alphonse Daudet. Daudet became famous when he started to publish letters from Provence which forged its image as an idyllic refuge from the stresses of urban life. Daudet lived in a windmill and described his life and the quaint characters he came across in his *Lettres de Mon Moulin*, a book that Van Gogh loved. The Provençal landscape might be magnificent, but it did not cure either Daudet or Van Gogh of their morbid anxieties. Daudet was often very depressed in his windmill and suffered from hallucinations. Charcot treated him with morphine.

Charcot's teaching style was flamboyant, to an extent that now seems deeply dubious. His Tuesday lessons were exercises in showmanship, his treatments as theatrical as his patients' symptoms. Often he would press on what he called the 'hysterogenic zones' and the pliant patient would respond dramatically. The hysterics would convulse, strike bizarre poses or even masturbate. In women, one such zone was on the lower belly, near the womb.

After nearly four months Freud received a longed-for invitation to a soirée at Charcot's house. The company would be dazzling and he did not want to be intimidated: predictably enough, he bucked himself up for the evening with a dose of cocaine. The guests included Léon Daudet, the son of the writer, Isador Straus, who worked for Louis Pasteur, and Gilles de la Tourette.

On February 20th Freud was invited to a second soirée, and again, fortified himself with cocaine. That evening he argued with Gilles de la Tourette, stressing that as a loyal Austrian, he objected to French policy towards his homeland. Freud finished the night in confident mood and wrote to Martha: 'I feel in my bones that I have the talent to bring me into the upper 10,000', by which he meant that he would rise to the highest ranks of his profession.

A week later, Freud was invited to another evening at Charcot's palace. He was more at ease this time and does not seem to have taken cocaine to prepare himself. Charcot's influence on Freud was enormous and he noted some of his hero's maxims, including the odd claim:

'*Mais, dans des cas pareils c'est toujours la chose génitale, toujours . . . toujours*' ('But in such cases, it is always the genital thing . . . always, always.')

Freud never forgot Charcot's phrase. The 'genital thing', or 'genital fixation' became – I mix the metaphors deliberately – the heart of psychoanalysis. Charcot had no interest in introspection and at this point, Freud did not dream that introspective methods might allow patients to discover the origins of their 'genital thing'.

Charcot had a sharp eye for detail and observed his patients carefully. Freud said, he 'used to look again and again at the things he did not understand to deepen his impression of them till suddenly an understanding dawned on him. In his mind's eye the apparent chaos ... then gave way to order: and the new diagnostic picture emerged. 'He was not a reflective man, not a thinker: he had the nature of an artist– he was, as he himself said, a *'visuel* – a man who sees', Freud said.

Indeed, Charcot loved to draw when he was a child and became an accomplished amateur artist. It has been suggested he learned how to observe his patients so well because of that passion for drawing – and he liked, incidentally, to draw under the influence of hashish. One dramatic contemporary account of Charcot claims:

'As soon as he was under the influence of the narcotic, a tumult of phantasmogoric visions flashed across his mind. The entire page was covered with drawings: prodigious dragons, grimacing monsters, incoherent personages who were superimposed on each other and who were intertwined and twisted in a fabulous whirlpool bringing to mind apocalyptic visions.'

Freud ended his visit to Paris with a small triumph. Charcot agreed to let him translate some of his works into German, but when Freud returned to Vienna, he had to face the familiar problem of poverty. On March 19th he wrote to Martha that he needed between 1000 and 2000 florins to continue living in Vienna – an amount his earnings did not provide. He would not borrow from usurers 'but where can semi-unselfish capitalists be found willing to lend money at a normal rate of interest with no more guarantee than a human head and two hands?' he asked.

Yet he somehow managed to raise the fare to visit Martha. He found it hard to leave her and they both cried at the railway station, saying their farewells. Just after his 30th birthday on May 6th, Freud fretted that he would have to move from Vienna because the city was so expensive and he had only two patients who paid fees.

In August, Freud for once turned up to perform his military duties and went on manoeuvres in Olmütz, Moravia. He was promoted from Oberarzt to Regimentsarzt and now supervised the medical services for a regiment. The former deserter was now amused by military life; Freud wrote to Martha that the generals strutted like peacocks, which led to an incident in a café. Freud shouted he too might be a general one day so would the waiters please bring him a glass of water?

But at least the army paid. When his military duties ended on September 11th 1886, he had managed to save money by not going to restaurants and taking the radical step of sometimes cooking his own meals. It made a difference, as somehow Freud now had enough cash to rent a respectable apartment for him and Martha. This expense would not have been covered by a single month's army pay, nor the economy of eating at home, so it seems likely that Freud must have ignored Polonius' wisdom, and been, yet again a borrower.

Finally, after a four-year engagement, Martha and Freud were married. The wedding was not held in a synagogue. Freud even had enough money for a honeymoon in Holstein on the Baltic. When their first son was born in October 1887, Freud named him Jean-Martin in honour of Charcot. His younger brother was named Ernst, in honour of Ernst Fleischl. None of Freud's boys were named, as one might have expected, after his father Jacob.

The critics of cocaine were now winning the debate. In 1887, the *British Medical Journal* commented that the 'undeniable reaction against the extravagant pretensions advanced on behalf of this drug had already set in'. In America, after studying 17 cases, J.B. Mattison warned there was a genuine danger of replacing an opium or morphine habit with a cocaine habit, when cocaine was used in an attempt to combat opiate addiction.

Freud was now 'subjected to grave reproaches' for championing the drug. His response was again one of stubborn denial. Freud's paper '*Beiträge über die Anwendung des Cocaïns*' (*Wiener Medizinische Wochenschrift*, 28, pp. 929–932, July 1887), was a passionate defence of cocaine. Freud wrote:

'All reports of addiction to cocaine and deterioration resulting from it refer to morphine addicts, persons who, already in the grip of one demon are so weak in will power, so susceptible, that they would misuse, and indeed have misused, any stimulant held out to them. Cocaine has claimed no other, no victim on its own. I have had broad experience with the regular use of cocaine over long periods of time by persons who were not morphine addicts, and have taken the drug myself for some months without perceiving or experiencing any condition similar to morphinism or any desire for continued use of cocaine. On the contrary, there occurred more frequently than I should have liked, an aversion to the drug.'

Freud never expanded on this contradictory statement and insisted that the accusation that users became addicted was simply wrong, though this 'aversion' had not prevented his own use becoming regular. Again, his attitude towards his own drug use suggests cognitive dissonance: it's not addictive, I take it all the time!

The 1887 article was the last Freud ever wrote about cocaine. He was not winning any converts to his position, and began to realise it would be wiser to dissociate himself from the drug. Eventually, Freud suppressed the compromising articles. He never mentioned *Über Coca* or the other cocaine papers amongst his lists of publications. Using cocaine to cure morphine addiction, Freud finally admitted, was 'like trying to cast out the Devil with Beelzebub.'

Ernest Jones claimed Freud stopped using cocaine in 1887 and that he did not find it hard to do so because he did not have an 'addictive personality'. Jones either did not know, or chose not to reveal, that Freud in fact continued, when under stress, to use what he deemed 'modest' doses of cocaine, 30 to 50 milligrams, for the next 15 years or more. Sometimes it seems Freud relished fooling his biographer.

Between 1887 and 1891 Freud finally began to establish his reputation as a doctor, independently of cocaine research. He published interesting material on cerebral palsy and aphasia and visited the celebrated Bernheim who used hypnosis as a therapeutic technique. Freud took an aristocratic woman patient to meet the great hypnotist, because she had proved too difficult a hypnotic subject for Freud to 'put under' himself. Given his chronic shortage of cash, it was useful that his growing reputation attracted more patients, but, once again, he had to face a number of family and other difficulties.

In 1891 Freud's brother-in-law, Eli Bernays, had to flee Vienna because he owed so much to pressing creditors; Freud wrote begging letters to all his friends, asking them to give Eli and Anna some cash and somehow scraped together 500 florins for them himself. No sooner had Eli and Anna left for America than Pauline, Eduard Silberstein's young wife, committed suicide by throwing herself from the upper storey of Freud's building at 8 Maria Theresien Strasse.

When Freud celebrated his 35th birthday, he knew all too well that he had not yet achieved the fame he craved. Traditionally, Jews believed that when a man reached that age, half the Biblical three score and ten, he became a full adult. Freud's ailing father presented him with a fine Bible to mark the occasion. He inscribed it in Hebrew and begged his son never to forget he was a Jew. Jacob knew, of course, that his son did not believe in God, but Freud did as his father requested. Indeed, Freud was to become an archetypal secular Jewish intellectual, divorced from the practice of religious Judaism, but nonetheless proud of its traditions of literacy, exegesis and inquiry. Freud was no believer, but he certainly adopted the traditional Jewish stance, exemplified by the Book of Job, of asking ultimate questions.

In the summer of 1891 Freud climbed the Dachstein, a peak some 9800 feet high, not far from Salzburg. This was no mean achievement, and it is tempting to speculate that as he knew Christison had climbed Ben Vorlich on cocaine, Freud might also have used the drug to speed and ease his climb. If so, he made no record of the fact.

Freud returned to Vienna to find Fleischl had deteriorated further. The Greek temple was now crumbling fast and there was nothing anyone could do to prevent its ultimate collapse. After years of suffering, Fleischl died on October 22nd 1891. He was only 45 years old. His friend Exner described the end tenderly, writing:

'When I was called on the 22nd of October to (his) bedside and saw a corpse before me, my first comforting thought was that "at last he has found rest". How many times in the last years have I left his room under the shadow of the tragedy that was playing itself out there. Peace had come there now. For those of us who were his friends, Ernst was already lost to us much earlier. Not all at once but from year to year gradually the relationship of lively mutual friendship turned into deep and one-sided pity.'

Exner spoke of Fleischl's brilliant gifts, which had made a deep impression on both men and women, and blamed the 'illness', as he called it, for the fact Fleischl had not ' made a bond for life with a woman'.

Freud, as he had predicted, had seen his 'temple', Fleischl, destroyed. It is of course possible that Fleischl would have died from drugs – morphine – regardless of the 'cocaine intervention', but the increased stress inflicted on his body by cocaine seems likely to have at least sped up his terminal decline. Had Freud treated cocaine with greater objectivity, and not been so quick to accept the claim that it could treat addiction, Fleischl might well have lived longer.

Freud seems to have fallen prey to a mistake common amongst clinicians experimenting with novel pharmaceuticals: when side-effects emerge, there is a strong tendency to 'blame the disease and not the drug.' So convinced of cocaine's virtues by his own experience, Freud could not, or perhaps simply would not, acknowledge that the fatal 'moral weakness' which killed Fleischl might not have been his 'addictive personality' but Freud's own failure to recognise the dangers of the drug in which he had invested so much time and effort. It would be wrong to claim that 'Freud killed Fleischl' – but he certainly did not heal him. And he violated the central tenet of the Hippocratic Oath: for with high doses of cocaine, such as those that he prescribed his teacher, it is impossible to 'do no harm.' Perhaps some part of Freud did recognise this: in later years, he would keep a photograph of Fleischl on his desk.

Fleischl died and was forgotten by the world – for a time. There is no mention of him in the letters Freud wrote between 1888 and 1897. But when he started to analyse his own dreams, the man who had lost his thumb, his self-control and then his life, came back to both haunt Freud and inspire him.

Chapter 8

Fliess and the Nose Obsession

Freud's relationship with Wilhelm Fliess was 'the only really extraordinary episode in Freud's life', Ernest Jones declared, adding that he was astonished by Freud's 'extreme dependence' on Fliess. Nevertheless, he made no attempt to explain it. The letters between the two men would make it possible to follow the friendship in detail, but none of Fliess' letters to Freud have survived. Freud destroyed them, but never explained his reasons, so scholars have been obliged to make sense of the friendship on the basis of Freud's letters to Fliess alone. It is reasonable to suppose Freud realised that the letters showed him at his most neurotic, and were frank about his cocaine use. Once he was famous, he did not want people to see those aspects of his personality.

The two men met in 1887 when Breuer suggested Fliess attend Freud's lectures on anatomy and the nervous system. A few days later, Freud wrote to Fliess 'you have made a deep impression on me' and expressed his hope that they would become more than professional acquaintances. Though they lived in different cities – Fliess was based in Berlin – they wrote to each other often. They arranged their holidays so they could meet and Freud described these meetings as 'congresses'. He was fond of puns, so he would have been well aware of the double entendre; 'congresses' can be diplomatic, scientific ... or sexual.

Fliess came from a family of Sephardim, Jews who could trace their descent from Spain. Like Freud, he lived a secular life, but retained a strong sense of Jewish identity and, like Freud, he had lived through many tragedies. His parents had a stillborn child. Then Fliess's younger sister, Clara, died of pneumonia when Wilhelm was twenty. Fliess told Freud about these deaths but he never admitted the most devastating; his father had committed suicide when Wilhelm was nineteen years old.

No one is sure who devised this obvious visual pun on Fliess's obsession
with the nose.

Even his children did not learn of their grandfather's suicide until after Fliess was dead.

In 1883, Fliess started to work as a general practitioner. He married Ida Bondy who had grown up in Vienna – her parents were patients of Breuer's. Ida's sister married Oscar Rie, yet another doctor of their circle, who treated Freud's children.

All Rie's correspondence with Freud is sealed for perpetuity in the Library of Congress in Washington; it seems likely that it contains not just details of the illnesses of Jean-Martin and Freud's five other children but also of his friendship with Fliess, a friendship Freud eventually came to see as very embarrassing.

The letters Freud wrote to Fliess are an odd mix. There is much in them about domestic matters; Freud discusses the triumphs and illnesses of his children, for example. At one point he wrote: 'Much joy could be had from the little ones if only there were not also so much fright.'

Freud outlined his anxieties and symptoms to Fliess who became his doctor at a distance. The letters also contain many drafts of ideas Freud was developing and a few very revealing remarks. He confided that he had become a therapist 'against my will' and 'I should like to go back to anatomy for a while, that is, after all, the only gratifying thing.'

The letters are often intimate. In 1897, for example, Freud confessed his dream about his daughter Mathilde in which he was 'over affectionate'. The letters make it very clear Freud used cocaine throughout the 1890s.

Freud had some sense of why he always needed a close friendship. Freud's half brother Emanuel had two sons, Sam and John. The latter was a year older than Freud and became his first playmate. Freud wrote to Fliess of him:

'I have also long known the companion of my misdeeds between the ages of one and two years; it is my nephew, a year older than me ... The two of us seem occasionally to have behaved cruelly to my niece, who was a year younger. Until the end of my third year we had been inseparable; we had loved each other and fought each other.' (Freud to Fliess 1985c, p. 268)

This close friendship influenced all his later relationships with his peers and he always had to have 'an intimate friend and a hated enemy' in his emotional life.

What Freud did not tell Fliess, though, was that his childhood 'companion' John disappeared from Manchester when he was in his early thirties. There is no mention of John in any letter Freud wrote after 1890. It does not seem far-fetched to suggest that 'losing' John made Freud eager for a new intense friendship. In his dealings with Fliess, however, Freud never felt himself to be an equal; though two years older than Fleiss, he always deferred to him.

Fliess became an ear, nose and throat specialist by name – but seems to have had comparatively little interest in the ears and throat. Never in the history of medicine did anyone make such grandiose claims about the nose as Fleiss. It was, he argued, connected to the genitals on many levels and one could only understand human beings through the nose. During pregnancy and menstruation, women often suffered from nasal congestion. There were many reports of coitus being interrupted when one lover suffered a nosebleed. A sick nose could lead to heart trouble, respiratory difficulties, painful periods, migraines and, of course, hysteria in women, Fleiss argued. The nose, he maintained, was of primary importance in almost all bodily matters. In retrospect, this theory would appear to be a classic piece of pseudo-scientific Victorian medical nonsense.

From the start of their friendship, Freud referred patients who had nasal problems to Fliess for treatment. Ignoring the growing evidence of the dangers of cocaine, Fliess believed it could heal nasal dysfunctions, and, since the nose was paramount, also fix just about every human ailment in the process. The nasal reflex, as Fliess called it, could be cured by cauterising or anaesthetising 'genital spots' in the nose with cocaine. Freud's letters also gave detailed, at times even poetic, descriptions of how much pus streamed out of his own nose. We do not know if Fliess reciprocated. Later analysts took these descriptions of matters probuscular on Freud's part as 'evidence' of a homoerotic element to the friendship, and Freud's gushing enthusiasm for Fleiss when they first met does read rather like the words of a man in love – of a kind.

The 'Fliess Syndrome,' as it became known, created a flurry of interest in 'naso-sexual medicine.' Over 220 articles and books were published on the subject in the next twenty years. Compared to Freud at the time, Fliess was very successful and developed other, often fanciful ideas, of which the most bizarre was the claim that we are ruled by 'periodicity'. The cycles of the moon rule us, Fliess argued. He presented no meaningful evidence for this literally lunatic conviction, but Freud believed so totally in these 'laws of periodicity' that he worried himself sick about the likely date of his own death, a date he could predict by studying 'critical periods' in his life. Freud could calculate those thanks to Fliess' magic numbers, 23 and 28, which reflected the 23-day and 28-day cycles in the body and of the moon. The letters between the two men often contain calculations and, sometimes, Freud called his friend a 'great astrologer'. This 'astrology' also bears some resemblance to traditional Hebrew numerology, 'Gematria', a system used extensively in Kabbalistic mysticism which is not generally thought to be a scientific discipline.

In the context of his time, Fliess may not, however, have been as peculiar as he seems to modern sensibilities. Issues of journals such as the *Chemist and Druggist* from the 1880s advertise a staggering array of potions and elixirs that now look much like snake oil. Victorian medicine was certainly not, in contemporary terms, scientific, and Fliess's 'nasal reflex' theory was no more arbitrary or absurd than many other medical conceits of the time – for example, the then orthodox view that masturbation could cause permanent physiological damage. It was only in the early 1970s that homosexuality ceased to be classified as a form of mental illness, and the 'multiple personality disorder' epidemic of the 1980s and 90s shows psychiatry remains perfectly capable of hallucinating 'disorders' into existence.

For example, I once interviewed a Canadian psychiatrist who claimed one of his patients had over 300 separate selves. Multiple Personality Disorder (or Dissociative Personality Disorder) has since been subjected to more rigorous examination, leading many to conclude it never actually existed. As an applied science, medicine is a social activity – and will always reflect the prejudices of its time. Medicine remains to some extent an art – and Fliess a strikingly original artist. One might even describe him, mischievously, as a medical surrealist.

In his *Freud: The Biologist of the Mind*, Frank Sulloway claims Freudians have exaggerated the oddity of Fliess's ideas and were wrong to insist that the Freud-Fliess friendship was either a platonic homoerotic affair or a product of transference. It was equally wrong for Ernest Jones to claim that Freud's total faith in Fliess was due to powerful unconscious forces. The well respected historian of analysis Paul Roazen, argued in *Freud and His Followers* that 'good grounds remained for Freud's immense admiration for Fliess.'

Fliess was certainly not alone in championing the supremacy of the nose. A respectable Baltimore laryngologist, John Noland Mackenzie, for example, had proposed the nose-sex connection in the 1880s. When Fliess' ideas became well known, Mackenzie was delighted, as they appeared to confirm his own ideas. By the end of the century, Sulloway wrote, 'the Mackenzie-Fliess naso-genital theory had come to be a common topic of discussion among rhinologists.' Two famous sexologists, Richard von Krafft-Ebbing and Havelock Ellis, thought there was good evidence for the nasal theory as some women suffered nosebleeds during menstruation. Drawing on Darwin's theory of evolution, which suggested a link between sexuality and the sense of smell in lower animals, Sulloway judged there was an 'important grain of scientific truth in Fliess's now-defunct nasal theories'.

Both Roazen and Sulloway also accept that there was some small truth in Fliess's ideas about 'vital and sexual periodicity (which) were becoming fashionable by the mid-1890s'. Darwin had recognised the importance of periodicities in nature and was fascinated by weekly cycles which he found 'in virtually all temporal aspects of growth, reproduction, and disease known to life science'. They were linked, Darwin suggested, with the rhythm of the tides. Our ancestors lived in the sea and depended on its ebb and flow. The stages of evolution made that clear. Long before our ancestors were apes, we were sea creatures and our life in the womb recalls that, as foetuses develop gills about three months after conception.

Even Fliess' 23-day cycle was not wholly absurd as Sulloway

'discovered' the work of John Beard, a lecturer in comparative embryology and vertebrate zoology at the University of Edinburgh who argued for the existence of this less obvious cycle. In his 1897 monograph *The Span of Gestation and the Cause of Birth*, Beard argued there was a 23-day cycle between the end of menstruation and the start of the next ovulation, making it a critical number. He also suggested that 46 days after conception – i. e twice the magical 23 – 'the embryo is recognisable in all its essential parts.'

The number 23 also seized upon the imagination of a figure now familiar to readers of this book: William S. Burroughs Senior, who maintained that there was a universal significance to the number 23 and thus to the number 5 (2 + 3), which could be observed in the alleged regularity with which these numbers showed up, in all sorts of apparent coincidences. This branch of drug-addled numerology has proved persistent, with the legendary underground sound system 'Spiral Tribe', who put on some of the most famous British raves of the early 1990s, presenting themselves as part of 'Network 23'. Exactly what the '23 conspiracy' is supposed to be is never clear, but it has proven to be a remarkably durable trope of underground culture.

There was nothing new about Fliess' third preoccupation – the idea of bisexuality being universal – as Plato had discussed it in ancient Greece. Sulloway concluded there was:

'... enough method and consistency to Fliess's madness to convince many – Sigmund Freud included – from a whole generation of scientific contemporaries that he had made a series of profound scientific discoveries. Above all, to those contemporaries who shared Fliess's biological assumptions, his ideas seemed to occupy the visionary forefront, not the lunatic fringe, of hard science.'

I cannot tell if Sulloway was making a pun on lunatic, but the point remains: much as they now seem absurd, Fleiss's 'biological assumptions' were not outrageous for his time.

In 1892 Freud was sent a patient whose treatment would bring a major breakthrough, a breakthrough that owed something to Fliess' ideas and support. There are three reasons for describing this case at some length. It features the nose, as the main symptom was an olfactory hallucination, a 'phantom scent'; then Freud's account of his methods shows how he was feeling his way towards a therapeutic system, trying one technique than another in a process of trial and error.

Finally, what I am tempted to call *The Curious Case of the Burned Pudding* reads like a Victorian tale of thwarted love and Freud relates it with the skill of a good storyteller. The case study has echoes of Charlotte Brontë's *Jane Eyre*, and is a neat demonstration of the oft-repeated claim that Freud's case studies read more like fiction than conventional medical histories.

Lucy was a 30-year-old English woman serving as a governess in the house of a successful and recently widowed Vienna businessman who she called the Director. She was plagued by a phantom stench of burnt pudding, which distracted and perplexed her. Lucy was depressed, tired 'and tormented by subjective sensations of smell.' Freud immediately examined her nose which did not have 'the perception proper to a sense organ.'

When Freud asked her what smell troubled her most, she replied it was the smell of burnt pudding. He had never before come across a case in which a dessert seemed to have triggered a neurosis.

Freud tried to put Lucy in a deep hypnotic state, but she was a poor hypnotic subject, and he failed to entrance her. He then asked her when she had first experienced the smell of burnt pudding. Lucy had been playing at cooking with the Director's two little girls when the postman delivered a letter for her. The children stole it and teased her, joking it had to be a gift for her birthday, which was coming soon. The letter, in fact, was from her mother. Lucy told Freud she had been thinking of going back to England because her mother was very lonely.

'When the children were having this game with me,' Lucy told Freud, 'there was suddenly a strong smell.' As she begged the children to give her back the letter, the pudding cooked, forgotten, and began to burn. Lucy explained: 'Ever since then, I have been pursued by the smell. It is there all the time and it becomes stronger when I am agitated.'

Lucy was also upset because she was unpopular with the other household servants, and quarrelled with them frequently. Freud managed to get to the bottom of that easily by making a nice intuitive leap. 'I believe that you really are in love with your employer, though perhaps you are not aware of it yourself and that you have a secret hope of taking their mother's place in actual fact,' he told her. The other servants were upset because they sensed Lucy's infatuation with the master of the house, and were jealous of her.

Lucy answered, Freud noted, 'in her usual laconic fashion.'

'Yes, I think that's true,' she said.

'But if you knew you loved your employer, why didn't you tell me?'

'I didn't know or rather I didn't want to know. I wanted to drive it out of my head and not think of it again and I believe latterly I have succeeded.'

Freud asked why Lucy had not told him about this; she replied very sensibly that the Director was her employer, distinguished and much richer than she. One day he began to talk to her about how his children should be brought up and became very 'cordial'. He told her how much he depended on her for the care of his children and 'as he said this he looked at her meaningfully.' Lucy's hopes had been raised, but nothing similar ever happened again. Freud, the good agony uncle, now suggested to Lucy that the 'intimate exchange' and the meaningful look 'had probably sprung from the Director's 'thoughts about his wife.' He would have talked about their children with her: now he found himself talking to Lucy, who had adopted the maternal role, and so he looked at her 'meaningfully' too.

Freud hoped this insight would cure Lucy of the smell hallucinations but it did not quite work. She still suffered from depression and, sometimes, from the burnt pudding smell, though less often than before – it now only plagued her when she was agitated. The persistence of the smell hallucination suggested to Freud that it was linked to other traumas.

After Christmas, when they picked up treatment again, Lucy reported that she was plagued by another 'similar smell resembling cigar smoke', but the aroma had been covered by the smell of the pudding.

Freud placed his hand on Lucy's hand, as Breuer had done with Anna O, and slowly Lucy revealed the truth.

Lucy was in the dining room. She was waiting with the children for the Director and another man to come to lunch from the factory.

'Go on looking at the picture; it will develop and become more specialised,' Freud suggested.

'Yes there is a guest. It's the chief accountant. He's fond of the children as if they were his own grandchildren,' Lucy said. But the man often came to lunch so there was nothing special about that.

'Be patient and just keep looking at the picture. Something is sure to happen,' Freud said. He was clearly prompting his patient.

'We're getting up to go from the table. The children say their goodbyes and then they go upstairs as usual to the second floor.'

'And then?'

Then, Lucy added, 'the accountant tries to kiss them. My employer flares up and shouts at him 'Don't kiss the children'. I feel a stab in my heart and as the gentlemen are already smoking, the cigar smoke sticks in the memory.'

Freud did not need much technique to probe deeper and he now struck 'gold'. This incident took place two months before the burning of the pudding and made Lucy see that the Director she adored could be horribly rude to a lovely old man.

Freud again employed the pressure of the hand technique and soon Lucy described a third distressing scene. A ladyfriend of the Director had come to visit. The lady kissed the children, not just on the cheek but on the mouth. The Director 'managed to restrain himself' and did not shout at the woman but the moment she left, 'his fury burst on the head of the unlucky governess.' Unjustly, he blamed Lucy for allowing such an outrage to happen and 'if it ever happened again he would entrust his children's upbringing to other hands.' Lucy told herself that it was mad to harbour hopes of ending up happily married to a man capable of flaring into fury at mild accountants and polite acquaintances.

Two days later, Lucy came to see Freud again. She was cheerful. She had accepted that she had no real prospect of being loved by her employer. 'And I shan't make myself unhappy over it,' she said.

'Are you still in love with your employer,' Freud asked.

'Yes, I certainly am but that makes no difference.' Stoically, she said 'I can have thoughts and feelings to myself.'

Lucy's nose was now no longer numb, when Freud examined it, and it was sensitive to pain. She was able to identify smells as long as they were strong. The treatment, Freud noted, lasted nine weeks in all. Later he met Lucy and she had maintained her recovery. Freud's success with Lucy added to his faith in Fliess, a faith that would soon be tested.

In 1893, Freud went through a spell of ill health; there seemed to be something wrong with his heart. Experiencing palpitations and shortness of breath, he turned to Fliess for help. From Berlin Fliess gave his friend very conventional advice – stop smoking. On November 17th 1893 Freud replied 'I am not obeying your smoking prohibition' and justified that by adding: 'Do you really consider it such a great boon to live a great many years in misery?'

Freud's last doctor, Max Schur, analysed Fliess' advice to Freud on his cardiac condition. He noted there were uncharacteristic mistakes in the letters Freud wrote when Fliess was urging him to stop smoking. Schur gives examples of words Freud invented such as 'Pressung', which does not exist in German. Something was the matter but Schur was not sure if it was Freud's heart, his unconscious or both.

By March 1894, Freud was certain something was badly wrong and wrote to Fliess that when he ran up the stairs he 'was unable to talk for five minutes and had to admit I was ill.' He went to have a massage but that was of no help, and wrote in despair: 'this morning I once again wanted to die relatively young'. By April 19th he accused Fliess of hiding the truly serious nature of his condition.

One consolation at least gave Freud '. . . some pleasure because it emphasises once again that the condition of the heart depends on the condition of the nose'. Fliess had diagnosed Freud's condition, and said that it was not a new problem. 'It is just the old focal pus accumulation which now happens to feel inclined to produce eruptions like Mount Etna.' In other words, when Freud sneezed like a volcano, it confirmed his friend's astuteness. Fliess urged Freud not to exaggerate and again told him to give up cigars. Freud responded:

'Last time you still explained it as being nasal and said that the percussive signs of a nicotine heart were missing. This time you show great concern for me and forbid me to smoke.'

Freud leapt to a dramatic conclusion. 'I can understand this only if I assume that you want to conceal the true state of affairs from me and I beg you not to do this.' Freud was imagining he was at death's door when probably he had a minor heart condition, perhaps a sometimes irregular heart rhythm, Schur argued. Schur did not consider a second possibility: that the palpitations were caused, or exacerbated, by Freud's use of cocaine.

Freud continued to write in melodramatic and hypochondriac terms, telling Fliess he did not think he was indispensable and promising to endure 'with great dignity' the fact that he would die young. What bothered him most was that he was unable to work. Then he suddenly changed the subject, saying: 'Rascals and wife are well; the latter is not a confidante of my death deliria.' Obviously, Freud knew he was exaggerating the extent of his illness but that did not stop him persisting in the macabre fantasy that he was close to death. Freud was in a volatile state, and told Fliess on January 24th 1895:

'Dearest Wilhelm,
I must hurriedly write to you about something that greatly astonishes me; otherwise I would be truly ungrateful. In the last few days I have felt quite unbelievably well, as though everything had been erased – a feeling which in spite of better times I have not known for ten months. Last time I wrote you, after a good period which immediately succeeded the reaction, that a few viciously bad days had followed during which a cocainisation of the left nostril had helped me to an amazing extent.'

Freud was continuing to use the drug. He added:

'The next day I kept the nose under cocaine, which one should not really do; that is, I repeatedly painted it to prevent the renewed occurrence of swelling; during this time I discharged what in my experience is a copious amount of thick pus; and since then I have felt wonderful, as though there never had been anything wrong at all. Arrhythmia is still present, but rarely and not badly; the sensitivity to external pressure is slight, the sensations being between 0 and −0. I am postponing the full expression of my gratitude and the discussion of what share the operation had in this unprecedented improvement until we see what happens next.'

The episode which reveals the most damaging aspects of Freud's dependence on Fliess was their treatment of Emma Eckstein. Eckstein first met Freud in 1892, when she was 27. She came from a prominent socialist family in Vienna and went to Freud complaining of stomach pains and depression which she believed were related to the pattern of her periods. Freud diagnosed her as suffering from hysteria as well as 'masturbating to excess', as he put it. Inevitably, he suspected Fliess' favourite malady was the cause of all this, 'nasal reflex neurosis'.

Fliess travelled to Vienna at Freud's request to examine Emma Eckstein. He diagnosed the nasal reflex and recommended cauterising her nose. The operation was carried out on February 22nd. Fliess then returned to Berlin. His departure had an impact on Freud's nose as a letter dated March 4th 1895 attests:

'On the last day you were here, I suddenly discharged several scabs from the right side, the one not operated on. As early as the next day there appeared thick, old pus in large clots, at first on the right side only and soon thereafter also on the left. Since then the nose has again been flooded; only today has the purulent secretion become somewhat less dense. Light but regular symptoms: in the morning a stuffed nose, vile head, not better until large amounts have been discharged; in the interval occasionally migraine; everything by the way, not very severe. During the first of these days, I noticed with pride that I can climb stairs without dyspnea; for the last three days pain in the heart region, atactic pulse, and beautiful insufficiency.'

133

The results revealed Fliess, Freud felt, to be a genius.

'Though not designed to make one feel at ease, this information affords some pleasure because it emphasizes once again that the condition of the heart depends upon the condition of the nose. I cannot regard the latter as a new infection; I have the impression that I really still have, as you surmised, a focal pus accumulation (right sphenoid bone), which now happens to feel inclined to produce eruptions.'

Freud repeated the volcanic image, describing his nose as 'like a private Etna.'

But while Freud obsessed about his nose, two weeks after her operation, Emma Eckstein's was bleeding profusely and producing a foetid odour that 'was very bad.' Freud obviously felt he could not cope on his own. On March 8th he asked a well-known local doctor, Robert Gersuny, to help, but he could not come to see her till the evening; so Freud called his old school friend, Rosannes, who came at noon. Rosannes cleaned an area inside Emma's nose and removed some sticky blood clots. Suddenly, he found himself pulling on a thread. 'Before either of us had time to think at least half a metre of gauze had been removed from the cavity. The next moment came a flood of blood,' Freud wrote. Emma turned white, 'her eyes bulged and she had no pulse. It lasted about half a minute but this was enough to make the poor creature unrecognizable.'

Rosannes packed the cavity with fresh gauze and Emma stopped bleeding. Freud was frightened and understood the horror of what had happened; Fliess had forgotten to remove some 50 centimetres of surgical gauze from Eckstein's nasal canal. The material had been in Emma's nose for 15 days, causing her bleeding.

'I felt sick,' Freud said. As soon as Emma's nose had been 'packed', 'I fled to the next room, drank a bottle of water and felt miserable.' He was given a small glass of cognac and 'I felt myself again.'

Rosannes arranged for Emma to be taken to a sanatorium to have the second parcel of gauze removed. When Freud went to see her, he was, understandably, uneasy and remorseful: Fleiss's mistake had nearly killed her. Emma noticed his anxiety and was in no mood to comfort him. Freud wrote to Fleiss: 'She greeted me with the condescending remark, "So this is the strong sex".'

Leaving gauze inside a patient after an operation is a very basic surgical error but Freud could not bring himself to blame Fliess. Instead he reassured him 'that this mishap should have happened to you, how you will react when you hear about it, what others could make of it, how wrong I was to urge you to operate in a foreign city where you could not follow through on the case ... all this came over me simultaneously.' Freud was so intent on protecting Fliess that he blamed Rosannes, saying that he should have sensed that there was an obstruction in Emma's nose, and therefore cancelled the operation.

Five days later Freud again consoled Fliess; he told him he had discussed what had happened with Breuer, who called it 'a minimal oversight.' It was time Fliess forgave himself for such a minor error.

On March 20th Freud was in good spirits, but poor Emma felt much worse. She was in great pain and her face was terribly swollen. 'At noon when they lifted the packing to examine her,' she had such a severe haemorrhage 'so that she almost died.' Gersuny, who was now available, made a new incision the next day to find the source of the bleeding but without success. Again, her nose was packed with fresh gauze. Astonishingly, Freud seems to have been almost more worried for Fliess than for Emma as he wrote:

'In my thoughts I have given up hope for the poor girl and am inconsolable that I involved you and created such a distressing affair for you. I also feel very sorry for her as I had become fond of her.'

The next week Emma had recovered somewhat and was 'tolerably well' though she was 'hysterical' but Freud the brave felt he could cope with that. When they removed the gauze 'we hope to be safe from new surprises.' On April 11th, however, the furious bleeding started again and Rosannes re-examined the cavity. 'As soon as the packing was partly removed there was a new life-threatening haemorrhage ... It did not

135

spurt, it surged.' Freud and Rosannes thought they had pierced a large blood vessel and struggled to pack Emma's nose with gauze again. 'Add to this the pain, the morphine, the demoralisation caused by the obvious medical helplessness and the tinge of danger,' Freud wrote. Again Emma could have died, but Freud told Fliess that he was '... very shaken that such a mishap could have resulted from an operation that was meant to be harmless.'

This catastrophe affected Freud's mood, his libido and his heart, he confessed to Fliess. 'My libido has long been subdued,' he said. He took one gram of digitalis, an herb-based medication used in treating irregular heartbeats, but the arrhythmia persisted and Freud became depressed; he could not sleep or work.

If word of Fliess' incompetence got out, his career would probably be ruined. Freud told Fliess, however:

'The writer of this letter is very miserable but also offended that you deem it necessary to have a testimonial certificate from Gersuny for your rehabilitation.' He stressed to Fliess that he did 'not reproach you with anything.' He wanted to come to Berlin to see his friend but could not afford to spend the 1000 to 1500 florins needed for the journey. It is remarkable that Fliess did not make the journey to Vienna to assist in Eckstein's treatment − or, bluntly, to clean up the mess he'd made. As ever, when upset, confused or uncertain, Freud reached for his favourite remedy: 'Today I can write because I have more hope. I pulled myself out of a miserable attack with a cocaine application.' The drug worked its magic. 'I cannot guarantee that I will not come for a day or two for a cauterisation or galvanization but at the moment that too is not possible.' The cauterisation would inevitably require yet more cocaine.

On April 26th cocaine had put an 'end to the last horrible attack.' Since then Freud had been well 'and a great deal of pus had been coming out.' Freud was not often callous but he now added that Emma − 'my tormentor and yours now appears to be doing well.' This description of Eckstein, who had almost died at the hands of Freud and Fliess, as their 'tormentor', suggests an interesting area of research, the hostility of doctors towards patients they fail to cure. Patients should really think more about their doctors' needs.

The next day, Freud claimed that his experience had shown him yet again the value of cocaine. 'Since the last cocainisation three circumstances have continued ... 1. I feel very well 2. I am discharging ample amounts of pus. 3. I am feeling very well. Thus I want nothing more to do with a heart condition, only the facilitation with nicotine.' By this, he meant that he intended to carry on smoking.

The intensity of the correspondence and the constant references to cocaine are striking, but the Emma Eckstein crisis did not stop Freud working. He was more driven than ever and concentrated on drafting *The Project for a Scientific Psychology*, a complicated theory of how the brain worked which is generally seen as Freud's first attempt to map the flow of conscious and unconscious forces in the mind. *The Project* was conceived in late March 1895. Fliess commented on draft after draft and those comments influenced Freud as he wrote during the summer. Freud used cocaine to keep his nose 'clean' (!) and his energy levels high. He wrote to Fliess on May 25th that he had 'discharged exceedingly ample amounts of pus and all the while felt splendid; now the secretion has nearly dried up and I am still feeling very well. I propose the following to you: it is neither the congestion nor the flow of pus that determines the distant symptoms.'

On June 12th Freud continued his self-observation on cocaine, writing to Fliess about the 'nasal' case of a Mrs R:

'You are right that I am overflowing with new ideas, theoretical ones as well. My theories on defense have made an important advance of which I shall give you an account next time. Even the psychological construction behaves as if it would come together, which gives me immense pleasure ... I am feeling I to IIa. I need a lot of cocaine. Also, I have started smoking again, moderately, in the last two to three weeks, since the nasal conviction (*that his cardiac problems had a nasal cause – my note*) has become evident to me. I have not observed any ensuing disadvantage. If you again prohibit it, I must give it up again. But do consider whether you can do this if it is only intolerance and not etiology.'

It's astonishing that Fliess, who was utterly sensible about the harmfulness of tobacco, never warned Freud to, at the very least, reduce the amount of cocaine he took.

'I began it (tobacco) again because I constantly missed it (after fourteen months of abstinence) and because I must treat this psychic fellow [*psychischenkerl*] well or he won't work for me. I demand a great deal of him. The torment, most of the time, is superhuman.'

Although Fliess had nearly killed Emma through his incompetence, Freud did not become less deferential to his friend. In fact, Freud now told Fliess how grateful he was to him and almost offered him homage.

'I am putting together all sorts of things for you today – several debts, which remind me that I also owe you thanks, your case history of labour pains, and two notebooks of mine. Your notes reinforced my first impression that it would be desirable to make them into a full-fledged pamphlet on the nose and female sexuality,' Freud wrote. In fact Fliess would have been well-advised to shut up about the nose.

In his dreams, however, Freud was more troubled. In August he had his famous dream of Irma's injection, the dream which pushed him towards some of his key discoveries. One critic has argued that the dream is not hard to understand as it is a perfect example of cynical wish-fulfilment; a doctor who has made a tragic error wants to be washed clean of blame.

Almost as soon as he had the dream, Freud described it to Fliess and suggested a cosy domestic arrangement. 'We can share quarters, live and take walks together, insofar as our noses permit it,' Freud wrote on August 16th 1895 before leaving for a short holiday in Venice. He then arranged to go to Berlin where he and Fliess discussed *The Project*. On the train back to Vienna Freud began writing his notes up. On October 8th, he sent Fliess two notebooks which contained his work on it so far and on January 1st 1896 he sent Fliess what is known as 'the Draft'. It is especially interesting because it deals with two issues which would be at the heart of psychoanalysis – anxiety and pleasure.

First, Freud argued we need psychological strategies to protect ourselves and introduced the 'principle of inertia'. The mind uses 'quantity-screens' made up of 'nerve-ending apparatuses' as a first line of defence against the powerful stimuli of the outside world. When the screens fail, we feel both pain and high levels of excitation, which often lead to anxiety.

Like a novelist introducing new characters, Freud now brought in the X, Y and Z neurons which each had a different role and, then, went on to explain the 'pleasure/unpleasure principle'. Human beings can't stand too much stimulation. When we make love and especially at the point of orgasm, we feel both pleasure and pain. Freud suggested the 'experience of satisfaction' was a reaction to the 'filling' of the neuron by pressure, resulting in a motor discharge.

One might have expected him to develop these ideas with reference to sex but, instead, he talked of how babies screamed. The baby first cries when he or she is hungry and so gets mother or nanny to feed them. The toddler then learns to say she is hungry. The scream has become language. But the old memory of screaming for food still lurks in the brain's layers of neurons, churning, unforgiven, and ready to erupt again.

Freud was prescient about this, as much current work on the development of language shows children's first words express desires, but babies then learn fast. The speed of this learning process led Freud to marvel at how the 'little primitive' developed so quickly.

The best evidence for the fact that children first talk about desires comes from the work of present-day child psychologists like Henry Wellman and John Flavell. Wellman and Karen Bartsch, for example, recorded over 20,000 conversations of children under the age of five. Many talked of desires from when they were just 18 months old. For example Eve and Mark, both aged 18 months, were the first to use expressions like 'I want'. Soon very young children begin to offer reasons for their desires. Abe (aged two years and five months) heard his mother ask his father if he enjoyed the cranberry muffin. The boy said 'I wanna a cranberry muffin. I like them.' 'I like' is, of course, a psychological explanation for his desire. By the age of 36 months many toddlers could talk about wishes and desires appropriately.

Wellman and his colleague Karen Bartsch found that about 1 in every 40 utterances had to do with wishes, while only 1 in 120 utterances concerned thoughts or beliefs. Rather more surprisingly, Wellman and Bartsch found that some children began to talk about thinking when they were very young. One dialogue shows this:

Adam (2.11): I ... just thinking.
Adult: You're just thinking?
Adam: Yes.
Adult: What are you thinking about?
Adam: Thinking 'bout leaf.

As they learn a more complex language of feelings, beliefs and thoughts, toddlers start to understand that other people are well ... other. I am me and you are you. Freud was right to marvel at the little primitives. Though it contained interesting ideas that anticipated his later work, Freud did not allow *The Project* to be published in his lifetime – the reasons for this restraint are unknown.

In March 1896, Freud wrote to Fliess that he would be bringing to their next 'congress' several handkerchiefs, cordial greetings from all the Freuds, the dream analysis, the aetiology of the neuroses of defence and a psychological conjecture. He was looking forward to meeting and hoped 'you would lend me your ear for a few metapsychological questions'.

After he got back to Vienna, Freud wrote to Fliess on April 26th that Fliess had helped him a great deal 'in moderation in regard to tobacco just as I feel more resolute and in better shape since our entrevue'. Then Freud returned to the subject of Emma Eckstein and said something bizarre and unkind, 'so far I know only that she bled out of longing'. As a child Emma had been 'a cutter' – Freud does not explain the phrase which today suggests someone who deliberately harms themselves as a 'cry for help' – and suffered from bad nosebleeds. Before she had her first period, Emma had headaches and was told she was malingering. Freud again showed himself to be a master of denial. Emma Eckstein's near-death, he claimed here, was a product not of Fliess's error in failing to remove the gauze, but of her own hysteria, which made her

The many forms in which cocaine became part of the first consumer society.

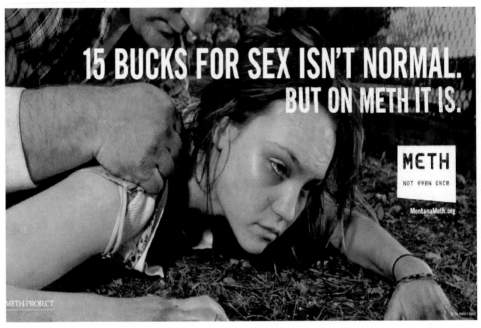

One of the best anti-drug posters.

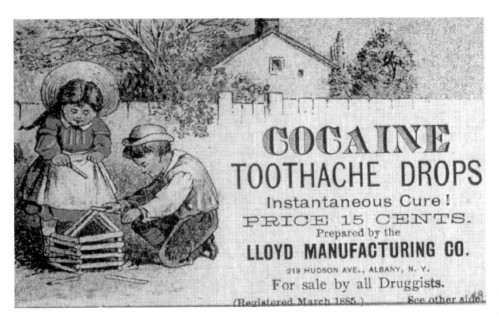

Cocaine could solve any ill. Queen Victoria used these.

Freud divided and sub-divided the mind into many compartments
– the theory inspired many artists.

This was drafted as an ad for an anti-psychotic drug in the 1960s ... truly.

'bleed out of longing'. Once again, neither the doctor nor any bungled treatment, but the patient was at fault.

But when he saw Emma again, Freud did not think he betrayed any hostility and wrote that she was moved when she saw how upset he was by her bleeding. It was a good thing Emma could not read his mind, for he wrote later that she experienced his concern 'as the realisation of an old wish to be loved in her illness and in spite of the danger she was in, she became happy as never before. When she went to the sanatorium because of an unconscious wish to entice me to go there, she started to bleed again as unfailing means of re-arousing my affection.'

There is nothing that can be said in Freud's defence here. The *physical reality* of the surgical gauze that Fliess had left behind in Eckstein's head did not cause her bleeding, he insisted: the true causes were psychological, her desire to 'arouse his affection'. Eckstein's 'treatment', was not merely far worse than the stomach pains and depression that originally brought her to Freud: it very nearly killed her. But Freud's response to Fliess's bungling was to condemn the patient as a hysterical manipulator and tormentor.

Emma Eckstein was not merely slandered by a guilty Freud: she was left with a slightly disfigured face for the rest of her life by the repeated operations, none of which served any therapeutic purpose. The woman had been put through hell on the basis of the 'nasal reflex' theory. Neither Fliess nor Freud ever offered her a word of apology.

Again Freud faced many stresses. He famously wrote that his father's death freed him to develop psychoanalysis. Jacob died in November 1896 – and Freud's reaction shows that he was deeply conflicted about his father's death. He certainly did not behave like a good son should. He was late for the funeral. A Jewish biographer would have asked whether Freud wanted to avoid leading the mourners, as Jewish custom required of him, in reciting the Kaddish, the prayer for the dead. A Jewish son who does not do so expresses contempt not just for God but for his father. Jones, a non-Jew, never raised the question. Freud's excuse for arriving late was lame; he had to wait a long time at the barbers' and did not dare ask to be shaved first.

Freud told Fliess he had come to respect his father but said very little about any grief he may have felt. He soon switched to an old topic, saying that 'with heart and nose I am satisfied again.' Jacob's death, however, may not have been the key reason for Freud's 'liberation'. The reality may have been more prosaic. After years of struggling, his practice was finally picking up. This is evident from his notebook for 1896, 1897 and 1898 in which he recorded all his patients, their basic problems and the fees he charged. I found this book in Box 50 of the Freud Archives in the Library of Congress; there does not seem to be another such notebook there, which suggests some documents are missing or buried in the closed files.

In 1896, Freud recorded that he had 388 patients' visits and made 63 house calls. In 1897, he had 864 patients' visits and made 192 house calls – his practice had virtually trebled. Unfortunately, the notebooks don't specify what his patients' symptoms were. Freud's financial position improved to the extent that he was now able to buy a few small terracotta figurines, beginning the collection that would mean so much to him.

At the end of 1897, Freud was well into his self-analysis, which journey of discovery was praised by Jones for its fearless honesty, and was proposed by Freud to be, along with the case of Anna O, the origin of psychoanalysis. Though he did not see himself as an addict, he did reflect on the causes of addiction and came to the simple conclusion that it was down to the 'genital thing'. In a letter to Fliess dated December 22nd 1897, Freud wrote:

> '... it has dawned on me that masturbation is the one major habit, the primal addiction and that it is only as a substitute and replacement for it that the other addictions – for alcohol, morphine, tobacco – come into existence.'

Freud asked 'whether an addiction of this kind is curable or whether analysis and therapy are brought to a stop at this point and must content themselves with transforming a case of hysteria into neurasthenia?'.

The main symptoms of neurasthenia were tiredness, anxiety, headaches and depression. Americans were particularly prone to the condition; William James nicknamed it 'Americanitis,' which was caused by the stress of living in overpopulated cities, with congested railways – psychiatrists discovered early on that people who were injured in train accidents suffered traumatic stress. Neurasthenics were prone to suffer – or perhaps enjoy – frequent nocturnal emissions, Freud said. In the light of this, his claim that cigars gave him self-control is especially interesting. The implication seems to have been that Freud thought smoking stopped him masturbating too much.

Freud did not reveal how either cocaine or his self-analysis affected his sex drive, however. He told Jones he lost all interest in sleeping with Martha when he reached forty. That was also, of course, the year his father died. The father dies and the great scientist stops having sex – any therapist would be intrigued by this course of events, but Freud's followers, characteristically, do not seem to have analysed the connection, if any, between Jacob's death and Freud's celibacy from such an early age. The usual explanation given for this abstinence is that Martha was finding pregnancy increasingly difficult and Freud hated using condoms. He would not compromise about wearing what he later called 'Turkish overcoats' and so he gave up intercourse. Freud had fathered six children in nine years of marriage which does not suggest he had a particularly low sex drive. I would like to suggest that Freud made a bargain, just as Faust had done – but not with any literal devil. He knew that many saints and mystics believed chastity allowed them to concentrate on developing their spiritual side. Freud, the great atheist, behaved like a monk because he believed – unconsciously, we presume – that 'the old and dirty gods' would reward his sacrifice.

By 1897 Freud had begun his self-analysis, which formed the basis for *On the Interpretation of Dreams*, the book that changed his life. Although published at the end of the 19th century, the book has long been recognised as one of the most influential and defining texts of the 20th century, a work that fundamentally changed how we think about the mind and motivation. It is a book that has been widely read and studied, subjected to almost as much critical analysis as the greatest Shakespearian tragedies.

Yet more than a century since it first saw print, it remains a book of shadows, and is not always frank about the influences on Freud's own dreams and their origins. It was the dream-interpretation business that would, in time, make Freud a household name. Yet again, cocaine played a crucial part, one that has long been suppressed by Freud's disciples.

Chapter 9

The Interpretation of (Cocaine) Dreams

The central claim of *On the Interpretation of Dreams* is that *all* dreams are wish-fulfilments, but the wishes are disguised and censored by the puritanical Super-ego. A man could hope for the insights of *On the Interpretation of Dreams* only once in a lifetime, Freud wrote. Critics of analysis see this as a grandiose boast while the faithful praise it as yet another example of his modesty; he did not expect to have a second revelation of this significance.

One of the most influential of post-Freudian analysts, Erik Erikson, was surprisingly cynical about the book and said that one key dream 'may, in fact, carry the historical burden of being dreamed in order to be analysed, and analysed in order to fulfill a very special fate' (p. 239). That special fate was to provide Freud with material he needed to confirm his theory of dreams as wish-fulfilments, which would finally make him famous. The paradox is that *On the Interpretation of Dreams* is a text about dreams being wish-fulfilments which fulfils the author's wish to prove that dreams are wish-fulfilments. Freud never discussed those paradoxes, though there are slips and asides which suggest he was not wholly blind to the ironies.

In the preface, Freud admitted he could not be totally honest with his readers, which would oblige him to 'reveal to the public gaze more of the intimacies of my mental life than I liked, or than is normally necessary for any writer who is a man of science and not a poet'. Intimacies, however, could not be avoided, which made for a 'painful but unavoidable necessity'; so Freud compromised. He held back some secrets he felt were too private for publication, but he knew the compromise was flawed, as he wrote:

Advertisement in the *Chemist and Druggist* from the days when cocaine was deemed no more of a public menace than vinegar.

'Naturally however I have been unable to resist the temptation of taking the edge off some of my indiscretions by omissions and substitutions. But whenever this has happened the value of my instances has been very definitely diminished. I can only express a hope that readers ... will put themselves in my position and treat me with indulgence.'

One must look at the cocaine dreams in the book bearing this admission in mind. The information we have about Freud's sleeping habits does not come from his own writings, but the memoirs of the family maid, Paula Fichtl. Freud would read a book, often a detective novel, before going to sleep and usually woke around 7 am. Freud never said how long after awakening he recorded his night's visions, yet current research on dreams and memory suggests time is a key variable in dream recollection. In most studies today, psychologists wake the dreamer up soon after they emerge from the stage of sleep in which dreams occur, Rapid Eye Movement sleep (REM). REM sleep was not discovered till the 1950s; in 1896, the most substantial work on memory was on how people remembered nonsense syllables. The nature of dreams is such, however, that even if Freud had used the most precise methodology, we still would not know whether he remembered his dreams accurately.

The most harrowing dream Freud recorded was one in which voices ordered him to dissect his own legs and pelvis. He saw them in front of him as if they were in the dissecting room, but he did not notice he had lost any limbs and was struck by the absence of pain. As a doctor, he knew there was something else wrong; his pelvis had been eviscerated and he could see thick protuberances which looked like piles. Dissecting his own body symbolised dissecting the deepest secrets of his self, Freud said, but he did not make public everything uncovered in this process of dissection.

The question of how much to disclose bothered him and he sometimes quoted Goethe's maxim: 'The best of what you know, you could not tell your students.' This, after all, came from the same pen as 'If I knew myself, I'd run away.' Freud's favourite writer was astonishingly ambivalent about the value of honesty. Anti-Freudians would no doubt say that Freud and Goethe had something in common here. A cheap shot, perhaps, but Freud did admit that there were dreams and meanings he felt compelled to conceal.

After the preface, Freud reviewed the existing literature on dreams. He began with the great dream interpreters of the Bible, Joseph and Daniel, whose ancient settings made for rather simpler dreams than those of the industrial age unconscious of Freud's Vienna. God did not go in for deeply disguised latent content. His message was as subtle and repetitive as a foghorn. He wanted the stiff-necked Israelites to behave, pray more, sin less, worship Him more fervently and reject all other gods. Freud then covered the extensive Victorian literature on dreams.

In his short book, *Freud und Das Kokain*, Von Scheidt suggested that cocaine did influence Freud's analysis of his own dreams. This idea needs to be developed fully, especially as Freud did not comment on the possibility that cocaine influenced his dreaming. This makes it all the more striking that the dream Freud uses to introduce and explain his technique of analysis was a dream in which cocaine played a crucial part.

Surprisingly, it seems that no one has to date performed a simple content analysis of the number of dreams described by Freud in which cocaine played a part.

The book includes accounts of some 144 dreams, of which only 39 were Freud's own, 27% of the overall dream count. In addition, a number of Freud's 39 dreams were very briefly outlined in the text. Some were mere fragments, half-developed images skated over in some haste. Five of his dreams were related in just two sentences apiece. In one dream Freud keeps a woman waiting, in another he sees a woman and her daughter – Mama, Freud suspected, was making it difficult for her daughter to continue in treatment. There was also a dream in which Freud receives a political pamphlet from a Social Democrat; one of his school friends had, in fact, become an important local politician.

Freud loved word-play and his unconscious indulged this taste, which suggests, given his theory, that he indulged himself. A number of dreams concerned words; one was 'norekdal' which Freud saw was a muddle of the names of two characters from Ibsen's *A Doll's House*, Nora and Ekdal. Freud sometimes reported seeing words, or even equations, appear in his dreams.

Some short dreams could still be significant. Freud wrote of one that he recalled from childhood, in which his mother was carried into a room by people wearing beaked bird masks. Freud's interpretation was very different from that of Marianne Krull, who claimed this showed Freud's mother was having an affair with his half-brother. In Freud's eyes, the dream expressed his terror of his mother's death.

When one excludes these fragments or short dreams, it becomes clear that only 17 of Freud's 39 dreams are fully developed, narrative dreams involving more than just one scene. Of these 17 long dreams, eight involve cocaine. We have seen that Freud was taking cocaine quite often so this is not that surprising: drug users frequently dream of their favoured drug.

Freud's second chapter dealt with a specimen dream, the dream of 'Irma's injection', a cocaine-saturated dream, which Freud described to Fliess in August 1895. Freud sets the scene skillfully, beginning: 'During the summer of 1895 I had been giving psychoanalytic treatment to a young lady who was on very friendly terms with me and my family.' That was not easy for the analyst because he had to cope with many pressures which 'may be a source of many disturbed feelings in a psychotherapist.' There is a trade-off. If he knows the patient his 'personal interest is greater, (but) his authority is less; any failure would threaten the old-established friendship with the patient's family.' There is a book to be written on Freud's attitude to, and obsession with, authority.

Freud's treatment had some success as 'the patient was relieved of her hysterical anxiety but did not lose all her somatic symptoms. At that time I was not yet quite clear in my mind as to the criteria indicating that a hysterical case history was finally closed, and I proposed a solution to the patient which she seemed unwilling to accept.'

With doctor and patient at odds, treatment had to stop for the summer holidays. Freud went off, walking in the hills, picking mushrooms and, no doubt, chewing the bark of trees. A few days later his colleague Otto came to see him and said he had visited Irma. She was better, but not totally recovered. Freud was annoyed by what Otto, in reality Oscar Rie, said because it implied a criticism of his failure to resolve the case. After Otto left, Freud wrote out Irma's clinical history, intending to send it to Breuer in order to justify himself. This shows the extent to which Freud, before the success of *On the Interpretation of Dreams*, still needed the good opinion of his seniors.

The cast of the dream has to be explained.

Irma, a 'hysterical' widow was, in fact, Anna Hammerschlag, daughter of Freud's schoolteacher. Freud had given the eulogy at her father's funeral.

Otto was Oscar Rie, doctor to Freud's children, brother-in-law of Fliess.

Königstein was Freud's friend and colleague in the cocaine research of the early 1880s.

M. is Dr Breuer, co-author of *Studies on Hysteria*. Breuer usually sported a splendid beard which Marx would have been proud of. In Freud's dream, however Breuer had finally gone to the barber's and was clean-shaven. Freud does not comment on the significance of this 'exposure' of Breuer.

The dream began in a large hall, where Freud was welcoming guests to a party. As soon as Irma arrived, Freud took her to one side 'as though to answer her letter in which Irma had expressed reservations' about Freud's approach. But Freud also wanted 'to reproach her for not having accepted' his solution – and he was very forceful about it. He said to her: 'If you will get pains, it is only your fault.' Don't blame the doctor, he's only human. Freud added that he might have said something like that to her in reality. But Irma was a feisty Jewish woman and snapped back: 'If you only knew what pains I've now got in my throat and stomach and abdomen – it's choking me.'

Freud was alarmed. Irma seemed pale and puffy and he noted 'I thought to myself that after all I must be missing some organic trouble.' These were not the symptoms for which she had been consulting him and he wondered why they were so 'prominent in the dream'. He was worried he was losing some of his basic medical skills, because, by this point he was only seeing neurotic patients. If Irma had a physical problem, it would be unreasonable to expect a specialist in nervous disorders to spot it.

Freud then took Irma to the window and looked down her throat. She was not pleased – after all, this examination took place in the middle of a party – and showed signs of 'recalcitrance ... like women who had artificial dentures'. The comparison is unexpected. Freud then wondered if Irma's problem was that she just had bad teeth.

Freud was not sympathetic in the face of Irma's recalcitrance and complained of her behaviour. 'She then opened her mouth properly and on the right I found a big white patch'; the adjective 'white' was left out in one version, Freud's translator, James Strachey noted. At another point, Freud saw grey patches, which were curly structures like nasal bones.

Immediately, Freud called in the freshly-shaved 'Dr M' or Breuer who peered into Irma's mouth and agreed with Freud. But 'Dr M' did not look his normal self: and not just because he'd been to the barber's. Breuer, who we last saw running off to escape Anna O's passion, now walked with a limp. Freud again does not offer any explanation for this detail, but one leaps readily to mind. The limp could well be a thinly-veiled metaphor for erectile dysfunction: Freud's subconscious was calling Breuer impotent. By the time he had this dream, Freud's attitude to Breuer was becoming hostile, as sometimes happened with figures he had once deferred to. Breuer's daughter complained that when the two men saw each other in a park, her father walked towards Freud and tried to embrace him; Freud just walked away.

One of two other doctors in the dream now took centre stage. Leopold Königstein was 'percussing Irma through her bodice' so she was now partly undressed. Both he and Freud also noticed that her shoulder was partly 'infiltrated'.

'Dr M' or Breuer now declared: 'There's no doubt, it's an infection but ... dysentery will intervene and the toxin will be eliminated'. That should have been the end of the matter, but the white patches reminded Freud of a serious illness his daughter Sophie had suffered two years earlier 'and of the fright I had in those anxious days.' But there was more – and here Freud was frank about his own use of cocaine.

The scabs on the turbinal bones in the nose, Freud said, 'recalled a worry I had about my own state of health. I was making frequent use of cocaine at the time to reduce some troublesome nasal swellings and I had heard a few days earlier that one of my women patients had developed an extensive necrosis of the nasal mucous membrane.'

The four doctors then agreed that they knew the origin of Irma's infection. It was Otto/Oscar who had given her an injection of a preparation of propyl.

Freud now produced dashes and gaps.

'Propyl ... propionic acid. trimethylamin.. (and I saw before me the formula for this printed in heavy type.

4. propyl–>trimethylamin [$(CH_3)^3CNH_2$]).'

Freud smiled at the senseless idea of an injection of proprionic acid, because it was inert. In English 'proprionic' would, of course, suggest 'priapic' – the very opposite of 'impotent'. Freud's English was good enough to make that link, and he may have suspected that the doctors wanted to give Irma a rather different kind of injection. The dream did not develop the erotic theme, however and the doctors just said: 'Injections ought not to be made so thoughtlessly, and probably the syringe had not been clean.' Poor Fleischl, recipient of so many injections, including those of cocaine administered by Freud, seems rather conspicuous by his absence at this point.

Mentions of cocaine recur in the dream. The scabs and nasal bones remind Freud of his own use of cocaine to reduce nasal swelling, and of a female patient who had developed an 'extensive necrosis of the nasal mucous membrane'. Talking with one of the doctors, Freud remembers how his treatment of a woman patient led to a 'severe toxic state', which led, in turn, to her death. The patient was called Mathilde, like Freud's eldest daughter, about whom he had an 'over affectionate' dream.

Though the dream has a story, it rather peters out, something that Freud never comments on. There has, in fact, been less commentary on the most famous dream in psychoanalysis than one might expect. Erik Erikson, as noted above, argued the dream was material Freud needed to press on with his work on dreams themselves.

Perhaps the most interesting commentary on the Irma dream is that of the cultural critic Slavo Zizek. In 2005 he analysed Irma's dream and made some interesting points about the 'logic' it exposes, at the heart of psychoanalytic dream-interpretation, logic which reminds him of an old Soviet joke:

'Did Rabinovitch win a new car on the state lottery?'
'In principle, yes, he did. Only it was not a car but a bicycle, it was not new but old, and he did not win it, it was stolen from him!'

Is the dream of Irma's injection a dream about unconscious sexual desire? In principle, yes. But in the dream Freud's desire is not sexual not unconscious, and, the desire doesn't even belong to him. The surface or superficial wish is clear enough and convincing given the issues raised in the cases of Anna O and Emma Eckstein. Please don't blame me for what went wrong when we treated Irma. And don't blame my friend Fliess, who couldn't do a nose job to save his life.

And I didn't kill Fleischl – he did it himself, with his 'dirty' syringes.

Zizek claims that the dream's true meaning is different. Freud's associations, Zizek argues, suggest he had fantasies about several women. He struts in his dream, fantasies fulfilled, the great patriarch, the potent Casanova, the phallus with a world-class brain.

When Freud examines Irma's throat, he remembers a governess, who was a 'picture of youthful beauty' until he looked into her mouth. Then disillusion sets in. The way Irma stands by a window reminds Freud of a meeting with an 'intimate woman friend' of Irma's of whom he 'had a very high opinion'. As I have pointed out, there is also the matter of the doctors giving injections. These associations, Zizek suggests, make it simplistic to think of the dream as a mere wish to escape being blamed for medical negligence. The dream parades and obscures a deep, dark blend of guilt, sexual longings and urges to dominance. As the dream peters out inconclusively one wonders if Freud wrote his memory of the dream in full.

The Botanical Monograph

The second cocaine dream is The Dream of the Botanical Monograph, which Freud interpreted as justifying his extravagant habit of buying too many books, books he couldn't afford. But Freud knew this was just the surface, not the latent, content. In the dream he had written a botanical monograph about cyclamens, a genus of perennials known for the brightly-coloured flowers that emerge from their tubers. In reality, Freud's one 'botanical monograph' was not, in fact, so floral. His true 'botanical' paper was *Über Coca*.

In the dream, however, the monograph featured attractive coloured plates. Freud wrote that he dreamed:

> 'I had written a monograph on a certain plant. The book lay open before me and I was at the moment turning over a folded coloured plate.
>
> Bound up in each copy there was a dried specimen of the plant, as though it had been taken from a herbarium.
>
> That morning I had seen a new book in the window of a book-shop, bearing the title The Genus Cyclamen – evidently a monograph on that plant.
>
> Cyclamens, I reflected, were my wife's favourite flowers and I reproached myself for so rarely remembering to bring her flowers, which was what she liked . . .
>
> Once, I recalled, I really had written something in the nature of a monograph on a plant, namely a dissertation on the coca–plant . . .
>
> I saw the monograph which I had written lying before me. This again led me back to something. I had had a letter from my friend [Fliess] in Berlin the day before in which he had shown his power of visualization: "I am very much occupied with your dream-book. I see it lying finished before me and I see myself turning over its pages." How much I envied his gift as a seer! If only I could have seen it lying finished before me!'

An interesting analysis of the monograph dream was written by Immanuel Velikovsky, who is best remembered for his book *Worlds in Collision* which suggested that Venus split off from the earth. Long before he developed his bizarre theories about the solar system, Velikovsky was a well-respected psychoanalyst. He studied under William Stekel, one of Freud's early 'disciples', and then went to Palestine where he found enough neurotic Central Europeans to make a living. The native Arabs seem to have had little interest in being analysed.

Velikovsky published a number of interesting papers, including an analysis of Freud's dreams, and pointed out that Freud mentioned plants called 'crucifers' three times in the botanical monograph dream. Velikovsky argued that 'crucifers' suggested the Crucifixion and also pointed out that the German word for 'leafing through' – *unschlagen* – does not just mean idly turning the pages of a book, but is a term for religious conversion. Paul Vitz also commented that Freud's failure to associate the Christian significance of 'cross' and 'cross-bearer' to 'crucifers' was indeed a telling omission.

It is worth noting another of Velikovsky's observations, Vitz added: 'Trimethylamin remained a riddle for Freud in another dream. Tri – three; amin – Amen: hence belief in the Trinity, and baptism.'

Velikovsky suggested Freud was depressed by his failure to win academic advancement to the title of professor and blamed this on anti-Semitism. The dream recalled the Crucifixion and the temptation of Christ. The devil took Christ to the top of the mountain and offered him the world. If Freud would only convert, he too would become a professor and the world would lie at his feet. Given his promise to his dying father that he would remain a Jew, this guilty wish for religious conversion is certainly one that Freud would have wanted to remain unconscious of. My interpretation is, of course, just a hypothesis, which in the best Freudian tradition, is impossible to refute.

Freud was frank about the link between cocaine and the monograph but not about the complex associations it evoked. These emerge more fully in the third, and darkest, cocaine dream.

The dream of non vixit

Freud started by describing a conversation with Fliess about Joseph
Paneth, a colleague at the University who took Freud's place as one of
Brücke's assistants. 'I tried to explain to Fliess that Paneth could not
understand anything because he was not alive. But what I actually said
and I myself noticed the mistake – was, 'non vixit' instead of 'non vivit'.
I then gave Paneth a piercing look. Under my gaze he turned pale – and
finally he melted away.' Freud should have been upset but instead 'I was
highly delighted at this...'

On the pedestal of the Kaiser Joseph Memorial in the Imperial
Palace in Vienna the following impressive words are inscribed:

> Saluti patriae vixit
> non diu sed totus
> ('For the well-being of his country, he lived not long but fully').

Paneth died too young and obscure to merit a stone memorial, but
the University had honoured Brücke and Fleischl, commissioning statues
after their deaths, which stood proudly on campus. The dream made
Freud angry. Paneth was brilliant but 'he was guilty of an evil wish [for
self promotion] ... I annihilated him.' The person who in real life Freud
had helped annihilate was, of course, Fleischl, but he did not make that
association and said nothing about his own powerful ambitions either.
Freud then remembered that he had played Brutus in a school play. He
now quoted Shakespeare's lines:

> 'As Caesar loved me, I weep for him;
> as he was fortunate, I rejoice at it; as he was
> valiant, I honour him; but as he was ambitious, I
> slew him.'

When Paneth was buried, the eulogist said he was irreplaceable.
'His remark was the starting-point of the following dream-thoughts: "It's
quite true that no one's irreplaceable. How many people I've followed
to the grave already! But I'm still alive. I've survived them all: I'm left in

possession of the field." ... This satisfaction, infantile in origin, constituted the major part of the affect [feeling] that appeared in the dream. I was delighted,' Freud admitted.

It was not 'survivor's guilt' that Freud felt but 'survivor's joy'. He had already survived baby Julius and Fleischl as well as Paneth. Freud's own cocaine adventures had not led to his death – nor the death of his career, only that of one patient. His delight in this fact does not make Freud likeable but, even if he did not plumb the dream's darkest meaning, he was brave to publish his interpretations.

Five other long dreams in the book involve either cocaine or Fleischl. The most surreal is the dream of the Three Fates or of the *Knödel*. Freud dreams he is going into a kitchen for a snack – the *Knödel* is a dumpling, a staple of the Austrian diet. Three women are in the kitchen, one of whom is Freud's landlady. She tells Freud he must wait until she finishes turning something in her hand, the dough for the dumplings. Freud is hungry and doesn't want to wait. His next act does not seem illogical within the dream. Freud puts on an overcoat. The first is too long and trimmed with fur. The second is covered with Turkish markings. The overcoat, Freud tells us, obviously signifies 'a piece of sexual equipment', one of those condoms he refused to use, and referred to as 'Turkish overcoats'.

Freud's first association is that the three women in the kitchen are the Three Fates of Greek mythology, the Furies, who decide men's destinies. The landlady is also really his mother who gave him 'my earliest nourishment. At the woman's breast love and hunger meet.' When he was six years old he saw his mother rub the palms of her hands together, as if she were making dumplings, till her hands became black. Amalie was making the point that we are made of earth and to earth we are bound to return.

The dream then turns, yet again, on word-associations. *Knödel* reminds him of the name of a man a friend had sued for plagiarism. This evokes Freud's schooldays, where he was taught to suck at 'wisdom's breasts, which every day give more pleasure'. Through the simplest of associations, the dream then evoked memories of Fleischl. As Freud put it: 'And finally there arose the recollection of another dear teacher

157

whose name Fleischl ("meat" in German) sounds like something to eat and of a distressing scene in which the epidermis scales (my mother and the inn hostess had blackened skin) played a role as well as madness and a substance which removes hunger; cocaine.' Freud added that he would desist from pursuing these associations further because they were too personal. So a dream that starts with Freud watching dumplings being made ends with his memories of cocaine and Fleischl. Freud missed one obvious interpretation: that his Super-ego was rebuking him for 'consuming' Fleischl with cocaine, which could be said to have eaten him alive.

Velikovsky saw it differently and wrote: 'It is a dream about the death of his mother and his father. Freud correctly recognised his mother in the hostess. She is the mother of a Jewish home. Dumplings are a specifically Jewish dish. She replies I should wait until she is finished' – not with the dumplings, but with her life. (The implication is he should not have revealed these intimacies until Amelie was dead.) Velikovsky also links the dream with the story of Freud's father being insulted when a Christian threw his hat in the gutter but does not discuss the points Freud makes about either Fleischl or cocaine.

Cocaine also features in the dream of the myopic son. The son of a professor needs an eye operation. In real life Freud took his father to be operated on by Koller, who used cocaine to anaesthetise the old man's eyes. In the dream the roles are reversed. The father takes the son to the eye doctor.

The dream of the attack on Goethe also has elements of cocaine. Freud interprets the dream as a riposte to those who criticised Fliess for his nasal theory, in which cocaine played a key part.

Two other dreams also suggest cocaine. The dream of warships puts Freud in the middle of a sea battle. Freud finds himself on a 'breakfast ship', where he tucks into one of the most delicious breakfasts he has ever eaten. There is a dream within the dream as Freud mentions the 'botanical monograph', *Über Coca*.

Finally, there is the dream of his dead father. Freud reveals both that his father was drunk in the dream and that one of his teachers, the physiologist Meynert, used to take chloroform as an intoxicant and had to be placed in an asylum. The juxtaposition in this dream of drug use, ruin and death needs little interpretation.

Freud was as committed to his new theory of dreams as wish-fulfilments as he had once been to cocaine, but older and perhaps a little wiser, he realised that his zeal posed dangers and that he sometimes tried to impose his interpretations on his patients. One woman 'the most intelligent of all my dreamers' annoyed him when she openly challenged his wish-fulfilment theory.

'On the following day she related a dream to the effect that she was travelling with her mother-in-law to the place in which they were both to spend the summer.' This was the last thing the woman wanted, as she hated her mother-in-law and had in fact 'succeeded in renting a house in a place quite remote from that to which her mother-in-law was going. And now the dream reversed this desired solution. Was not this a flat contradiction of my theory of wish-fulfilment?'

Freud was not merely a master of denial but marvellous at sophistry. No patient was to outwit him on his chosen territory:

'According to this dream, I was wrong; but it was her wish that I should be wrong, and this wish the dream showed her as fulfilled. But the wish that I should be wrong, which was fulfilled in the theme of the country house, referred in reality to another and more serious matter. At that time I had inferred, from the material furnished by her analysis, that something of significance in respect to her illness must have occurred at a certain time in her life. She had denied this, because it was not present in her memory. We soon came to see that I was right. Thus her wish that I should prove to be wrong, which was transformed into the dream that she was going into the country with her mother-in-law, corresponded with the justifiable wish that those things which were then only suspected had never occurred.'

It is this kind of circular and irrefutable logic – ah, *mein liebchen*, your wish was to prove me wrong! – which has made so many 'hard' scientists and philosophers of science disdain psychoanalysis. One can be both exasperated by Freud's logical, or illogical, games, predetermined to prove his interpretations were correct – and charmed by their deftness, and the deep humanity that motivates them. Freud needed, above all else, to be right – and believed what he had to, at times, in order to fulfil this wish.

The dream of the irritating mother-in-law made him think of an exchange with an old school friend who had become a lawyer. At school, Freud was always top of the class while his friend was merely average. Years later his friend came to hear a lecture in which Freud explained his novel theory of dreams (a lecture delivered in 1897 to the B'Nai B'rith, a Jewish organisation). His friend told him later that after the lecture, he 'dreamt that he had lost all his lawsuits – he was a lawyer and then complained to me about it. I took refuge in the evasion: "One can't win all one's cases"; but I thought to myself: "If, for eight years, I sat as primus on the first bench, while he moved up and down somewhere in the middle of the class, may he not naturally have had the wish, ever since his boyhood, that I too might for once make a fool of myself?"'

On the Interpretation of Dreams sold only a few hundred copies in the first year. Freud was bitterly disappointed, but over time, somewhat mysteriously, the book started to have a life of its own and became required reading for intellectuals. The book soon began to seep into popular culture. In *The Antarctic* (1904) Otto Nordenskjold noted the dreams of his crew when they explored the glacial continent, and found some anecdotal confirmation of Freud's thesis. Life in the Antarctic was harsh and wearing, and the crew's dreams often expressed a longing for the comforts of normal life.

> 'Eating and drinking formed the central point around which most of our dreams were grouped. One of us, who was fond of going to big dinner parties at night, was exceedingly glad if he could report in the morning "that he had had a dinner consisting of three courses." Another dreamed of tobacco – of whole mountains of tobacco; still another dreamed of a ship approaching on the open sea under full sail.'

The sailors dreamed of receiving comforting letters from home.

Nordenskjold added: 'It would surely have been of great psychological interest if all the dreams could have been noted.'

There were some flattering reviews and the *Interpretation* made an impact on young psychiatrists like the Swiss Carl Jung. Psychoanalysis had made its debut and Freud was on the way to becoming famous: more, he had begun his long mutation into the iconic Freud of legend, the bold explorer of inner space, who would prefer not to remember or dwell upon certain errors of his youth.

On the Interpretation of Dreams was seen as a brave book owing to Freud's honesty about some deeply personal experiences, including an account of what analysis calls 'the Primal Scene' – witnessing his parents making love. This is true, in part – but such *half-honesty* is the Freudian paradox, for he concealed as much as he revealed. We have seen that Freud was ambivalent about being totally honest and he did not mention one event that he sometimes dreamed about – the criminal career of uncle Josef.

Freud admits to only one dream that mentions his uncle directly, a long dream of riding on a horse when Freud had problems with his scrotum. It would have hurt badly to ride, so he said that this dream expressed his wish to be free to ride. Velikovsky argued however, that the dream was about Freud's desperate longing for success. Rand and Torok point out that the dream has a very odd association; in German the normal word for boil is 'furuncle' but Freud could not bring himself to use the word as he was trying to repress memories of his uncle Josef. A crude interpretation is that uncle Josef was a pain in the balls. It seems that Freud found it easier, even after Fleischl's death, to talk and dream about cocaine than about his uncle.

Inevitably, *On the Interpretation of Dreams* revealed more, in places, than Freud may have intended. Cocaine and its wide-ranging associations 'leaked out' repeatedly into his dreams, indicating its deep significance for Freud, at perhaps the most fruitful and formative stage of his thought – a significance he could not consciously admit. The content analysis, above, shows the influence of cocaine on Freud's most famous book was far-reaching. Unlike Thornton, I don't suggest this invalidates his insights, but critics who ignore the link omit something important. Cocaine

161

formed the immediate, and dramatic, background to the development of psychoanalysis. Unlike later schools of psychotherapy, especially American ones, traditional Freudian analysis made no use of medication: in inventing psychoanalysis, Freud turned away from the use of drugs. Once again, it is frustrating that he wrote nothing on the subject.

A useful compilation of reviews of Freud's books appeared in his lifetime and re-printed some 25 reviews of *On the Interpretation of Dreams* – and only one of them made any mention of drugs. One critic at least realised that Freud's method of self-analysis could be traced back to de Quincey's *The Confessions of an English Opium Eater*. One review is especially generous, as it was written by Emma Eckstein's brother. Her family, somewhat unbelievably, did not bear a grudge about her nose tragedy and Emma herself even became a psychoanalyst, suggesting she did not blame Freud for Fliess botching her operation.

Freud's study of his own dreams inspired a number of imitators, of whom the most intriguing perhaps is the French neurophysiologist Michel Jouvet, some seventy years later. Jouvet showed that the range of brain activity in cats was identical to that of human beings when they dreamed. He then guessed that during paradoxical sleep, cats did not move because messages in the brain froze their motor system. He found he could undo this by sectioning the pons, a structure deep in the brain. Once they were lesioned, 'dreaming' cats made exactly the same movements they would make if they were catching prey. Cats were dreaming of eating mice and birds – wish-fulfilment indeed.

Despite that, Jouvet told me he found it hard to accept Freud's theory, because he believed it was not just the cat who dreamed, but the chick. 'I would say that we shall discover the function of dreaming activity in the end in the bird's egg.'

Jouvet himself constructed a far-reaching theory of dreams. He believed that dreaming allows the DNA code to replay and refresh itself. If people are deprived of sleep for any length of time, they begin to experience not just exhaustion, but agitation and eventually, a temporary psychosis. This, Jouvet claimed, has nothing to do with lack of sleep, but everything to do with lack of dreams. When we don't dream, Jouvet argued, our personality fragments, because, as it were, our DNA dries up. In normal circumstances, 'in the night the choleric person will be reprogrammed to be choleric again ... In that sense you can find a place for the ideas of Freud. His unconscious, for a neurophysiologist like me could be part of the genetic code.'

Jouvet went on to record 1400 instances of his own dreams and told me he planned to record 2000. He remembered an average of 1.4 dreams a night. He found that many of his dreams incorporated events of the previous day but also 'that there is a peak with events that took place 7 to 8 days before.' He made a further intriguing finding. Jung argued one could never be certain of correctly identifying people in a dream, including oneself, but Jouvet found he could divide his dreams into those which seemed to have a clear message and those in which he could recognise the characters. He described one dream in which his sister appeared. 'I recognised her face and her clothes and I said to her 'What language are you speaking?' The explanation Jouvet offered was not psychoanalytical but neurological; he believed that during dreaming the normal connections between the left and the right hemispheres of the brain break down. Thus we dream in a 'split brain' condition.

Jouvet's interest in dreams was not merely academic; he used his research findings to change some aspects of his life:

'Since I became conscious of my dreams ... after certain depressive dreams I know that this part of me is in play. It can then affect my behaviour during the day so that I avoid certain depressing circumstances.'

Jouvet is no Freudian, but he was left with some respect for the man.

While Freud was studying his 144 dreams, Havelock Ellis, a man he admired for his work on sexuality, embarked upon an experiment to see how a drug – a very different substance – affected him. The 19th century had seen introspective reports on nitrous oxide, opium, hashish and cocaine. By the 1890s, there was a new, or rather, re-discovered, artificial paradise on offer. Havelock Ellis produced a brilliant and rather neglected study of the effects of an ancient substance – the peyote cactus, containing the drug mescaline. The introspective drug-using tradition was about to embark on a new, and brightly-coloured, journey.

Promotional poster for John Huston's 'Freud: The Secret Passion'. The first draft of the screenplay, written by Jean-Paul Sartre after Freud's death, ran to over 500 pages. The finished film was considerably less ambitious, portraying Freud as a conventional Hollywood hero.

Chapter 10

Artificial Heavens from 1900 to 1950

Ernest Jones claimed that Freud lost all interest in the passionate side of marriage after he was forty, yet he was a veritable Don Juan in comparison to another pioneering sex researcher. When he married in 1891 at the age of 32, Havelock Ellis was still a virgin. He remained one as his wife, Edith Lees, was a lesbian. After their honeymoon, Ellis moved back into his bachelor apartment. During the early 1890s he began to study homosexuality and published *Sexual Inversion* with John Addington Symonds. The book described the sexual relations of homosexual men and boys, relations that Ellis did not consider to be either a disease, immoral, or a crime – a radically enlightened position for a doctor of his time. It took almost a century for American psychiatry to catch up.

In his autobiography, *My Life*, Ellis admits his friends were amused at his being considered an expert on sex, when he suffered from impotence until the age of sixty. Then he saw a woman urinating and was aroused for the first time in his life.

Ellis published his findings about what he called 'mescal' in two different journals. 'Mescal', in this case, meant 'mescaline' – the active ingredient in the hallucinogenic cacti peyote and San Pedro, not the liquor of the same name, said to be filtered through the peyote cactus. For our purposes, the terms mescal/mescaline/mescalin will be used interchangeably, to signify the drug. He described the physiological symptoms in a paper on 'The phenomena of mescal intoxication' in *The Lancet* on June 5th 1897. A year later he published a longer account in *The Contemporary Review*.

The Kiowa Indians of New Mexico had taken peyote during religious ceremonies for centuries. In 1893 a botanist, Louis Lewin isolated mescaline from peyote and established the basis for modern research into hallucinogens, which he dubbed 'Phantastika'. James Mooney of the United States Bureau of Ethnology learned of Lewin's work and procured a supply of mescaline. In 1894 Mooney gave some to two Washington doctors and a number of volunteers.

The Washington experiment, Ellis wrote, 'showed, for the first time, the precise character of mescal intoxication and the remarkable visions to which it gives rise.' The Native Americans used it even though Washington had made buying and selling of the drug illegal and the crime carried severe penalties. A later Supreme Court ruling lifted the prohibition on Native American use of peyote for sacramental purposes. The peyote ceremonies usually took place on a Saturday night, around a large camp fire. The leader handed each man four buttons taken from a peyote cactus. Each man chewed and swallowed about ten or twelve buttons between sunset and daybreak 'and they all sat quietly round the fire in a state of reverie while attendants sang and played the drums.' In the morning, the spell was broken and the men went 'about their business, without any depression or other unpleasant after effect.'

Ellis managed to get a small sample of mescaline sent to London. Like Freud, he chose a significant date, Good Friday, to take his first dose of three buttons. Alone in his rooms in the Temple, he took these between 2.30 and 4.30 pm. The first symptom observed during the afternoon was 'a certain consciousness of energy and intellectual power.' An hour later he felt 'faint and unsteady; the pulse was low, and I found it pleasanter to lie down.'

Ellis could still read but 'a pale violet shadow floated over the page around the point at which my eyes were fixed.' Objects he was not looking at directly, 'show a tendency to look obtrusive, heightened in color, almost monstrous, while, on closing my eyes, afterimages were vivid and prolonged.' He compared the images to what one saw in a kaleidoscope, 'symmetrical groupings of spiked objects.'

Soon Ellis saw a field of golden jewels, studded with red and green stones which delighted him. The jewels turned into butterflies or the wings of wonderful insects. Ellis then found himself staring into a vast hollow vessel whose surface was made of mother-of-pearl. 'Every conceivable color, streams of red, with scarlets, crimsons, pinks, sprung up together, or in quick succession.'

The images were most vivid when Ellis' eyes were closed, in a room lit only by firelight. After nine hours he started to feel faint and went to bed. As he undressed he was struck 'by the red, scaly, bronzed, and pigmented appearance of my limbs whenever I was not directly gazing at them.' Ellis was alarmed to be changing colour while his skin turned lizard-like. To make that worse, every slightest sound 'seemed magnified to startling dimensions.'

When Ellis turned on the gas, he found the ordinary gas jet 'seemed to burn with great brilliance ... I was even more impressed by the shadows, which were in all directions heightened by flushes of red, green, and especially violet. The whole room ... became vivid and beautiful.'

About 3.30 in the morning the effects were fading, but Ellis was still seeing human figures which were 'fantastic and Chinese in character.' He finally fell asleep and woke up with no hangover of exhaustion or nausea. His eyes, though, seemed unusually sensitive to colour, especially to blue and violet. 'Ever since this experience I have been more aesthetically sensitive than I was before to the more delicate phenomena of light and shade and color,' he wrote.

Ellis then expanded his research, testing mescaline on friends. The first was a painter who felt 'attacks of pain at the heart and a sense of imminent death.' It was terrifying. The painter told Ellis: 'I saw an intensely vivid blue light begin to play around every object. A square cigarette box, violet in color, shone like an amethyst. I turned my eyes away and beheld this time, on the back of a polished chair, a bar of color glowing like a ruby ... I was nevertheless somewhat alarmed when this phenomenon took place.' It seemed to him 'like a kind of madness beginning from outside me, and its strangeness affected me more than its beauty.'

The artist collapsed into an armchair, started to shake and '... felt as though I were dying.' His legs tingled, he felt nauseous and choked by gas. This gas seemed to burst into flame in his throat. The painter's legs became heavy, the back of his head 'seemed to open and emit streams of bright color; this was immediately followed by the feeling as of a draft

167

blowing like a gale through the hair.' He added that he had a strange sweet metallic taste in his mouth which he associated with the colour green. Next he heard singing in his ears and felt his eyes and the palm of his left hand start to burn.

Daylight 'seemed to fill the room with a blinding glare' and the artist could not keep his eyes open as he wanted to as, when his eyes shut, he saw parts of his body changing. He felt 'pranks' were being played on his body and that 'my reason appeared to be the sole survivor of my being'. He started to tremble and felt nauseous, so Ellis gave him some brandy, coffee, and biscuits which helped a little.

Ellis offered his friend another biscuit, leading to a fiery fantasia that challenged all the laws of physics – and baking. When the artist held the biscuit close to his leg, his trousers seemed to catch fire and a blue flame enveloped his whole body. When he finally put the biscuit in his mouth, it burst out in blue fire and 'illuminated the interior of my mouth.' It didn't do much for his complexion, for his skin seemed to get thinner till it had 'no stouter consistency than tissue paper.' Then came the Oriental touch. 'To my amazement I saw myself as though I were inside a Chinese lantern, looking out through my cheek into the room.'

After 24 hours the artist had a normal night's sleep, but then hardly slept for the next three nights. Grotesque images flicked through his mind, figures with prodigious limbs, or strangely dwarfed creatures, 'or impossible combinations such as five or six fish, the colour of canaries, floating about in air in a gold wire cage.'

The artist recovered as 'the whole outer and inner world of reality came back, as it were, with a bound … my body had become in a manner a stranger to my reason – so that now on reasserting itself it seemed, with reference to my reason, which had remained perfectly sane and alert, for a moment sufficiently unfamiliar for me to become conscious of its individual and peculiar character. It was as if I had unexpectedly attained an objective knowledge of my own personality. I saw, as it were, my normal state of being with the eyes of a person who sees the street on coming out of the theatre in broad day.'

Ellis next experimented on two poets. The first barely reacted to the drug at all; the second poet saw 'the most delightful dragons' and then a monument in Westminster Abbey, but in front of it, to the left, knelt a figure in Florentine costume, like someone out of a picture of Botticelli.' Mescaline, it turned out, was a cross-cultural hallucinogen, playing on whatever pictures its users' brain had stored.

Later, on the Embankment, the poet was fascinated by an advertisement for Bovril, 'which went and came in letters of light on the other side of the river'. This is now the Oxo Tower. 'I cannot tell you the intense pleasure this moving light gave me and how dazzling it seemed to me,' the poet said.

'It would be out of place here to discuss the obscure question as to the underlying mechanism by which mescal exerts its magic powers,' Ellis wrote, which was realistic, given the limited knowledge of the brain at the time. He compared mescaline intoxication with the effect of other drugs. Hashish, Ellis claimed, made users highly emotional and prone to sudden, violent movement (this conflicts with the image of the sedentary, stoned 'couch potato', and the general association of hashish with relaxation, rather than excitation), but 'the mescal drinker remains calm and collected amid the sensory turmoil around him; his judgement is as clear as in the normal state; he falls into no oriental condition of vague and voluptuous reverie.' Mescaline was 'the most purely intellectual' of drugs and so it would not easily develop into a habit.

In this claim, Ellis seems to have been correct. Hallucinogens appear, for the most part, to cause no addiction or physical withdrawal syndrome. Indeed, of all drugs used recreationally, the more powerful hallucinogens, such as LSD and mescaline, seem to be the least likely to be consumed with any regularity, owing in part to the intensity and long duration of their effects.

Ellis finished with a paean to the drug. The mescaline-containing cactus was 'the most democratic of the plants which lead men to an artificial paradise.' Wordsworth would be the favourite poet of those who took mescaline as many of his 'most memorable poems and phrases cannot – one is almost tempted to say – be appreciated in their full significance by one who has never been under the influence of mescal. On all these grounds it may be claimed that the artificial paradise of mescal, though less seductive, is safe and dignified beyond its peers.'

In 1899, a year after Ellis published his paper in the *Contemporary Review*, H.G. Wells wrote *The Sleeper*, whose hero has taken many drugs including cocaine. The once magical elixir was, Wells said, a 'thug helper ... one of those alkaloids that stifle natural fatigue and kill rest.' The thug helper, cocaine, was about to claim another victim, the only woman who belongs to the early introspective tradition. Annie Meyers' *My Cocaine Hell* has no intellectual pretensions, but she had some insight into her own thoughts and feelings on and about the drug. Her cocaine experience was very different from Freud's: Annie Meyers ended up on the street.

Annie Meyers was a respectable widow. In 1895, she had a bad cold and went to her local chemist. He gave her a catarrh remedy that was full of cocaine. The first glug turned the widow into an addict. She soon spent all the money her husband had left her and resorted to what we now see as typical addict behaviour. She became a practiced thief.

Meyers' book is well worth reading, 100 years on, and it seems very odd that it is never cited in accounts of the literature. Annie also had a hat obsession, and collected headwear with a slightly feverish zeal. One of the many things she regretted about her cocaine use was that it had made her neglect her hats. Despite such oddities, she gave an excellent description of how the drug affected her. She wrote:

'Cocaine gives an exhilarating feeling, brightens up the intellect for the time being and makes one very fluent in conversation. I am informed that a great many of our speakers use cocaine before they step on the platform.'

Annie took high doses of cocaine and suffered from paranoid delusions which she described vividly. Once she imagined people wanted to kill her for trying to find out the secrets of their lodge and she ended up fighting invisible lodge members all night. The drug made her 'half crazy with fear of arrest'. Under the influence, she feared the police were chasing her all over Chicago, sometimes using searchlights. She fantasised that one Lieutenant Elliott was especially determined to catch her, but Annie eluded him, even when he turned up at her lodgings.

Annie charted the physical horrors of prolonged cocaine use well. She said it was the only drug that will soften the bones and eat the flesh; she thought she had leprosy as she lost her teeth and part of her jaw bone while using it (these may have been the consequences of malnutrition – unlike Freud, most cocaine users experience a near-total loss of appetite on the drug).

To feed her habit, Annie became a prolific shoplifter, driving one store detective to scream: 'You bad woman don't come in this store again.' He was an optimist to think she'd listen: a few days later she was back, stealing a pair of fur gloves. When the store detective grabbed her and asked how much she would sell the gloves for, Annie said for fifty cents to get cocaine. He was outraged; they were worth at least two dollars. Annie sometimes tried to pull off impossible stunts; she was accused of trying to steal a stove – quite how she would have carried it away without anyone noticing is not clear. She was more sensible in stealing a pram, which she wheeled away and sold before she was caught. Silk was one of her favourites and she managed to steal 90 yards of it from a store called Marshall Fields.

Annie was not always the most reliable witness. She remembered assisting in 'an operation performed on the eye of a lady friend and they used cocaine to deaden the pain while they took the eye out, cleaned it and put it back!' Despite cocaine's anaesthetic properties, such an operation is obviously impossible.

She did not admit to working as a prostitute, though it seems likely that she may have done so at times, but she was proud to have invented 'The Cocaine Dance'. Annie would go to 'sporting houses' and dance 'and a collection would be taken up and given to me. I would run without a hat to the drug store immediately to get my idol; as I used to pet it and call it my baby and my only friend and laugh and cry over it like an insane person.'

Finally Annie's sister managed to persuade her to turn to the Church and she was saved. William James, in his *The Varieties of Religious Experience*, argued that conversion-experience was one of the most successful means of substance abuse rehabilitation: the same is clear from the spiritual emphasis of the 'Twelve Step' programmes of Alcoholics Anonymous,

Narcotics Anonymous, and the other 'Anonymous' groups, all of which invoke a 'higher power'. God may or may not exist: but he/she/it has certainly sobered up many a drunk and addict.

Wells's story, Meyers' book and critical reports in the medical journals such as that by Broderau demonstrate the growing concern at the time about the physical and psychological dangers of cocaine. Freud would have been all too aware of this controversy. It is a pity that he never wrote a word to explain what persuaded him to stop using a drug that had been a feature of his life for much of the 1890s. It's reasonable to suggest a combination of causes. He had more confidence than ever before and he may have asked himself whether some of the symptoms he had experienced might be due to a phenomenon he had once denied, the toxic effects of cocaine. He was no doubt also eager to leave his memories of Fleischl and Fliess behind.

If Freud said nothing about cocaine after the 1890s, he was very frank, however, about his need for cigars, and must have been aware of the health issues involved. That other great writer/doctor of the period, Anton Chekhov, certainly was as he wrote a brilliant dramatic monologue, *On the Harmfulness of Tobacco*. There was no lack of evidence for tobacco's dangers at the time. Although we tend to think the link between lung cancer and smoking was made by Doll's research in the 1950s, he was building on the work of earlier researchers.

Turn-of-the-century statisticians noted an increase in lung cancer and suspected that smoking was the cause. Animal research supported their suspicions. In a series of experiments, guinea pigs were put in smoke filled rooms and soon developed cancers. As a result of the publicity, the states of Washington, Iowa, Tennessee and North Dakota outlawed the sale of cigarettes. The Supreme Court suspected many cigarettes contained more than mere tobacco, leading one judge to thunder 'there are many [cigarettes] whose tobacco has been mixed with opium or some other drug, and whose wrapper has been saturated in a solution of arsenic.'

It is, in fact, the case that cigarette smoke often contains arsenic – but not, so far as is known, cigarette packs. Despite this official suspicion of tobacco, it would be generations until the American government officially accepted the carcinogenic effects of smoking, and much of the medical establishment was just as slow to be persuaded.

In 1902, Sears, Roebuck and Co advertised a 'Sure Cure for the Tobacco Habit', which seems to have been the first commercial product to promise to cure smoking. It was sold with a cute tag-line, 'Tobacco to the Dogs'. The product 'will destroy the effects of nicotine', Sears boasted.

Freud was never going to buy the Sure Cure and continued to joust with Fliess about his smoking. Once, when he was not smoking, Freud wrote to him: 'I have not smoked for seven weeks since the day of your injunction. At first I felt, as expected, outrageously bad. Cardiac symptoms accompanied by mild depression, as well as the horrible misery of abstinence. These wore off but left me completely incapable of working, a beaten man. After seven weeks I began smoking again . . . Since the first few cigars, I was able to work and was the master of my mood; before that life was unbearable.'

A caring doctor could hardly demand that his patient give up smoking when he had been told cigars had a 'magical' effect on that patient's moods. Freud tried to make Fliess guilty about telling him not to smoke:

'I was deprived of the motivation which you so aptly characterize in one of your previous letters: a person can give something up only if he is firmly convinced that it is the cause of his illness . . . For the first time I have an opinion that differs from yours on some matter . . . You have been so absolute and strict in your smoking prohibition, the merit of which is all relative . . .'

In this not-so-subtly hostile response, Freud made it clear he was not going to abandon the habit that gave him the most pleasure in life and which he felt facilitated his incredible capacity for work. When he visited America, Freud hated the country and just about the only positive comment he made was that the Americas had given the world tobacco. Without Columbus he could never have smoked cigars.

I have suggested that the young Freud lacked confidence and

needed the approval of both Breuer and Fliess well into his forties. Writing *On the Interpretation of Dreams* made Freud less dependent on any mentor and more sure of himself. Freud finally got a very public accolade from the Kaiser. On October 13th 1902, Freud had the pleasure of boasting to Fliess that he had an audience with Franz Josef I. The Kaiser had finally granted Freud the rank of Professor Extraordinarius. Freud wrote to Fliess:

'Congratulations and bouquets keep pouring in as if the role of sexuality had been suddenly recognised by His Majesty, the interpretation of dreams confirmed by the Council of Ministers and the necessity of the psychoanalytic therapy of hysteria carried by a two thirds majority in Parliament.'

Now Freud did not need either cocaine or Fliess so much to bolster his self-belief, and their friendship was already waning. They hardly exchanged any letters in 1902 or 1903. A year later, the break came when Otto Weininger published a book about bisexuality. Fliess suspected Freud had spoken about his ideas to Weininger's 'analyst', Hermann Swoboda, and that Swoboda in turn had outlined Fliess's ideas on bisexuality to Weininger. On July 20th 1904, Fliess accused Freud of conspiring to steal his ideas. They had not exchanged letters for some time, Freud complained, and now Fliess accused him of being 'a robber.' Freud was no longer willing to appease his friend and pointed out Swoboda was not a pupil but a very sick patient. Fliess deserved credit for developing the idea of bisexuality but 'it was a close run thing', Freud sniped. Others had written about bisexuality. He denied that he had given Swoboda 'any details from your communications' and in any case, Weininger's work was 'shoddy' and no one would take it seriously. Freud admitted he had 'freely scattered suggestions without asking what will become of them', but he had never 'appropriated something belonging to others.' He refused to apologise. Neither Fliess nor his wife ever forgave Freud.

Two years later, the dispute became public when Fliess published a self-justifying memoir; he claimed he had been shocked by Freud's attitude and explained why to the wife of a band leader, of all people. Fliess invited readers to contact this Frau Schalk, who would confirm that Freud was madly jealous of him. It was an extraordinary, and rather undignified, outburst.

Freud fought back in November 1906, writing five letters to Karl Kraus, the editor of *Die Fackel*, Vienna's great satirical paper, to ask for his backing against Fliess. Though Kraus did not wholly agree with Freud's ideas, he thought he was right in this instance and wrote an article saying so. Fliess felt humiliated; he and Freud never spoke again, and their correspondence ground to an absolute halt. By this point, of course, the balance of power and success in their relationship had been reversed, with Freud by now the more eminent figure: Fliess's accusations suggest that he could not bear being surpassed by his once-deferential admirer.

The success of a book can change a man – and Freud was changed deeply by *On the Interpretation of Dreams*. The forty-year-old who needed reassurance about his heart condition and volcanic, pus-spewing nose now had followers who all but sat at his feet. From 1902, every Wednesday, Freud welcomed a group of his colleagues to 19 Berggasse. These meetings were the origins of the Vienna Psycho-Analytical Society, the world's first group dedicated to the study of Freud's ideas.

Freud always waited until all the guests were assembled and until Martha had finished serving black coffee and cigars; she gave every man his own ashtray. Only then did Freud make his entrance. Freud's son Martin described the room as 'so thick with smoke it seemed a wonder that human beings had been able to live in it for hours, let alone speak in it without choking.'

When Freud started to speak, his colleagues scribbled notes and puffed on their cigars. The pleasure of cigar smoking was part of the pleasure of psychoanalysis, the analyst E.J. Elkin suggests and adds that 'cigars and smoking are central to understanding Freud's life, his work and his own personality. And given Freud's conviction that he could not work without them, without cigars there may not have been psychoanalysis.'

Two small details show the remarkable change in Freud's reputation after *On the Interpretation of Dreams* was published. His 'disciples' had a special medal made for him to celebrate his 50th birthday in 1906. The medal showed Oedipus and the Sphinx and on its reverse was printed: 'He solved the famous riddle and was a man most mighty.' The second accolade was one of the first signs of the far-reaching cultural influence Freud would wield. When George Bernard Shaw was giving notes to actors for the first production of *Major Barbara* in 1905, he told them that in one scene 'the Oedipus Complex must be very apparent here.'

Freud became so intent on developing psychoanalysis that he ceased to follow the latest research in his once-favourite discipline of anatomy. There is a certain irony to this. In *The Project for a Scientific Psychology*, Freud had looked forward to the day when the study of body and mind, or brain and mind, would be unified in one 'hard' objective science, yet he concentrated entirely on studying and treating neurotic symptoms alone.

Freud was familiar with Descartes, who argued body and mind were separate, one a machine, the other a soul. The once brilliant anatomist had by 1902 chosen mind over body.

But choosing the mind above all else would also cause problems in time, for Freud was to insist that one need not qualify as a doctor in order to become a psychoanalyst. Such 'lay analysts' would be inclined to assume all physical symptoms had a psychological root cause. When this assumption was mistaken, patients could be left vainly searching for the deep childhood cause of a simple physical illness, which might, in many cases, have been better treated by a physician. Sometimes, as Freud admitted, a cigar is only a cigar, and sometimes a physical symptom reflects nothing but a physical illness. Analysts, however, were to become increasingly reluctant to admit as much, ironically at the same time as the foundations for the modern understanding of the brain were being laid down.

In 1903, Otto Loewi was 30 years old and a reasonably successful physiologist. He suddenly wondered if nervous impulses in the brain might be transmitted by chemical rather than electrical means. He had no idea how to research this notion, and let the idea slip to the back of his mind for 17 years, until he had a dream described in his auto-biography.

'The night before Easter Sunday of that year I awoke, turned on the light, and jotted down a few notes on a tiny slip of paper. Then I fell asleep again. It occurred to me at 6 o'clock in the morning that during the night I had written down something most important, but I was unable to decipher the scrawl. The next night, at 3 o'clock, the idea returned. It was the design of an experiment to determine whether or not the hypothesis of chemical transmission that I had uttered 17 years ago was correct. I got up immediately, went to the laboratory, and performed a single experiment on a frog's heart according to the nocturnal design.'

It took Loewi ten years to carry out the experiments which became the foundation for the theory of neurotransmitters. Loewi noted: 'Most so called 'intuitive' discoveries are such associations made in the subconscious.' In 1936, thirty-three years after that momentary inspiration, Loewi achieved something Freud never did; he shared the Nobel Prize for Medicine.

If Freud took cocaine after his final quarrel with Fliess, he left no evidence of it and his last doctor, Max Schur, never wrote on the subject. Any lingering temptation almost certainly faded in 1904, when Freud became embroiled in another cocaine cataclysm. The story once again reveals Freud as a master of denial, a term whose modern, psychological meaning was of course defined ... by Freud.

Hans Gross was one of Europe's leading criminologists and bullied his son Otto for most of the boy's childhood. Otto escaped to South America in 1900, just after he had qualified as a doctor. In South America he became a heavy user of coca leaves and cocaine extracts. He sailed back to Europe and began to practice psychiatry in Munich in 1903. Otto was gifted and soon published his first papers, which had a more political edge than most psychoanalytic writings. He was attracted to anarchism and soon became involved with radical artistic movements like Dada.

Despite these enthusiasms, Freud was impressed by the young Otto and in 1904, Gross was accepted into the Vienna Society. Four years later Gross announced: 'Soon, in Salzburg, there will be the first congress of the Freud school. I will propose for it a talk on cultural perspectives in which I will express the program for my life. This is a moment like no other. Through a practical method, through a technique of examination we can suddenly see into the essence of spiritual and mental life. Those who have eyes can see in this new perspective the future at work.'

Freud was not pleased by this emphasis on 'culture' and told Gross: 'We are doctors and must remain doctors.' He still respected Gross, telling Jung that the young man was 'a valuable person and has a good head', but was dismayed by the young man's political passion. Freud rejected Gross's premise that the 'psychology of the unconscious is the philosophy of revolution' and that the aim of analysis was 'to make people inwardly capable of freedom, to prepare the way for revolution'. Freud had struggled too much to risk being seen as some kind of political revolutionary – and inasmuch as he held any political views himself, they were of a far more moderate kind than Gross's.

Soon after the Salzburg congress, Freud suggested to Gross that he needed treatment and recommended Jung take him on as a patient. Freud told the latter that Gross 'urgently needs your medical help; what a pity, such a gifted resolute man. He is addicted to cocaine and probably in the early phase of toxic cocaine paranoia.' (This was remarkable, coming from the man who had once insisted that cocaine induced no cravings.) Jung began to treat Gross in April and, as with Fleischl, at first it seemed to go well. By June, Freud was telling Jung 'I cannot underestimate the importance of your having been obliged to analyse him. You could never have learned so much from another case.'

The truth, again, was darker than Freud's words suggested, though more comic than in Fleischl's case. Gross fled from the hospital, going over the wall with a spectacular leap. Outraged, Jung said Gross was suffering from 'dementia praecox' – schizophrenia. Gross's oppressive father now went to court and had his son declared mentally incompetent.

Gross both practised and preached sexual liberation. In 1903 he had married Frieda Schloffer, but almost at once started an affair with Else Jaffé, born Else von Richthofen. Both Frieda and Else bore him children, which did not stop Gross bedding Else's sister, Frieda Weekley, who later married D.H. Lawrence. Marriage was a fetter. Free love should rule between men and women, women and women and men and men. Gross went so far so to claim that no man could know why a woman loved him if he did not understand his own homosexual leanings. Freud might well have been in partial agreement with him on this point.

After escaping the asylum, Gross went to live in Italy, where he established a commune that soon became notorious for its orgies. This did not endear him to the Italian government, and Gross was kicked out of the country, returning first to Berlin and then to Vienna.

In 1914 Gross finally managed to get the judgement that had declared him incompetent quashed. He resumed work as a doctor and soon became head of a typhus clinic in Temesvar, Romania. He had not abandoned his political ambitions, however, and published *Die Freie Strasse* (*The Free Road*) which outlined his ideas for sexual revolution.

In November 1918, Gross developed his radical ideas into the realm of the fantastic and suggested the Kaiser's Government set up a 'Ministry for the liquidation of the bourgeois family and sexuality.' Freud both thought this ludicrous, and understood the danger of psychoanalysis taking on a political character: he expelled Gross from the analytic society, with what amounted to a decree of excommunication.

Gross died of pneumonia in Berlin on February 13th 1920, after having been found near-starved and frozen on the street. Freud ignored the death of the young man he had once praised. The only eulogy at Gross's funeral was given by William Stekel, who had treated him after his escape from Jung. Stekel had himself quarrelled with Freud by then, partly because he'd dared to write two books about dreams, *Die Sprache des Traumes* (*The Language of Dreams*; 1911), *Die Träume der Dichter* (*The Dreams of Poets*; 1912). Freud did not welcome competition on 'his territory', as we have seen.

As usual, Freud never healed the breach with Stekel and, predictably enough, did not attend Gross's funeral. It is plausible to suggest that the death reminded him uncomfortably of Fleischl and his own use of cocaine. It even took four years before Ernest Jones announced Gross's death at the Eighth International Psycho-Analytical Congress.

Gross was not the only analytic casualty of the time. In 1919 Freud was treating Helene Deutsch, who became a famous analyst herself. He had told her to treat a brilliant but disturbed analyst, Viktor Tausk. In July Freud reversed himself, telling Deutsch that she had to choose. If she carried on treating Tausk, he would stop treating her. She had to decide between the two men and, naturally enough, for a disciple, she chose Freud over the patient he himself had sent to her. On the morning of July 3rd, 1919, after Deutsch had told him she would not continue as his analyst, Tausk shot himself; he had also tied a cord round his neck, to ensure that he would die of asphyxiation, should the bullet fail to kill him. This was no plea for attention: Tausk clearly meant to end his life.

Freud wrote to his friend Lou Andreas Salomé that: 'I confess that I do not really miss him; I had long realised that he could be of no further service; indeed that he constituted a threat to the future.' Tausk was trying to use analysis not just with patients who suffered from neurosis but with those suffering from psychosis, such as schizophrenics. Freud believed such patients were too severely disturbed to be helped by analysis and that Tausk's attempt would fail.

Freud's own words are damning, as Roazen argued in *Brother Animal*. It was another Faustian bargain but this time with another man's soul. It was a far, far better thing for Tausk to die at his own hand than for his continued existence to show psychoanalysis had its limits. The story is shocking. The reputation of analysis mattered more than a man's life. Freud did not even seem curious as to whether his order to Deutsch, terminating Tausk's treatment, might have played a part in his suicide, though he did later meet Tausk's son and told him how much he regretted his father's death.

Meanwhile medical and political opinion had turned, decisively, against cocaine. In America in 1906, the Pure Food and Drug Act controlled the contents of all patent remedies and banned the use of opium and cocaine except for medicinal purposes. China also started a campaign against opium. The government wanted to modernise the country and, also, was reacting to America's conquest of the Philippines. In America, the Temperance movement was campaigning vigorously to ban alcohol, so it was hardly surprising there was also pressure to stop the evil of the East, opium, debauching a new American colony. Washington convened a meeting of thirteen countries to discuss the control of 'narcotics'.

The International Opium Commission met in Shanghai in February 1909 but did not agree on any concerted action. Three years later, when he became President of the USA, William Taft was handed a report that claimed cocaine posed the most serious drug problem America had ever faced and that it affected poor blacks most of all. The American doctor Charles Towns wrote:

'Most of the cases of the cocaine habit have been admittedly created by the so-called catarrh cures, and these contain only two to four percent of cocaine. In the end, the snuffer of catarrh powders comes to demand undiluted cocaine.'

It was also widely claimed that most black men who raped white women had taken cocaine. The same claims would later be made about Mexicans and cannabis, and demonisation of the 'Heathen Chinee' had been used in the campaign against opium. These drugs were not merely dangerous to the body and mind: they came from dirty foreigners, intent on despoiling white women. To some extent, the 'War on Drugs' began as a war against miscegenation, a campaign to preserve the modesty and dignity of white womanhood.

A new conference was convened in The Hague and this time a decision was reached. On January 23rd 1912, twelve nations signed a Convention. Each country would bring in domestic laws which banned the use of opium, morphine and cocaine without prescription. This was the first time nation states agreed to control the behaviour of citizens all over the world.

After much lobbying and counter-lobbying, the Harrison Act became Federal law in 1914. Cocaine, heroin, morphine and opium could now only be obtained with a prescription signed by a doctor, though this decision radically changed constitutional law. States had the power to regulate medicine, not the Federal Government, leading some historians to argue that the true agenda behind prohibition was to expand the power of the Federal regime. Not a single milligram of cocaine or the stronger opiates would be allowed in patent remedies and every gram would be tracked and taxed from the moment it entered the States to the moment it was consumed. Bureaucracy triumphed.

Every history has its unsung eccentrics. In 1916 in Calcutta A.P. Bhargava was selected for duty as Excise Preventative Officer for Bihar and Orissa. He would be more effective in tracking down cocaine smugglers, he thought, if he knew something about the drug. He gathered as much information as he could and was appalled that 'the public was in a state of complete ignorance' about the dangers of cocaine. He quoted as an authority Professor Berkeley of Johns Hopkins, who said he would trust 'a morphine maniac more than a cocaine debauchee'.

Bhargava organized raids on cocaine dens and was impressed not just by the depravity of cocomaniacs but by their ingenuity. They stashed cocaine in the collars of dogs, in consignments of tea, in rubber dolls and in shoes. One Burmese woman was arrested smoking a cigar, which turned out to contain cocaine. In the French protectorate of Pondicherry south of Madras, shameless European prostitutes concealed packets of cocaine in their knickers and offered the drug to their clients.

During the First World War, there were many reports of 'crazed soldiers', and alarming stories about cocaine's addictive potential and propensity to induce paranoia. In the negotiations for the Treaty of Versailles, the British and American governments proposed adding the Hague Convention on drugs to the Versailles Treaty. The British Parliament then passed the Dangerous Drugs Act of 1920 which finally outlawed heroin, cocaine and morphine. These drugs could now only be obtained on prescription.

The scientific consequences of the prohibition of heroin and cocaine were considerable. For 30 years no major scientist followed in the footsteps of Christison, William James, Freud or Havelock Ellis: the use of drugs without prescription was now solidly associated with vice, making such research politically sensitive and even dangerous. At the same time, developments in psychology were making introspective research methods taboo. A crude behaviourism became orthodoxy after John B. Watson was sacked by Johns Hopkins University for sleeping with a student. Watson's predecessor as professor of psychology had been found in 'a negro brothel' and the university did not want another scandal. Dismissed, Watson had to make a living in advertising and nearly all his academic friends shunned him.

It was soon forgotten that while Watson had argued psychology should study behaviour, he was not dogmatic in excluding subjectivity from his research. In fact, he often talked to his experimental subjects about what they were thinking, because one could observe what they said about their thoughts. But from 1920 to 1970, any psychologist who expressed an interest in introspection was deemed to have committed the ultimate crime of being *unscientific.*

The new prohibitions had little impact on the drug-using classes of Hollywood or Paris's Left Bank, but their continued self-indulgence contributed little to the systematic study of either drugs or the brain. Actors and artists consumed formidable quantities of cocaine, heroin, alcohol and mescaline, but few were interested in methodically recording the drugs' effects on their mood and behaviour. The scientific aspirations of the Hashish Club, Freud and Ellis were forgotten.

By the 1920s Hollywood was in a swirl of drugs. The most significant death in terms of drug politics was that of Wallace Reid who got his big break playing the blacksmith in D.W. Griffith's famous *The Birth of a Nation.* Reid often played a 'male flapper,' a daring and thrill-seeking young rake. The titles of two of his films said it all – *Watch My Speed* and *Double Speed.* The title of a third even has an innuendo of substances, *Excuse My Dust.* For the sake of accuracy, 'speed' had not been coined as a term for amphetamines at the time.

Reid became a drug addict after he was injured on location and treated with morphine by studio doctors, who kept him supplied. One day he collapsed on a film set and started to cry. He was sent to hospital and vowed he would 'come back cured or not at all.' On January 18th 1923 Reid took a morphine overdose and died. Splendid material for a movie, his studio, Famous Lasky Players, realised, but for the fact that Will Hays, the cinema censor, had banned all references to narcotics. He now made an exception and let Reid's widow make a propaganda film, *Human Wreckage,* about the evils of drug addiction.

We have seen that Freud liked Sherlock Holmes; he was also a fan of Agatha Christie's books in which illegal drugs often feature. In *The Murder of Roger Ackroyd*, published in 1926, Hercule Poirot discovers a goose quill which was used to carry 'snow,' or heroin. In one of his last cases, *The Twelfth Labour of Hercules*, Poirot meets an old flame in a night club called Hell. Undercover cops are watching Hell, which they suspect is the hub of a cocaine ring and the club is duly raided. The cops are right. The climax comes when Poirot tells his old love the Countess to get her dog to drop what it has in its mouth. A small packet of cocaine falls to the ground.

Freud almost certainly also read Dorothy L. Sayers's famous *Murder Must Advertise*, first published in 1933. The mystery starts with a murder on a spiral staircase which turns out to be the work of a major drugs ring that has infiltrated the advertising agency. The anti-drug message had penetrated popular culture – it was certainly a great gift to the authors of crime novels.

But these novels did not reflect the true situation in Britain after the First World War. In 1924, the Home Office's Rolleston report found that cocaine and heroin addiction were rather modest problems. Two psychiatrists made that clear. Sir Frederick Hogg, who ran the Dalrymple Retreat in Rickmansworth, said that during some 20 years of practice he had treated 1300 alcoholics but only 100 drug addicts, of whom a mere 26 were addicted to cocaine. Sir Frederick Buzzard told the Committee he had treated no more than 30 cocaine addicts in his long career. The Rolleston Report concluded that heroin and cocaine could be supplied to registered addicts as a maintenance treatment. Sustaining their addiction with prescription drugs, preventing physically traumatic withdrawals, would stop desperate addicts committing crimes to fund their habits. This report was to be the cornerstone of British policy on drugs for the next 50 years, and it seems to have been largely successful, for some decades, in limiting the spread of addiction.

Freud had taken cocaine for some 17 years without inflicting obvious damage on his body but, by 1923, his cigar habit had taken its toll. Freud developed a leukoplakic growth in his mouth, which turned out to be cancer of the soft palate. Freud waited years before showing anyone the growth. He was afraid smoking would, as he put it, '. . . [be] accused as the [cause] of this tissue-rebellion.'

After the operation to remove the growth, Freud had to wear a prosthesis in his mouth. He could not speak or eat properly without it. If he kept it in all the time, the prosthesis hurt; if he took it out for long periods, the device might shrink and not fit back properly. Freud told his Manchester nephew Sam that his speech 'may be impaired but my family and my patients say it is intelligible.' A small antiseptic room was set up in 19 Berggasse so that his daughter Anna could clean and replace the prosthesis every day. She was still being analysed by Freud, so father and daughter were each other's analyst and nurse, respectively.

Over the next 16 years, Freud had 30 operations to excise pre-cancerous and cancerous lesions. He kept hoping someone would design a better prosthesis as wearing it made for 'a life of endless torture,' Max Schur (his last doctor) noted in *Living and Dying*.

But Freud thought the torture was worth it. Cigars, he said, have 'served me for precisely fifty years as protection and a weapon in the combat of life . . . I owe to the cigar a great intensification of my capacity to work and a facilitation of my self-control.' He recommended smoking to his nephew Harry, saying: 'My boy, smoking is one of the greatest and cheapest enjoyments in life, and if you decide in advance not to smoke, I can only feel sorry for you.'

Max Schur called in a pathologist to examine Freud's mouth and nose. The pathologist found widespread inflammation of the mucous membrane and recommended Freud stop smoking. When he showed Freud the pathologist's report, Schur said Freud 'shrugged his shoulders' and Schur asked himself whether he 'was entitled or even obliged' to insist more strongly that Freud give up cigars. But 'I could not, and in retrospect I realize that I should not regret this fact.' He doubted anyway whether 'such an attempt would have been successful.' There was no question now of cauterising Freud's nose with cocaine as Fliess might have suggested.

In 1923 Freud underwent another operation which suggests Ernest Jones may have been wrong in accepting Freud's 'confession' that he had lost all interest in the passionate side of marriage when he was forty. Freud had his sperm ducts tied. This peculiar 'rejuvenation' treatment was then rather fashionable. An endocrinologist, Eugen Steinach, had discovered that the interstitial cells of the testicles produced the male sex hormone testosterone and suggested that tying up the sperm ducts would atrophy the cells that produced the hormone. Steinach became world famous and there is a cartoon of him standing alongside Einstein and Freud.

As cancers, like Freud's cancer of the jaw, were thought to be the result of ageing, rejuvenation treatment should help, so the argument went, as it delayed the ageing process. Today, the whole thing seems a bizarre fantasy. When Schur asked Freud who had suggested this treatment to him, Freud insisted it was his own idea and that he hoped it would not only cure his cancer but revive his sex life. He and Martha were still sharing a double bed and she was, of course, past child-bearing age so he would not have to use the condoms he hated.

In 1926, three years after his sperm ducts were tied, Freud was asked to write an introduction to the German edition of the works of Dostoevsky, whose place in literature Freud assessed as being 'not far behind that of Shakespeare'. Dostoevsky was a lifelong compulsive gambler, and of all behaviour that does not involve the actual use of drugs, gambling appears to most closely resemble addiction. Dostoevsky, no slouch at introspection, knew perfectly well why he loved gambling: for the rush, the thrill of putting one's fate in the random hands of a roulette wheel. This compulsion was the subject of his novella *The Gambler* – written to a tight deadline, the text was mostly dictated to a stenographer, who later became Dostoevsky's second wife.

The novella itself had to be finished at great speed because Dostoevsky had gambled, betting all future earnings from anything that he would ever write against his ability to deliver the manuscript to one of his many creditors by a tight deadline. He very nearly lost the bet. As the wily creditor shut up shop early, Dostoevsky was forced to request a dated and time-stamped receipt for the manuscript from a local police station to prove he had delivered on time.

The Gambler tells the story of a young tutor, in love with his master's mistress, who falls prey to the gambling compulsion at the tables of Monaco. He eventually buys the affection of his beloved with his winnings but her love and loyalty last only as long as his takings from roulette. At the book's conclusion, *The Gambler* is reduced, inevitably, to *The Loser*, of both love and money.

Dostoevsky, in Freud's words, was 'astute enough to recognise the fact and honest enough to admit it and knew the chief thing was gambling for its own sake – *le jeu pour le jeu.*'

'The main thing is the play itself,' Dostoevsky wrote, 'I swear that greed for money has nothing to do with it, although Heaven knows I am sorely in need of money.' Like all true compulsives, Dostoevsky never stopped gambling until he had lost everything. The losses drove him and his wife to 'the direst need': but neither of them, of course, could understand the latent causes of his gaming. These, however, were self-evident to Freud. Dostoevesky gambled out of pure masochism, Freud claimed, adding that the great writer 'could scold and humiliate himself before her (his wife), invite her to despise him and to feel sorry she had married such an old sinner'. The wife herself noticed 'the direst need' spurred her husband to write and that, strangely, the writing 'never went better than when they had lost everything and pawned their last possessions'.

But there was no trace here of 'the genital thing', and so Freud was moved to exercise his imagination further to explain the novelist's vice. He claimed that Dostoevsky was punishing himself by gambling, because his father had been murdered. The murder is a matter of historical record – Dostoevsky's father, described as something of a tyrant, was killed by his own serfs when Dostoevsky was a boy, away from home at boarding school. To Freud, however, Dostoevsky must have felt, on a subconscious level, guilt at his father's death, owing to his own Oedipal urge to kill him – a wish the serfs had conveniently fulfilled.

Thus, Freud argued, Dostoevsky's urge to lose money, time and again, was a ritual expiation of suppressed guilt at his own patricidal longings – 'losing it', repeatedly, as his father had lost everything. Freud went on to diagnose Dostoevsky's lifelong epilepsy also as psychosomatic in origin. As an exercise in psycho-biography, Freud's essay on

Dosteovsky stretched known facts to breaking point with wild leaps of the imagination. When you read Freud in detail, you are struck by a paradox. He can be at times very precise and logical and, at other times, a wild writer who will stop at little to make the facts fit the theory. His essay on Dostoevsky is a master-class in the selective use of evidence to reach a patently absurd conclusion, which, in Freud's hands, is made to seem almost plausible. Like the most skilful authors of detective stories he knew how to spring a surprise plot twist.

Chapter 11

The Fliess Letters

A few weeks after Wilhelm Fliess died in 1928, his son Robert visited Freud. Robert had trained as an analyst and had come to believe his father had abused him both physically and sexually. He had 'clarified the picture of my father in two expert and thorough analyses, the last in middle age'. Robert had 'an extended conversation with Freud himself about his one time friend'. Perhaps as a result of Freud's willingness to talk to her son, Ida Fliess did not raise the question of Freud's letters, which were in her possession, for another three years. She may also have felt constrained while Oscar Rie, her brother-in-law, was still alive, for Rie had been doctor to Freud's children.

Once Rie died, Ida felt free. Her husband Wilhelm had been bitter about Freud's growing famous while he and his cherished naso-sexual medicine dwindled into obscurity. Ida decided to make use one of the most precious assets her husband had left – the letters Freud had written to him between 1887 and 1904. These letters, as noted above, not only testified to the many mistakes and absurdities of the Eckstein case, but recorded, in detail, Freud's use of cocaine, proving it continued beyond the turn of the century.

Ida wrote to Freud asking him to find her husband's letters. Freud had destroyed them, but pretended otherwise to a woman who in private he called 'the witch'. He made excuse after excuse, said he could not find them and promised to look for them again, but explained that his apartment had so many nooks and crannies that it could take forever to find them. Finally he had to confess, not that he had taken the dramatic step of destroying them, but that they had been mysteriously lost.

Witch or otherwise, Ida's desire to reclaim Fleiss's letters may have had more pragmatic than occult origins: she probably needed money. By

Princess Marie Bonaparte, Freud's friend and patient, who both paid for the Fliess letters and assisted Freud's escape from the Nazis, pictured with her husband, Prince George of Greece.

1932 the Great Depression was causing financial problems even for the wealthy, including the by-then quite affluent Freud. His maid, Paula Fichtl, noticed that he stopped buying new suits regularly because he had fewer patients than before. Freud, who sometimes charged exorbitant fees and sometimes nothing at all, wrote to a prospective patient in May 1933:

> 'You are right to assume that my greedy instincts will be strongly influenced by your future career in America. But, in addition, there are material needs to be considered. I am still forced to make a living. I cannot do more than five hours of analysis daily and I do not know how much longer I shall work at all. Thus a fee of $15 is my lowest rate per hour. The amount of $1500 which you have proposed for your analysis would cover 100 hours, that is four months. Even if for you I were to decrease this to $10.00, this would result in 150 hours, which would be about 6 months. I can make no other arrangements.'

Ida Fleiss knew that one of Freud's friends would not have been affected by the Depression. Princess Marie Bonaparte was Napoleon's great-granddaughter; Marie's paternal grandmother, Princess Pierre Bonaparte, was ruined during the Paris Commune of 1871. To restore the family fortunes, she arranged for her son to marry an heiress. It was a perfect match. The boy had class and the girl had money: her family owned a good chunk of Monaco, including the casino in which Dostoevsky set *The Gambler*.

Marie's mother died a month after she gave birth, and Marie was unlucky enough to be left in the care of her father, who was obsessed with mountaineering and not the most devoted of parents. Marie was handed over to be brought up by her grandmother, Princess Pierre, a monstrous snob. A girl who could trace her descent from Napoleon could hardly play with ordinary children, she decreed, and condemned Marie to a lonely childhood in grand palaces. Marie developed night terrors, a morbid fear of illness and enough obsessional anxieties to delight an orchestra of analysts.

When Marie was 25 years old, her father chose Prince George of Greece as a suitable husband for his daughter. George was not an ideal husband, as he was as every bit as neurotic as Marie. Their wedding night was not one of erotic bliss: before they consummated the marriage, he confessed 'I hate it as much as you do. But we must do it if we want children'. The fact they managed to have two sons shows that they were conscientious aristocrats, forcing their loins to do the necessary.

George was actually rather fond of Marie, as long as she did not insist on sex – which she did not, in fact, hate as much as he did. So the Princess took lovers, including Aristide Briand, Prime Minister of France. No man, however, managed to excite her greatly because 'she had a marked virility complex,' a French psychiatrist, René Laforgue told her. In other words, she was too masculine. Laforgue suggested she see Freud, and Marie left immediately, for Vienna.

Freud and Marie adored each other from the start. She was highly literate and kept detailed notes about their sessions. Freud sensed Marie would become very dependent on him and forewarned her of the inevitable transference: 'I am 69 years old and there are a few things that don't work so well. You must not get too attached to me.' Marie started to cry. The analysis began in the spirit of a great platonic love affair and the 'lovers' soon found common ground: both were completely devoted to their dogs. Freud even translated a soppy book Marie wrote about her dog, Topsy, and arranged for it to be published by his own Belgian publishers.

Within a few days, Marie admitted she loved Freud. It was not all one-way. Freud replied 'I have told you more than I tell most people in two years' though they had just known each other for two weeks, but he repeated she should not get too attached to him. At which point, Marie once more burst into tears. The idea of being let down by a man yet again, as she had been by her father, lovers, and a least one French prime minister, was unbearable. Freud promised not to let her down and, as proof of his devotion, doubled her time on the couch to two hours a day. No other patient was so privileged, but then, no other patient could pay as much.

Freud did not manage to cure Marie's alleged frigidity but he was, at least, sensible when she sought his advice. When Marie asked if he thought it would be a good idea for her to commit incest with her son, Freud advised against it.

Marie realised both the historic importance of Freud's letters to Fliess and that protecting Freud's reputation was not just a matter of appeasing his intellectual vanity. In January 1933 Hitler became Chancellor of Germany. Freud's books were burned as were those written by Einstein, Hemingway, Heine and thirty other 'decadent' writers. It would have been a huge propaganda coup for the Nazis, had they been able to denounce psychoanalysis as a Jewish science dreamed up by a degenerate 'cocamaniac'. Though the Nazi elite, other than Hitler himself, were often fond of opiates and methamphetamine, they did not advertise the fact.

Hitler had been cured of hysterical blindness in 1917, as we have seen, and that influenced his attitude, and so the attitude of the Nazis, towards psychotherapy. They hoped to convert Freudian analysis into an Aryan doctrine to help less than perfect Aryans become more efficient in their service to the state. The Führer was not the only ex-patient among the leading fascists; Hermann Goring, who was addicted to morphine and spent time in an asylum in the mid-1920s, had also been helped by a therapist. Göring's cousin Matthias was in fact a well-known psychotherapist whose main objection to Freud was not that he was Jewish, but a question of furniture. Matthias Göring argued that it demeaned the patient to make him lie down on the couch. The therapist should sit facing the patient and look them in the eye, an idea later adopted by Carl Rogers, the father of humanist psychotherapy or counselling.

Seventy years after Jacob Freud had not dared to protest when an anti-Semite knocked his hat into the gutter, his son still had to deal with hatred of the Jews. The Nazis drove a tough bargain. German psychoanalytic institutions would only be allowed to survive if Matthias Göring was allowed to run them. Hitler even sent supportive telegrams to the new 'Nazified' psychotherapy association.

The letters between Freud and Fliess were thus of great political importance. Ida Fliess wrote to Marie saying she had sold the letters to a dealer for 12,000 schillings. Marie contacted the dealer at once and had no trouble in persuading him to sell her the letters. At first Freud was ecstatic but Marie refused to destroy the letters, as he wished. In that she was wiser than her analyst, but she was also very tactful and did not read the letters herself.

Early in July 1936, Freud's cancer returned. On December 12th, he had yet another operation using 'short wave treatments with a portable machine.' He would be in pain for the rest of his life but refused to take anything stronger than aspirin: where cocaine had provided a sense of intellectual clarity and stimulation that Freud adored, opiates clouded his thinking and ability to write.

In March 1938 the Nazis took over Austria and declared it part of Greater Germany. Following much hesitation, three months after the Anschluss, Freud left Vienna for London. The complicated tale of how he arranged for all his furniture, his collection of figurines, the sacred analytic couch as well as most of his library to be transported to Britain was the subject of my book, *The Escape of Sigmund Freud*. Strangely, Freud was helped to escape by a committed Nazi chemist, Anton Sauerwald. Sauerwald had been a student of Freud's university colleague, Josef Herzig, and remained fond of his old teacher. Herzig may well have praised Freud to Sauerwald as a young man and though he was an active member of the Nazi party, Sauerwald seems to have decided that Freud's genius outweighed his Jewishness, and saw to it that the Freuds escaped the Reich.

Freud's collection of antiquities contained around 3000 objects and every one of them was dear to him. He wrote to Stefan Zweig: 'for all my well-known frugality, I have made many sacrifices for my collection' and 'actually read more archaeology than psychology'. The 'old and dirty gods' comforted Freud as he left the city where he had lived since early infancy.

Before leaving Vienna, Freud bequeathed his stock of cigars to his younger brother Alexander, who was fleeing to Canada. 'Your seventy-second birthday finds us on the verge of separating after long years of living together,' Freud said. 'I hope it is not going to be a separation forever, but the future – always uncertain – is at the moment especially difficult to foresee. I would like you to take over the good cigars which have been accumulating with me over the years, as you can still indulge in such pleasure, I no longer can.'

When he said he could no longer indulge, Freud was exaggerating – he in fact continued to smoke when he reached London. Marie Bonaparte commissioned a tobacconist to make him some cigars which had no nicotine but he found them disgusting; they may well have been no less carcinogenic than the real thing. It is not nicotine, but the tar produced by tobacco's combustion, that is the primary cause of smoking-related illnesses; herbal cigars and cigarettes may be nicotine-free, but they still contain high levels of tar. Proper cigars, as always, helped Freud write and he produced two books and an important paper during the last 15 months of his life.

First, he concentrated on writing *Moses and Monotheism*, a subject which he had pondered since 1914. Freud claimed Moses was not a Jew but an Egyptian prince, belonging to a small sect that rejected the old deities bearing the heads of cats, crocodiles and other animals; this sect worshipped the sun instead as a symbol of the one and only God. Moses needed followers for this new monotheistic faith and recruited the Jews, slaves whose own religion, at the time, was polytheistic. A mischievous critic might speculate that Freud's claim that Moses was not Jewish reflected his own guilty desire to be free of the anti-Semitism which had dogged his career. Psychoanalysis claims we can love and hate, be loyal to and betray the same person or idea at the same time. Those we identify with reveal a great deal. Freud never denied his Jewishness but he may well have imagined his life woud have been rather easier if he had been born a Christian.

Freud knew that the book would provoke outrage among both Jews and Christians, but he had waited a long time to write it, and, given his own identification with Moses, must have taken great pleasure in finally, as he saw it, revealing his own hero's secret – that he was not a Jew. He had not felt free to present such radical arguments while in Vienna.

Freud also wrote *An Outline of Psychoanalysis*, providing a final summary of his ideas. At the end of one chapter, Freud again predicted that yet-to-be-discovered drugs would provide cures for neurosis and psychosis, in time. Till then, analysis was the best means of reducing neurotic misery, but he looked forward to the day when an exact pharmacology would supersede the talking cure and chemical 'magic bullets' would fix the malfunctioning brain. Despite the claims of pharmaceutical companies over subsequent decades, that day has yet to arrive.

As his own death approached, Freud had no idea that a Swiss chemist had made a discovery on November 16th 1938. Albert Hoffman worked for the pharmaceutical company Sandoz and was searching for a drug to help women through difficulties in labour when he discovered LSD. Hoffman's discovery would revive the introspective tradition.

Drug historians often claim that the synthesis of LSD was a 'happy' accident but Hoffman stressed it was nothing of the sort and that he 'synthesised the diethylamide of lysergic acid with the intention of obtaining an analeptic.' An analeptic or stimulant would speed up labour by energising muscles in the womb, Hoffman's reasoned. Hence the range of chemicals that he was working with, including LSD itself, were structurally related to the amphetamines.

Hoffman also produced other compounds which he expected to possess different pharmacological properties. Hoffman's head of department, Professor Ernst Rothlin, studied these new compounds, including one which was given the laboratory code name LSD–25 because it was the twenty-fifth compound in the lysergic acid series. Laboratory animals reacted with 'marked excitation' to LSD–25, Hoffman noted, but 'work on LSD then fell into abeyance for a number of years.'

Even if Hoffman had published his results at the time, Freud would not have read them. By the middle of 1939, he was growing steadily weaker, and had no illusions about the terminal nature of his condition. Marie Bonaparte came to his home at Maresfield Gardens in London on August 6th to say her farewells and a few days later, Freud's doctor, Max Schur, moved into the house to be with his patient till the end. Schur had promised that when the time came, he would ease Freud into death with morphine. When Freud was in such pain that he could no longer think properly, he told Schur that the suffering no longer made any sense. Schur administered the first injection.

As he lay dying, Freud was tended by his wife, Martha, his daughter Anna and the household maid, Paula Fichtl. Fichtl noted the details of his final days, the meals they tried to feed him and the sadness shared by the three women at his bedside. On September 21st 1939, Freud said goodbye – to Martha, to his daughter Mathilde, to his sons and, finally, to Anna, who was herself becoming famous for her therapeutic work with children.

Freud then asked Schur to give him several large injections of morphine. It was what we now call 'voluntary euthanasia' or an 'assisted suicide'. Freud died shortly before midnight on September 23rd, 1939 and was cremated three days later in North London at Golders Green. In his funeral oration Ernest Jones said: 'It has been hard to wish him to live a day longer when he was suffering so much.' Jones paid respect to 'what in others expresses itself as religious feeling' but was, in Freud expressed 'as a transcendental belief in the value of life and in the value of love.' Jones recalled Freud's vivid personality and 'instinctive love of truth.'

He added that he felt no one could ever have lied to Freud. 'One can say of him that as never a man loved life more, so never man feared death less.' Jones finished in some style: 'So we take our leave of a man whose like we shall not know again. From our hearts we thank him for having lived; for having done; for having loved.'

One of Britain's leading analysts, Edward Glover wrote a tribute in *The Listener*. Freud's discoveries were not 'divorced from everyday affairs', but were concerned with the 'very mind of Everyman, with his happiness and more important with his miseries.' Glover ended eloquently:

'At a time when Europe has been thrown into a cubicle of war,' it is perhaps appropriate to see what ... is the message that his work has for a distracted generation, Freud was, of course, no manufacturer of cheap philosophies of life but all his work, his researches and discoveries bear witness to his profound belief in the value of truth.'

Glover added, a nuance, saying Freud offered the 'truth, however incomplete it may be.' He argued that if Freud attacked anything in the human mind, he attacked its tendency to unreason and to self-deception. Neither he nor Jones said anything about Freud's many failures and self-deceptions. Eulogies and obituaries are not the place for such critiques and Freud had suppressed evidence and burned letters which allowed his zealous followers to believe not just that he was 'a man most mighty' as the 1906 medal had been inscribed but a perfect man. Freud knew better himself but did not always say so. It is a pity the poet Hilda Doolittle was not asked to speak. She loved Freud but saw some of his faults.

It would be possible to end this book with Freud's death, but the introspective tradition to which his cocaine experiments contributed has continued, and its development provides an important context for the reassessment of Freud in, as it were, the light of cocaine. It is a story that has remained controversial, and grown ever-more complicated, with the production of successive generations of drugs – legal and illegal, 'therapeutic' and 'recreational', pharmaceutical and bootleg – following a process that closely maps Freud's, and the world's, experience with cocaine in the late 19th and early 20th centuries.

In the 70 years since Freud died, there has been an explosion in the range of legal and illegal drugs available, an explosion made greater by the distribution routes provided by the internet. All too often, despite great advances in pharmacology, the history of cocaine repeats itself with these new substances. The wonderful elixir turns out to be something of a curse: for example, the 'soft' drug ecstasy (MDMA) proved to have profound psychological consequences for some users. On the other side of the legal divide, despite the protestations of their manufacturers, new generations of anti-depressants initially welcomed as 'harmless' did not turn out to be 'non-addictive' or 'side-effect free'. Echoing Freud's claims for cocaine, it was said Prozac would not merely bring relief to the depressed but make normal users 'better than well'. It turned out, however, to be highly addictive to some users and prone to cause unpleasant side-effects including, according to much research, an increased risk of suicide.

When reports of such side-effects first emerge where a pharmaceutical is concerned, its medical proponents are highly reluctant to acknowledge the problem. As with Freud and Fleischl, the usual medical response is to 'blame the disease, not the drug.' We become attached to our poisons, and cognitive dissonance readily takes hold.

Economics reinforce the psychology. On the London and New York Stock Exchanges, the pharmaceutical sector accounts for approximately 8% of the value of all shares. When doubts about a drug are publicised, stock market values can plummet dramatically: and, if the drug has already been widely prescribed, especially in the USA, litigation and compensation claims are likely to follow, with class-action suits from groups of patients claiming to have been damaged. Of all drugs, those used in psychiatry are amongst the most likely to have unpleasant, psychological effects, as they target neurotransmitters whose function in the brain is still ill-understood.

Without being remotely dogmatic, it is possible to chart four stages of the cycle of illusion and disillusion with medications, which closely parallels a similar process with underground, recreational drugs:

First a drug is 'discovered', usually by accident, often decades after it was first created to solve an entirely different problem. Obvious examples include those drugs which were supposed to deal with tuberculosis and were then used for depression, or the 'anaesthetics' that eventually found their place on psychiatric wards, as anti-psychotics.

The second stage is euphoria. The new drug is heralded as a miracle-cure or tonic. Hopeless cases are said to have been spontaneously cured in clinical trials (generally funded and conducted by pharmaceutical companies themselves, raising serious questions about their objectivity). Some medications are proposed not only to heal the sick, but to improve the healthy – the 'Better than Well' effect, taken from the title of a rather evangelistic book on Prozac by Carl Elliott, subtitled, in a tone that echoes the young Freud writing of cocaine, 'American Medicine Meets the American Dream.' Psychiatrists are as prone to believe these claims as anyone else.

Thus the third stage of the cycle is anxiety as the drug turns out to have unexpected side-effects and to be less beneficial than it first seemed. In the case of psychiatric medications, patients may, for example find they have the shakes, sweat profusely, lose their teeth, become impotent, are constantly drowsy and no longer 'feel themselves'. Such side-effects are unsurprising, viewed historically, when the drug that fights the symptoms of depression or stops schizophrenics hearing voices was created to deal with physical problems. At this stage, pharmaceutical companies sometimes behave like neurotics, becoming defensive and sometimes deceitful – just like psychoanalysts have done at times. A particularly distressing side-effect is when the patient physically attacks the prescribing psychiatrist. I have known two patients sent to Broadmoor for such 'madness'. One was in for over 30 years having stabbed her shrink in the buttock.

The fourth stage can lead to a more realistic appraisal of the drug, or it can end in hostility, court cases, not to mention accusations that data were faked and counter-accusations that any critics of a drug are foolish, corrupt or obsessed. This cycle of illusion and disillusion does not help objective assessment of how psychoactive substances affect the brain, least of all when claim and counter-claim fly in an atmosphere of furious, and sometimes personal, attacks. Litigation and stock market prices further muddy the waters.

This four-stage cycle has recurred consistently since Freud's cocaine experiments. Reckless as Freud's behaviour with cocaine appears to us today, pharmaceutical companies and black market drug dealers can be every bit as reckless and irresponsible. Drug dealers are drug dealers and pill pushers are pill pushers. No one can deny that pharmaceuticals have cured millions of patients of physical illnesses and alleviated painful symptoms, but disturbances of the mind are more complex and claims that some new panacea can fix/heal/mend/improve the mind need to be judged with scrupulous care.

We can be both confused and dishonest about what we actually demand from doctors and pharmaceutical companies. The following list is, of course, impressionistic. We want drugs to cure specific diseases: but we also want tonics to keep us going and productive, be they stimulants, anti-depressants or aphrodisiacs. We want the opposite too, sedatives, painkillers and anxiolytics to deaden our misery and provide a pinch of oblivion. We also want drugs that control the obviously mentally ill. I can stand a lot of your pain, of course, because I'm not feeling it. If my neighbour hears voices which make him violent, I probably won't mind if his medication makes him drowsy and prone to tremors. With medications, the issues seem clear. We want drugs that heal without harming or, at least, without doing too much harm. With illegal drugs, the debate is more confused and produces more heat than light, more fog than clarity. Drug policy, however, remains a pressing social issue, growing all the more urgent as new drugs are invented, and their recipes disseminated online, at ever-faster rates. The failure of politicians and doctors to come to terms with this is astonishing. We can be sure of only one thing: drug policy is rarely tainted by a drop of rationality.

Five years after Freud died, Hoffman returned to his research on LSD. He insisted 'LSD was not the fruit of a chance discovery' but that it was 'the outcome of a more complex process.' He had made a chance observation which compelled him to design and perform 'appropriate experiments'. These led logically 'to the actual discovery.' He was a meticulous man, in contrast to the chaotic nature of 'the actual discovery', the bizarre and profound nature of which led to his dubbing LSD 'my problem child'.

In 1943, Hoffman prepared a new batch of LSD and carried out 'a planned self-experiment with this compound.' On Friday, April 16th Hoffman was forced to stop work in the middle of the afternoon and to go home, as he was seized:

> '... by a peculiar restlessness associated with a sensation of mild dizziness. On arriving home, I lay down and sank into a kind of drunkenness which was not unpleasant and which was characterised by extreme activity of imagination. As I lay in a dazed condition with my eyes closed (I experienced daylight as disagreeably bright) there surged upon me an uninterrupted stream of fantastic images of extraordinary plasticity and vividness and accompanied by an intense, kaleidoscope-like play of colors. This condition gradually passed off after about two hours.
>
> The nature and the course of this extraordinary disturb-

ance raised my suspicions that some exogenic intoxication may have been involved and that the Lysergic acid diethylamide with which I had been working that afternoon could have been responsible.'

Hoffman was puzzled and said:

'I could not imagine how this compound could have accidentally found its way into my body in a sufficient quantity to produce such phenomena. Moreover, the nature of the symptoms did not tally with those previously associated with ergot poisoning.'

Hoffman decided to conduct some experiments on himself with LSD–25. 'I started with the lowest dose that might be expected to have any effect, i. e., 0.25 mg LSD. The notes in my laboratory journal read as follows:

April 19, 1943: Preparation of a 0.5% aqueous solution of d-lysergic acid diethylamide tartrate.
4.20 P.M.: 0.5 cc (0.25 mg LSD) ingested orally. The solution is tasteless.
4.50 P.M.: no trace of any effect.
5.00 P.M.: slight dizziness, unrest, difficulty in concentration, visual disturbances, marked desire to laugh . . .'

Hoffman, alarmed by his intoxication, asked his laboratory assistant to accompany him on the ride home. (Hoffman was a keen cyclist.) What happened next led drug historians to dub the incident 'Bicycle Day', though in fact, Hoffman and his assistant cycled by night.

'While we were cycling home, however, it became clear that the symptoms were much stronger than the first time. I had great difficulty in speaking coherently, my field of vision swayed before me, and objects appeared distorted like images in curved mirrors. I had the impression of being unable to move from the spot, although my assistant told me afterwards that we had cycled at a good pace... Once I was at home the physician was called.

'By the time the doctor arrived, the peak of the crisis had already passed. As far as I remember, the following were the most outstanding symptoms: vertigo, visual disturbances; the faces of those around me appeared as grotesque, coloured masks; marked motoric unrest, alternating with paralysis; an intermittent heavy feeling in the head, limbs and the entire body, as if they were filled with lead; dry, constricted sensation in the throat; feeling of choking; clear recognition of my condition, in which state I sometimes observed, in the manner of an independent, neutral observer, that I shouted half insanely or babbled incoherent words. Occasionally I felt as if I were out of my body.'

The doctor found a rather weak pulse but an otherwise normal circulation. Six hours after Hoffman had taken LSD, he was in a much more normal state though he was still hallucinating. 'Everything seemed to sway and the proportions were distorted like the reflections in the surface of moving water. Moreover, all objects appeared in unpleasant, constantly changing colours, the predominant shades being sickly green and blue. When I closed my eyes, an unending series of colourful, very realistic and fantastic images surged in upon me. A remarkable feature was the manner in which all acoustic perceptions (e.g., the noise of a passing car) were transformed into optical effects, every sound evoking a corresponding coloured hallucination constantly changing in shape.'

Hoffman described what he saw just as Havelock Ellis had done, as being 'like pictures in a kaleidoscope.' Hoffman finally fell asleep at about 1 am and woke up the next morning feeling perfectly well.

Hoffman had provided a classic introspective account, as Davy, James, Freud and Havelock Ellis had done before him. Methodically, Hoffman then tested LSD on volunteers at Sandoz and confirmed 'the extraordinary activity of LSD on the human psyche.' It only needed a tiny dose of LSD, 0.03 mg to 0.05 mg, to produce these effects. 'In spite of my caution, I had chosen for my first experiment five times the average effective dose. LSD is by far the most active and most specific hallucinogen. It is about 5000 to 10000 times more active than mescaline, which produces qualitatively nearly the same symptoms.'

The power of LSD was 'not just a curiosity; it is in many respects of the greatest scientific interest.' It showed that 'certain mental illnesses that were supposed until then to be of purely psychic nature had a biochemical cause because it now seemed feasible that undetectable traces of a psychoactive substance produced by the body itself might produce psychic disturbances.'

Some people might be born with too much lysergic acid, or a similar compound, in the brain or might respond to particular crises by producing too much of such a compound. Hoffman realised he had stumbled on a psychoactive substance of extraordinary power which would become hugely important in psychiatry.

But the world was at war in 1943. It was only after 1945 that scientists outside Switzerland learned what Hoffman had discovered and even then it seems to have taken four years for Sandoz to supply anyone else with LSD. Generously the company did so without asking for payment. In 1950 Anthony K. Busch and Warren C. Johnson published the first report on the psychotherapeutic use of LSD on 21 psychotic patients. They concluded that 'LSD–25 may offer a means for more readily gaining access to the chronically withdrawn patients. It may also serve as a new tool for shortening psychotherapy.' The military showed some interest at once and American sailors who were depressed and suffering from post-traumatic stress were given the drug.

Hoffman's work also fascinated Aldous Huxley, the world-famous author of *Antic Hay* and *Brave New World*, which depicted a future where human beings were conditioned and controlled from birth, in part by the use of an LSD-like drug, 'soma'. Huxley took the name from Hindu literature, and some historians think it refers to the hallucinogenic *Amanita Muscaria*, a very different and more toxic fungus than the commonly used 'magic mushrooms' containing psilocybin and psilocin. *Amanita* has provoked a furious debate among a community few know exists – theologians who specialise in fungi. The debate concerns the Tree in the Garden of Eden. The forbidden fruit was, they argue, not in fact an apple but a fungus, the mushroom *Amanita*, which would make the Serpent in Genesis the first drug dealer in history and Eve, the mother of all humankind, the first drug user.

Fifty-four years after Havelock Ellis had taken mescaline in Harley Street, one of the world's great intellectuals would repeat the experiment in a city that remains a capital of drug use – Hollywood.

Cartoon by Tony Jadunath, artist and former Broadmoor patient,
depicting cocaine's dangers.

Chapter 12

The Chemical Muse 1952–1960

1952 was a special year in the cycle of pharmaceutical illusion and disillusion. It was the year of Aldous Huxley's first mescaline trip, in imitation of Havelock Ellis, and also the year in which three new legal drugs went on the market, medicines that changed psychiatry dramatically. This growing focus on psychopharmacology would also see later generations of psychiatrists go in the opposite direction from psychoanalysis, away from the mind and back to the body and brain, away with the analyst's couch and the talking cure – and back to the drugs. With it, some would allege, came a return to Charcot-esque 'objectification' of the psychiatric patient, reduced to a dysfunctional brain to be corrected by chemical means.

Huxley had gone to Hollywood in 1937 to write screenplays of, amongst other books, *Pride and Prejudice* and *Jane Eyre*. From an eminent family of scientists, he both became something of a prophet, in the Orwellian sci-fi style, and cultivated a deep lifelong interest in religion and mysticism. Mescaline and its traditional use in inducing visionary experiences appealed to his metaphysical side.

Huxley was '. . . willing, indeed eager, to be a guinea pig (so) one bright May morning, I swallowed four-tenths of a gram of mescaline dissolved in half a glass of water and sat down to wait for the results.' He asked the psychologist Humphry Osmond to stay with him and they kept a dictating machine switched on to record the experience. Huxley chose Osmond because he had argued there was a similarity between the effects of LSD and the early stages of schizophrenia: he was intrigued by the possibility of experiencing 'voluntary madness'.

Huxley had very poor eyesight and did not expect the drug to release a flood of images, so he was amazed when, 30 minutes after drinking the solution, he began to hallucinate visually, much as Ellis had done in 1896. 'I became aware of a slow dance of golden lights. A little later there were sumptuous red surfaces swelling and expanding from bright nodes of energy that vibrated with a continuously changing, patterned life,' Huxley wrote.

An hour later, Huxley was looking at a small glass vase and saw many tiny differences in colours, which prompted him to compare mescaline and the writings of mystics. 'Like mescaline takers, many mystics perceive supernaturally brilliant colors, not only with the inward eye, but even in the objective world around them,' he said. 'I was seeing what Adam had seen on the morning of his creation–the miracle, moment by moment, of naked existence.'

The great revelation was that 'the eye recovers some of the perceptual innocence of childhood.' Huxley quoted the famous Christian mystic Meister Eckhart who used the word 'Istigkeit' or 'Is-ness' which he described as 'a transience that was yet eternal life, a perpetual perishing that was at the same time pure Being, a bundle of minute, unique particulars in which, by some unspeakable and yet self-evident paradox, was to be seen the divine source of all existence.'

Mescaline had not made Huxley lose all sense of space, but space did not matter: nor did time. When Osmond asked about time, Huxley laughed: 'There seems to be plenty of it.' He could have looked at his watch; but his watch seemed to belong to another dimension.

Still Huxley preserved some detachment and found some of mescaline's effects on him amusing. 'Even the legs of the chair glowed with the Inner Light, and were infinite in its significance ... I spent several minutes – or "I" was not involved in the case, nor in a certain sense were "they" – being my Not-self in the Not-self which was the chair.'

Mescaline flung open 'The Doors of Perception', Huxley argued, because it stopped the brain acting as a filter which excludes all sense-impressions it has learned to define as 'irrelevant'. The drug reversed what Huxley called this 'reduced awareness' so that he could enjoy total perception. He had no idea how the drug accomplished this effect. Though the experience affected every aspect of Huxley's perception, he felt he could still 'think straight'. He joked that when he listened to recordings of what he had said 'under the influence of the drug, I cannot discover that I was then any stupider than I am at ordinary times.'

'The mescaline taker,' Huxley added, 'sees no reason for doing anything in particular and finds most of the causes for which, at ordinary times, he was prepared to act and suffer, profoundly uninteresting. He can't be bothered with them, for the good reason that he has better things to think about.' These better things were spiritual. Some users:

'... discover a world of visionary beauty. To others again is revealed the glory, the infinite value and meaningfulness of naked existence, of the given, unconceptualised event. In the final stage of egolessness there is an "obscure knowledge" that All is in all – that All is actually each. This is as near, I take it, as a finite mind can ever come to 'perceiving everything that is happening everywhere in the universe.'

Six hours after taking mescaline, Huxley was taken to the local drug store, which also sold books. To his surprise he found one on Van Gogh and stared at an illustration of the famous yellow chair 'which contained the essence of every chair'. Huxley could still make fun of himself, an English gent with sharp dress sense whose trousers now acquired metaphysical properties, saying:

'More even than the chair ... the folds of my gray flannel trousers were charged with "is-ness". To what they owed this privileged status, I cannot say ... "This is how one ought to see", I kept saying.'

His trousers were part of the great Scheme of Things – and that was even more true of 'the legs of my infinitely more than Van-Goghian chair'.

Osmond then asked Huxley to shut his eyes and think about what was going on inside his head. Huxley mused: 'What wonder, then, if human beings in their search for the divine have generally preferred to look within!' The Taoists and the Zen Buddhists had looked 'beyond visions to the Void, and through the Void at 'the ten thousand things' of objective reality.

Huxley agreed with Osmond that the experience conveyed a sense of madness, even a temporary model of what real mental illness might feel like, in part, writing: 'Schizophrenia has its heavens as well as its hells and purgatories.' Most people who took mescaline experienced only the heavenly part of schizophrenia, but depressives and the chronically anxious had disturbing visions and panic attacks on the drug. For healthy people 'mescaline is completely innocuous.'

Suddenly, however, like James after taking nitrous oxide, Huxley felt an intense fear, 'the fear of being overwhelmed, of disintegrating under a pressure of reality greater than a mind.' He then took down his copy of *The Tibetan Book of the Dead*, opened it at random and found this passage: 'O nobly born, let not thy mind be distracted.' That was the problem – to remain undistracted, by the memory of past sins and by imagined pleasures. Huxley's response to this lyrical outburst was to laugh – maniacally. 'I laughed till the tears ran down my cheeks.'

Then Huxley ate a hearty meal and was taken for a drive. The effects of the mescaline were wearing off, but when they reached Sunset Boulevard the stream of cars 'all bright and shiny like an advertiser's dream and each more ludicrous than the last,' seemed surreal. 'Once again I was convulsed with laughter. The Red Sea of traffic parted at last.'

Huxley then looked down at Hollywood which looked like a 'vast, dim panorama that was hardly different from itself.' For an instant the drug swept over him again and he seemed to see 'fragments' of William Blake's New Jerusalem 'unforgettably beautiful, empty but charged with all the meaning and the mystery of existence.' Tinseltown had become the Holy City.

Humankind would never 'be able to dispense with Artificial Paradises,' he maintained. Huxley remembered H.G. Wells, who claimed most of us only escape reality 'through art and religion, carnivals and saturnalia, dancing and listening to oratory which served ... as Doors in the Wall.' Chemicals could do the same but all the 'modifiers of consciousness are labeled Dope, and their unauthorized takers are Fiends.'

The world needed a new soma or ideal drug, Huxley said, which 'will relieve and console our suffering species. It had to be 'less toxic than opium or cocaine, less likely to produce undesirable social consequences than alcohol or the barbiturates, less damaging than the tars and nicotine.' This splendid chemical would free us from 'the wine-bibbing past, the whisky-drinking, marijuana-smoking and barbiturate-swallowing present.' It had to be better than 'goof pills' (barbiturates) and Christianity combined. From this and later writings, it would seem that Huxley's ideal soma would be a psychedelic like mescaline, but also something of a tranquiliser. Huxley wrote of the search for an ideal drug in lyrical terms, but his rhetoric could have been inscribed as a motto on the lab walls of every major pharmaceutical company. The world's largest drug manufacturers were about to launch a whole new generation of chemicals onto the market, compounds that would lead, in time, to drastic changes in the medical and popular perception of mental illness – and mental health.

While Huxley was taking mescaline on the West Coast, on the East Coast at Sea View Hospital on Staten Island in New York, Irving Selikoff and Edward Robitzek began clinical trials with two promising new drugs, isoniazid and iproniazid. Their patients suffered from tuberculosis. The story behind these drugs yet again emphasises the random element of pharmaceutical history. In 1938, Freud had thanked the Führer for forcing him to come to London. Ironically, Hitler also seems to deserve the thanks of the pharmaceutical industry.

The German nation contributed much to the market in what would become recreational drugs in the first half of the 20th century. Oxycodone, a powerful and highly euphoric synthetic opiate that is now sold on the street in the US at quite staggering prices (an 80mg pill can cost as much as $80), was first synthesised in Germany in 1916: MDMA, or ecstasy, was likewise a German invention. Then the Third Reich's scientists invented methadone, when seeking an alternative to morphine after the allies had blocked the Reich's access to opium supply routes. The German army suffered from a shortage of painkillers, and the resulting research led to the synthesis of methadone. It is often claimed that the drug was named 'Adolphine', in honour of Hitler, but this is, in fact, a myth that arose from an early brand of methadone being marketed under the name of 'Dolophine'. Methadone, by blocking the brain's opiod receptors, greatly reduces the euphoric effect of consuming other opiods, and has an extremely long half-life, hence its use as a maintenance therapy in the treatment of opiate (especially heroin) addiction.

Another German pharmaceutical discovery, though, was accidental, and had its beginnings on the battlefield. When ethanol and liquid oxygen ran low during the end of World War II, the Germans started using a chemical named hydrazine to propel their V 1 and V 2 rockets, many of which were fired on England. When the war ended, large stocks of hydrazine survived and these were given to chemical companies. Call it lateral thinking, but some pharmacologists wondered if rocket fuel might not also have medical uses. Chemists at Hoffman-La Roche began to play with variations on hydrazine, eventually synthesising isoniazid. They wanted doctors who would test the drug on patients. They found some across the Atlantic on Staten Island in a hospital for patients with tuberculosis.

The American doctors were surprised when patients given isoniazid perked up. Selikoff and Robitzek reported 'a subtle general stimulation ... the patients exhibited renewed vigor and indeed this occasionally served to introduce disciplinary problems.' Patients who could previously hardly get out of bed now tried to punch the nurses, ran wild and sometimes even ran away. The Associated Press released a photo of patients dancing in the wards. The caption read 'A few months ago, only the sound of TB victims coughing their lives away could be heard here.' The press did not know the victims were being given a derivative of rocket fuel.

The second and more influential psychiatric drug of the period also originated in Germany, though it had a less explosive history. In 1952 Jean Delay, head of psychiatry at Sainte-Anne Hospital in Paris, oversaw 200 doctors, 1000 nursing attendants and 4000 patients, including many who were deemed psychotic. The wards housing the most severely disturbed population, largely patients diagnosed as schizophrenic, were run by Pierre Deniker, whose brother-in-law had drawn his attention to a new compound made by the pharmaceutical company Rhône-Poulenc.

Again this had been first developed, almost at random, in the German dye industry at the end of the 19th century. By December 1950, researchers had refined this into chlorpromazine, tested it on rats and seen intriguing results.

Rats fed the drug displayed a marked detachment, and could not be induced to climb up a rope, even with a piece of cheese tied to its end. An experimental group was then selected for initial human trials of the drug, logically enough, a sample composed entirely of taxi drivers. On chlorpromazine, they ignored red lights and drove in a heavily sedated, rather dangerous fog. With logic worthy of *Alice in Wonderland*, some chemists now suggested that chlorpromazine would boost performance on the battlefield and persuaded the Pentagon to give the drug to American soldiers fighting in Korea. Call it lateral thinking again. The imaginative 'logic' here seems to have been that the drug which caused taxi drivers to ignore red lights might also help soldiers ignore stress under fire.

But the soldier-on-chlorpromazine did not turn out to be a superior fighting machine: in fact, he became detached to the point of uselessness. On the drug, soldiers were too apathetic to return fire, evacuate their wounded or otherwise function effectively. The drug sedated subjects without knocking them out, inducing a state of calm so intense that it seems to have overpowered all normal fight-flight reflexes. The military soon abandoned research into the drug.

What did not work on the battlefield, however, might revolutionise psychiatric wards. Patients were often unruly, violent towards each other and staff, likely to vandalise the wards and otherwise hard to control. A drug that could calm disturbed patients without the negative effects and connotations of opiates or barbiturates (psychiatrists did not want to be seen as merely 'doping' patients into docility) would be a great boon to psychiatry

Pierre Deniker found that the drug did indeed calm patients on his psychotic wards. A colleague said he realised that chlorpromazine was effective because no patients broke hospital windows in the week after its introduction. Even better, patients were not rendered comatose but 'semi-detached' by the drug; if nurses talked to them they could rouse themselves to say something. It was a massive improvement.

David Healy, in his definitive work *The Creation of Psycho-pharmacology*, analysed the complicated history of the development of psychiatric medications from the 1950s onwards. Harvard University, he stresses, had just set up a new course which taught bright young pharmacologists not merely how to analyse drugs but also to synthesise new ones. America's most distinguished university sensed that a new pharmacopeia would find an eager market-place.

By 1957, some 400,000 patients were being given the 'TB drug', isoniazid, for depression. By then chlorpromazine was also being widely used both in Europe and America. Henry Brill, who ran mental health policy for New York State, promoted the drugs for both good and bad reasons. Asylums were crowded and often inhumane and it was much cheaper to keep patients in the community. The new 'miracle' drugs made that possible. Brill promoted their use without understanding how they worked, but at the time, little was understood by anyone of their mechanisms of action. It was a kind of chemical magic – and a financial miracle, to boot. Branded as 'Thorazine', chlorpromazine sold well, and widely.

But chlorpromazine had no recreational appeal, or, as the medical profession puts it, 'abuse potential'; many experimental subjects complained they found the drug and its side-effects, including extreme dryness of mouth, distinctly unpleasant. Later research confirmed this 'dysphoric' (the opposite of 'euphoric') property of chlorpromazine: recreational drug users given it experimentally disliked the substance, and thought it 'not worth paying for.'

Today we have a clearer idea of the mechanisms by which these medicines work, progress that owes something to the work of Otto Loewi. They affect the process by which messages pass from one neuron to the next – the never-ending flow that the brain needs to work normally.

The brain is packed with neurons or individual cells. A good way to imagine this is to think of each cell as an island, connected by a series of bridges to other islands. The bridges are called 'dendrites' and the dendrites connect one neuron to another. Groups of neurons form 'neural networks'.

When a baby is born, the rapid flowering of these connections is a true miracle of nature. The dendrites – or in the image used above, the bridges – reach out to make contact between brain cells. Traditionally the dendrites are called 'branches'. The points of contact are called 'synapses' (from the Greek work for clasp). In the womb and during the first three years of life, the synapses are constantly developing. Researchers call this process, poetically, 'synaptic exuberance', as the synapses multiply so quickly.

The figures are astonishing. It is estimated that every brain cell has an average of 10,000 synapses or connections. Two brain cells will, therefore, have 1 million connections with other brain cells. There are 100 billion cells in the brain, each with some 10,000 connections. Yet every neuron is separate; neurotransmitters smooth the passage of signals, allowing them to move through the synapse of one neuron and then on to the next.

Dopamine is one key neurotransmitter. It was first discovered in 1910, seven years before Otto Loewi 'saw' messages in the brain were sent from one cell to another by chemical transmission. Dopamine is very sensitive to cocaine, nicotine and other such stimulants. The well-ordered brain needs neurotransmitters to work properly and if they do not, our behaviour changes drastically. Crudely put, if brain cells don't connect quickly enough, patients can become too lethargic; if brain cells connect too fast, patients can be overwhelmed with incessant frantic thoughts.

The process of discovery continued apace. In 1955, a Swiss psychiatrist, Ronald Kuhn, found a third compound, 'G 22355' which had been patented in America. Kuhn realised he had found something interesting when 40 seriously depressed patients suddenly became 'alive' on the drug. After taking G 22355, they jumped out of bed in the morning and started to take interest in life on the ward. A rich investor, Robert Böhringer, who liked to roam around the Geigy offices and ask people what they were working on, heard about this. He gave some to a depressed relative. Five days later Böhringer's relative was 'cured', and Böhringer encouraged Kuhn to carry out a formal study. The results were promising.

'Patients began to 'get up in the morning of their own accord. Their facial expressions become more vivacious ... they once again begin to seek contact with the outside world ... instead of being concerned about imagined or real guilt in their past, they become occupied with plans concerning their future ... suicidal tendencies also diminish, becoming more controllable or disappearing altogether.' Even their voices sounded stronger, Kuhn noted.

Geigy named the compound 'Imipramine' and began to market it aggressively. It had a 3-ring chemical structure, leading to its classification as the first of the 'tricyclic' anti-depressants.

In the space of five years, three important new psychiatric drugs had been discovered – and no one had yet spotted any major problems with their usage. There were great differences between European and American psychiatry, however. In Europe there was relatively little private medicine and most psychiatric patients were treated in huge Victorian asylums like Napsbury outside St Albans or the Bürgholzi outside Zurich. Napsbury housed over 2000 patients and was, in effect, a large private village with workshops and a farm.

There were large asylums in America too, but many psychiatrists were in private practice outside hospital. 'Office psychiatrists', as they were called to make it clear they never went near an asylum, were usually Freudians. They had to keep their patients functioning well enough to stay in work because only then could they have medical insurance and pay the all-important fees. When a new medication called Miltown (chemical name 'meprobamate') was launched, American psychiatrists snapped it up because patients could take it and still work. Miltown offered 'happiness by prescription', according to the press. 35 million prescriptions for meprobamate were written in 1957, making it the second fastest-selling drug in pharmaceutical history. Doctors felt under pressure to prescribe this new, and fashionable, medication. If a doctor declined to prescribe Miltown on request, a patient could always find themselves a physician more amenable to their demands, taking their business elsewhere.

One busy Hollywood shrink confessed he took Miltown to pep him up for 'the nerve wrenching drive home'. The shrink, who clearly had dangerous socialist inclinations, told the Hollywood tabloid *Uncensored:* 'I wish the government would subsidise slot machines for tranquilisers on every corner.' The tabloid reassured readers they could take Miltown confidently because it 'was not addictive' and 'a severe over-dose can't kill you.' The comedian Milton Berle quipped that Miltown worked such wonders for him that 'I'm thinking of changing my name to Miltown Berle.' Huxley himself thought Miltown was wonderful. In *Brave New World Revisited*, he wrote 'in a world where nobody gets anything for nothing tranquilisers offer a great deal for very little.'

In Britain, the new medications found an unlikely champion in the Tory (later to become an Ulster Unionist) Minister of Health, Enoch Powell. From 1959 onwards, he argued that the old Victorian asylums should be closed and psychiatric patients treated in the community. Today, Powell is best-remembered for his inflammatory 'rivers of blood' speech, in which he warned that immigration to the UK from the West Indies and India would lead to racial violence. Eight years before he prophesied the coming of 'rivers of blood', Powell gave another speech, which was every bit as radical – if rather more progressive – for its time. It became known as the 'Water Tower' speech, taking its name from the water towers which loomed over decrepit asylums like Napsbury. Powell argued:

> 'There they stand, isolated, majestic, imperious, brooded over by the gigantic water-tower and chimney combined, rising unmistakable and daunting out of the countryside – the asylums which our forefathers built with such immense solidity to express the notions of their day. Do not for a moment underestimate their powers of resistance to our assault.'

Powell spoke of the horrors of asylums and wanted to see psychiatric wards in general hospitals where the mentally ill would be less isolated. The new medications allowed psychiatric patients to be controlled outside locked wards and to live in the community. These changes would provide, Powell said, something 'different and better', more flexible services and freedom for the mentally ill to live fuller lives. 'The services would be more individual-centric,' he said. Powell did not foresee how much resistance such reforms would meet with, both from a public deeply prejudiced against, and frightened of, the mentally ill, and a conservative psychiatric establishment.

Powell was also unaware that many patients hated taking the new drugs, owing to their manifold and bizarre side-effects. Patients complained they suffered from increased heart rate, drowsiness, dry mouth, constipation, blurred vision, dizziness, confusion, intense sweating and sexual dysfunction. In the case of chlorpromazine and its derivatives, the side-effects, over time, turned out to include a severe motion disorder, tardive dyskinesia, characterised by involuntary movements, often including violent shakes and facial twitches, resulting from the drug's effect on dopamine receptors. This syndrome, classified as 'Parkinsonian' as its symptoms bear a close resemblance to those of Parkinson's disease, can be permanent, continuing to afflict the patient even when the drug is withdrawn.

Patients were now in a double-bind. If they didn't take the drugs, they might face involuntary committal to a locked psychiatric ward: if they did swallow the pills, unpleasant, and sometimes crippling, side-effects could follow. Some patients became cunning at convincing doctors and nurses they had taken their medications, while actually palming and discarding them, with occasionally tragic consequences.

In the early 1980s, I interviewed a patient in New York's Creedmoor Hospital who had stopped taking his anti-psychotic medication, owing to increasingly unpleasant side-effects. Shortly afterwards, 'the voice of God' told him to push a perfect stranger in front of a subway train. Britain has seen several cases of the mentally ill murdering perfect strangers in recent years, murders often committed by patients being 'cared for' in the community, who have gone off their drugs. Tabloid hysteria over such cases makes it necessary to point out that they are highly unusual. Overall, the mentally ill are less violent than the general population.

Additionally, the fact that a patient ceased to take a drug and then committed a crime does not prove that the drug would have prevented them, if consumed, from committing the crime in question. It is widely assumed that had these patients followed doctor's orders and taken their meds, they would not have become violent. Plausible as this may be, it remains an assumption. As some psychiatric medications are addictive, it seems possible that patients who become violent when off drugs may in part be suffering the agitation of a withdrawal syndrome – anti-psychotics, in particular, are heavily sedating, and their sudden withdrawal can cause extreme 'rebound anxiety'. In patients prone to psychotic episodes, such anxiety, untreated, could well have dangerous consequences. This too, of course, is a theory that cannot be easily tested.

Despite growing anxieties about side-effects, it was clear there was a huge market for anti-depressants and anti-psychotics – and discoveries of new compounds had to continue, in order for pharmaceutical companies to profit, as once a drug had gone off-patent, it could be manufactured by competitors.

In 1958 P. Janssen, who had inherited a small pharmaceutical company from his parents, produced a new molecule, R1625 which he called 'haloperidol'. He had a name, but no real idea what the drug might be useful for. Janssen gave a supply to some psychiatrists in Liège in Belgium, where it was promptly stored on a shelf. R1625 was not tested until the night the son of a local doctor was admitted, in the grip of a psychotic episode. The resident doctor was not sure what to do, remembered the compound on the shelf and gave the young man a 10 milligram injection of haloperidol. The effects were stunning. The doctor's son quietened down, stopped being a nuisance on the ward and became manageable, although he seemed dissociated and confused. The next day Janssen came to see for himself.

Janssen suggested 10 milligrams was too large a dose so it was reduced to 1 milligram. At this dose, the drug still worked and the patient went home. He continued to take haloperidol for seven years, married, qualified and worked as an architect and had children; every year Janssen, the patient and the patient's doctor father met to review the dose. After seven years they decided to stop the drug. The worst that could happen, they assumed, was that the patient would become psychotic again and would have to be put back on the drug.

After a few weeks without medication, the patient relapsed, but when he was given haloperidol again, the drug simply did not work as well as previously: indeed, it never did work well for him again. The patient's life had been saved by a drug and was now ruined by the same substance. It made no sense. Haloperidol was given to many thousands of patients. It did help many, but many also began to develop side-effects that were becoming all-too-familiar.

If Freud had been alive in 1960, he would have seen that some 80 years after his youthful work on brain anatomy, our knowledge had grown substantially, but theories of the brain were still rather simple-minded. Neurologists and psychiatrists tended to be impressed by the latest gadget and adopt it as a metaphor. For decades the brain had been compared to a telephone exchange. By the 1960s, scientists were seeing it more like a computer, though computers, at the time, were huge machines that filled a room. If the lines of the exchange or the valves in the computer had a fault which was then successfully repaired through the application of Chemical A, any logical engineer would expect Chemical A to always repair the same fault. Valves and phone lines wouldn't suddenly take against Chemical A, and cease responding to it, but Janssen's patient showed these metaphors had their limits: the brain was not a simple, predictable mechanism. Seven years after haloperidol had calmed the doctor's son 'miraculously', it no longer did so. This tragic case made it clear that no one really knew precisely how these drugs affected the brain. Both the drugs and brain itself remained far more mysterious than psychiatrists liked to admit.

Psychiatry needed a more reasoned approach which studied new drugs' mechanisms of action, their effect on patients' behaviour and also, asked patients how they felt while on the drug. Common sense demanded a mix of pharmacology, routine medical observation and introspection. However, partly for social and political reasons and partly as a result of a chance tragedy, the very opposite of common sense was to guide drug policy in the generation to follow. The next great drug-using 'intellectual' of the introspective tradition, Timothy Leary, would do more damage to the cause of a rational drug policy than thalidomide, the opium wars and a thousand whirling dervishes on magic mushrooms.

Chapter 13

The Search for Soma, 1960s

Timothy Leary portrayed himself as a trail-blazing psychedelic explorer, and quickly rose to guru status in the counter-culture. Yet even many fellow 'psychonauts' accused Leary of monstrous egotism and reckless advocacy of the unfettered use of LSD – as opposed to its careful consumption in controlled circumstances. Leary made a career as an LSD evangelist, transforming himself in the process from an unexceptional social psychologist, happy to devise an unexceptional questionnaire, into a celebrity who shared a bed with John Lennon and Yoko Ono.

This chapter tells the disturbing story of how and why research on psychedelics was suppressed and became a criminal offence. The reasons for this prohibition were very much of their era. The counter-culture may have caught the headlines and changed the mood of America but it was a movement without formal leaders, let alone institutions, and finally incoherent objectives. The USA National Security establishment, on the other hand, was supposed to make sober judgements and take responsible actions in the best interest of the state and it citizens. Leary's antics and the Cold War paranoia of the time worked together to the detriment of science. Virtually every decision made by the American authorities after 1965 hampered proper scientific work on LSD, work that could have both revealed a great deal about the brain and also helped thousands of alcoholics and terminal patients.

Timothy Leary was trouble from the moment he went to the United States MilitaryAcademy at West Point in 1940. He was caught drinking whisky, lied about it and was forced to resign. He then went to the College of the Holy Cross in Worcester, Massachusetts. If Freud used cocaine at least in part to fight depression, Leary used LSD to explore his spiritual side, much as Huxley had done with mescaline.

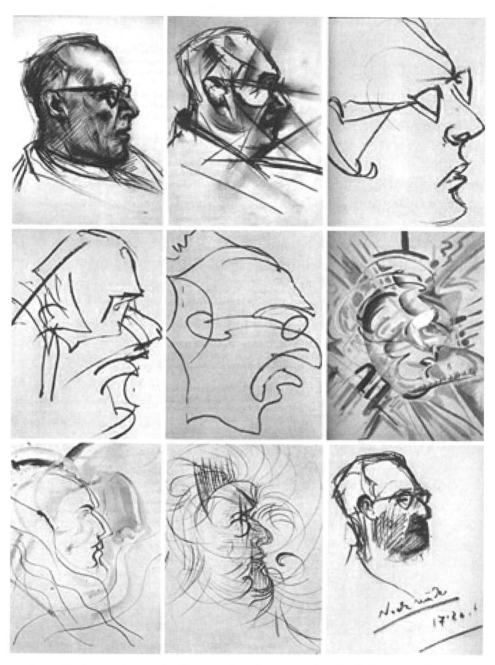

An artist's montage of self-portraits, drawn under the influence of LSD.

In 1950 Leary was awarded his doctorate at Berkeley with a thesis on 'The Social Dimensions of Personality: Group Structure and Process.' When he turned forty, Leary went to Mexico with a friend to experience the wonders of 'magic mushrooms' – fungi containing psilocybin and psilocin, generally considered to be gentler hallucinogens than mescaline or LSD.

'I learned more about ... (his) brain and its possibilities ... (and) more about psychology in the five hours after taking these mushrooms than ... (he) had in the preceding fifteen years of studying and doing research in psychology,' Leary wrote. He returned to Harvard and began an ambitious project, testing the effects of magic mushrooms and, later, LSD on prisoners and theology students.

It seems likely that Leary was influenced by John Allegro's book on the Dead Sea Scrolls, *The Sacred Mushroom and the Cross* (1956). Allegro argued that the early Christians used magic mushrooms to inspire religious experiences. Historians of drug use have made little of this book, though it provoked outrage at the time. Allegro linked Christianity to other ancient mystery cults such as the Eleusinian, Orphic, and Essenism, claiming they were all interconnected fertility cults that used naturally-occurring hallucinogens. Believers could achieve visionary encounters with divine entities, much like Native Americans did with peyote. Allegro claimed Jesus himself was not a historical character or even an allegory but a sacred mushroom, the Fly Agaric – perhaps, as noted above, the 'soma' of the Rig Veda, *Amanita Muscaria*.

In April 1962, Leary organised an experiment with 20 theology students in the basement of the Marsh Chapel at Boston University. They were given either LSD or a placebo, watched a Good Friday liturgy on television and filled in a questionnaire, a rather prosaic instrument for measuring contact with the divine.

Students who had taken LSD frequently reported mystical experiences and visions of Christ. Leary then gave LSD to 300 subjects and reported that 75 percent of them claimed to have undergone a revelation on the drug, describing it as one of the most educational experiences of their lives. The publicity that followed went to Leary's head and he ignored his duties as a lecturer. That gave the Harvard

President, Nathan M. Pusey, a reason to sack him on May 27th 1963. Pusey said Leary 'has failed to keep his classroom appointments and has absented himself from Cambridge without permission, to relieve him from further teaching duty and to terminate his salary.'

The loss of his Harvard post did not bother Leary, as his psychedelic research had attracted the interest of Peggy, Billy and Tommy Hitchcock, heirs to the Mellon fortune who bought him a rambling mansion in Millbrook, in upstate New York. Success did not agree with Leary, who became grandiose, arrogant – even messianic – as his 'enlightenment' unfolded:

'We saw ourselves as anthropologists from the twenty-first century inhabiting a time module set somewhere in the dark ages of the 1960s. On this space colony we were attempting to create a new paganism and a new dedication to life as art,' Leary wrote.

Outside the space colony, though, serious research into LSD continued, finding indications that the drug could be of great clinical use in the treatment of alcoholism. Some psychiatrists had noticed similarities in the experiences of people on LSD and those suffering delirium tremens. The 'DTs' often marked a 'rock bottom' or turning-point for alcoholics; researchers guessed that LSD might be able to trigger such a change without the terrible physical effects of the DTs.

Two significant studies on LSD and alcoholism took place in Canada, but the results were lost in the literature till a medical historian at the University of Alberta, Erica Dyck, did some detective work. She claims that the first Canadian study demonstrated that even one dose of LSD could help cure long-term alcoholics. She wrote: 'the LSD somehow gave these people experiences that psychologically took them outside of themselves and allowed them to see their own unhealthy behavior more objectively, and then determine to change it.'

Dyck interviewed patients who had been involved in the original studies – many of whom had not had a sip of alcohol since their LSD experience 40 years earlier. Some of her interviewees had taken part in a study in Saskatchewan in 1962 led by Huxley's friend, Humphry Osmond, this showed 65% of a group of alcoholics stopped drinking for at least 18 months after just one treatment with LSD. The trial was properly controlled and found LSD compared very well with other therapies. Fewer than 25% of alcoholics quit drinking after undergoing group therapy, and less than 12% did so after a course of traditional, one-on-one, psychotherapy. By comparison, LSD seemed highly effective. As a chronic condition, alcoholism had previously proven fairly drug-resistant. Barbiturates and benzodiazepines could alleviate withdrawal, sometimes a matter of life and death, as, in rare cases, severe alcohol withdrawal can lead to fatal convulsions. Other than such palliatives, chemical interventions in alcohol abuse had generally been limited, pre-LSD, to behaviourism-influenced aversion therapies such as 'Antabuse' – drugs that made the user violently ill if they consumed any alcohol. This was intended, in theory, to re-educate or condition the problem drinker to associate alcohol not with pleasure, but nausea. Of course, this led many patients to just stopping taking the drug so they could drink again. LSD seemed to offer an exciting new form of treatment, one that resulted in many patients losing the desire to drink, without the grotesqueries of Antabuse, a very crude implement.

The results of the study were published in *The Quarterly Journal of Studies of Alcohol*, but met with much scepticism, not least because of Leary's antics. By then he had broadcast his famous mantra to 'turn on, tune in, drop out' – take LSD, tune into the universal spiritual dimension it unlocked, and 'drop out' of American social norms, in particular, the materialistic 'American dream'. Leary, while thoroughly enjoying his notoriety, was accumulating bad publicity for the drug, which was tainted by association with his name. Touting its revolutionary potential, he proposed universal use of LSD, and seems to have been wholly blind to the drug's dangers, ranging from 'bad trips' and 'freak-outs' that passed once the drug wore off, to lasting psychotic episodes in a small minority of users. Fellow psychologists seem to have found Leary-as-celebrity insufferable, and many wanted nothing to do with any subject linked to him. He seems to have had a remarkable talent for alienating anyone and everyone who did not accept him as a guru, and to have believed, without a moment's self-doubt, in his own 'enlightenment' compared to 'lowly terrestrials'. Leary was the worst possible public face for LSD.

But a group in Toronto then replicated Osmond's study with one crucial change. They wanted to observe the effects of LSD in isolation, so they blindfolded subjects before giving them the drug; LSD did not seem to work under these conditions.

The Saskatchewan group argued alcoholics had to take LSD in a nurturing environment. However, the Toronto researchers were more credible, partly because the first group included Osmond, who seemed a little eccentric by 1962. Both papers, however, were forgotten which Dyck believes marked a real loss to science. She writes:

'The LSD experience appeared to allow the patients to go through a spiritual journey that ultimately empowered them to heal themselves, and that's really quite an amazing therapy regimen. Even interviewing the patients 40 years after their experience, I was surprised at how loyal they were to the doctors who treated them, and how powerful they said the experience was for them– some even felt the experience saved their lives.'

Such subjective reports supported the claim that LSD could affect a dramatic change in the behaviour of alcoholics, but did not begin to explain why LSD exerted this effect. Instead of trying to solve an important therapeutic question, the American government made it impossible and illegal for serious scientists to do serious research on LSD. Hoffman's 'problem child', as he dubbed LSD long after its discovery, was put behind bars, as it were.

'We accept all sorts of drugs, but I think LSD's "street" popularity ultimately led to its demise,' Dyck claims. 'And that's too bad, because I think the researchers in Saskatchewan, among others, showed the drug is unique and has some intriguing properties that need to be explored further.'

The Canadian psychiatrists were not the only serious researchers in this field. In 1963 a man was nearing the end of his career in a very conservative job as Vice-President of J.P. Morgan Bank. Wasson had been well and widely educated – his father made him read the Bible three

226

times before he reached the age of fourteen. After the First World War, he travelled, studied at the London School of Economics and became a journalist. In 1926, in London, he married Valentina Guercken, a paediatrician. The couple went on honeymoon in 1927 in the Catskill Mountains, where Valentina found mushrooms similar to those she had sampled in her native Russia – probably fly agarics, *amanita muscaria* or a closely related species such as *amanita pantherina*. It was the start of a lifelong passion for the couple. They became obsessed with magic mushrooms and studied the role of the fungus in history, linguistics, religion, mythology, art, and archaeology.

In 1955, Wasson and Valentina went to Mexico to research the magical and religious use of psilocybin mushrooms in aboriginal sacred rituals. Wasson and his circle realised it would be politic to give these drugs a new name and so coined the term 'entheogen,' to replace the loaded terms 'hallucinogenic' or 'psychedelic'. The term, however, makes a staggering claim – that these drugs *engender* encounters with *theos*, divinity or God. The claim may be sweeping, but it makes some sense in the light of recent research (and need have nothing to do with supernaturalism or 'belief' in the conventional sense). Newberg and Aquili (2002) have used the latest brain-imaging techniques to study Buddhist monks and Franciscan nuns; the authors claim that when the nuns and monks feel the presence of God or a transcendental experience, there is a massive pulse in a particular area of the brain, the posterior superior orbietal lobe. David Healy takes this to its logical conclusion and argues that religious experience is neurochemical in origin. God is not out there in the Heavens, but inside us – specifically, our brains.

On May 13th 1957, *Life* magazine ran a story by Wasson on the Mexican mushroom sessions with a witch-healer-wise woman, Maria Sabina. Around this time Wasson and Hoffman became friends and the two travelled to Mexico. In some ways Hoffman is the introspective drug-user who most resembled Freud. He was motivated by scientific ambitions, perhaps in a purer way than Freud had ever been. Hoffman described his reactions meticulously, as usual:

'Thirty minutes after my taking the mushrooms, the exterior

world began to undergo a strange transformation. Everything assumed a Mexican character. As I was perfectly well aware that my knowledge of the Mexican origin of the mushroom would lead me to imagine only Mexican scenery, I tried deliberately to look on my environment as I knew it normally. But all voluntary efforts to look at things in their customary forms and colours proved ineffective. Whether my eyes were closed or open, I saw only Mexican motifs and colours. When the doctor supervising the experiment bent over me to check my blood pressure he was transformed into an Aztec priest and I would not have been astonished if he had drawn an obsidian knife. In spite of the seriousness of the situation, it amused me to see how the Germanic face of my colleague had acquired a purely Indian expression. At the peak of the intoxication, about $1^1/_2$ hours after ingestion of the mushrooms, the rush of interior pictures, mostly abstract motifs rapidly changing in shape and color, reached such an alarming degree that I feared that I would be torn into this whirlpool of form and colour and would dissolve.

After about six hours the dream came to an end. Subjectively, I had no idea how long this condition had lasted. I felt my return to everyday reality to be a happy return from a strange, fantastic but quite real world to an old and familiar home.'

Hoffman isolated and extracted the active chemical ingredients from the mushrooms, naming the most potent component 'psilocybin', and an accompanying alkaloid, 'psilocin'. Psilocybin and psilocin were about 100 times more active than mescaline and about 100 times less active than LSD. All these substances caused 'psychic disturbances by acting on some common mechanism, or on mechanisms acting through a common final pathway'.

It is important to be clear about the distinctions between these substances:

Peyote is the cactus from which mescaline was extracted in 1890.

LSD was a derivative of lysergic acid that Hoffman synthesised as described.

Psilocybin was again discovered by Hoffman, and its effect is similar to, though much less powerful than, that of LSD. It is a very, very different drug, finally, from the highly toxic active ingredients of the 'other' kind of magic mushroom – red-spotted *Amanita*, which produces more of a feverish delirium than a transcendental trip, through the compounds muscimol and ibotenic acid. Amanitas are so toxic that their recreational use is very rare in most of the world, though it has been noted in contemporary Russia, and described in the fiction of contemporary Russian novelist Victor Pelevin. However, even many committed users of psilocybin, LSD and other such psychedelics 'draw the line' at *Amanita* and other such deleriants (i.e Datura, or 'Jimson Weed', containing scopolamine and atropine).

Hoffman found it more cost-effective to synthesise psilocybin and psilocin than to extract the compounds from the mushrooms. He tested this artificial version of the drug on Maria Sabina, Wasson's 'witch' and wise woman. 'She took a rather strong dose corresponding to the number of mushrooms she usually ingests . . . At dawn when we left the hut, our Mazateca interpreter told us that Maria Sabina had said there was no difference between the pills and the mushrooms. This was a final proof that our synthetic psilocybin was identical in every respect with the natural product.'

Later in 1963, Hoffman attended the annual convention of the World Academy of Arts and Sciences in Stockholm. He called LSD 'medicine for the soul' and admitted his frustration at its being pushed underground.

Some LSD users thought the drug might ease the suffering of terminal patients who'd reached the very end. As he lay dying, Aldous Huxley made a written request to his wife for an intramuscular injection of 100 mg of LSD. He put it in writing to protect her against prosecution. She did as he wished and he died peacefully a few hours later on November 22nd 1963, the day President Kennedy was assassinated. It would be nearly 40 years before doctors again took up research into the use of LSD in terminal patients. This was partly a reaction by the authorities to Leary's antics and partly, as we shall see, a horrified response to their own experiments with LSD.

Two years after Huxley died, Leary took his children and girlfriend to Mexico and was arrested for trying to smuggle cannabis on his return to the USA. He was sentenced to 30 years under the Marijuana Tax Act, the first law that aimed to control cannabis, was fined $30,000 and ordered to have psychiatric treatment. The sentence was extreme, and seems to have been politically motivated – he had smuggled in a mere three ounces of Mexican herbal cannabis for personal use. Leary, whatever his manifold faults, did not approve of commercial drug dealing, and three ounces of even the very highest quality cannabis would have a contemporary US value of under $1000. Leary appealed, claiming that the Marijuana Tax Act was unconstitutional, as it appropriated to the Federal Government the power of regulating medicine, a power traditionally reserved to individual states. Marijuana had not been included in the Harrison Act.

Leary then had what seemed a brilliant idea. The American Constitution guaranteed freedom of religion, so Leary founded LSD, the League for Spiritual Discovery. He failed, however, to get this organisation officially recognised as a new religion which used LSD as part of its Communion, although, as noted elsewhere, the American Government does permit the sacramental use of peyote – otherwise illegal – in Native American religious practice. But no administration was about to recognise the man who had told American youth to 'drop out' as the High Priest of a Church.

Leary did not just antagonise conservatives. Owsley Stanley was a famous underground LSD cook who produced an estimated half a kilogram of LSD, or roughly 5 million 100-microgram 'hits' of normal potency. He was not in it for the money as he gave away most of his LSD or sold it very cheaply, believing that in so doing he was spreading enlightenment. Stanley was also a brilliant sound engineer and worked with The Grateful Dead, creating their unique 'Wall of Sound' apparatus, which contributed much to the popularity – and cultish following – of their concerts, at which industrial quantities of LSD and cannabis were consumed. Owsley loved LSD – but had no time for Leary:

'Leary was a fool. Drunk with 'celebrity-hood' and his own ego, he became a media clown-and was arguably the single most damaging actor involved in the destruction of the evanescent social movement of the '60s . . . He would not listen to any of us when we asked him to please cool it, he loved the limelight and relished his notoriety. . . I was not a fan of his.'

Hoffman had told the World Academy that LSD had been used sensibly by some doctors in relieving pain. By 1965, it was estimated that between 30,000 and 40,000 psychiatric patients had received LSD therapeutically and the psychiatrist Sidney Cohen summed up the largely positive evidence. He told a 1965 conference that LSD could make patients less defensive and 'allow repressed memories and conflicted material to come forth.' They found it easier to understand repressed material 'because the patient sees the conflict as a visual image or in vivid visual symbols. It is accepted without being overwhelming because the detached state of awareness makes the emerging guilt feelings less devastating.'

After taking LSD, patients also felt closer to their therapists and their newly-won insights stayed with them after the effects of the drug had worn off. Despite such serious work that showed LSD could help patients in great distress, in 1966, the American government made the drug illegal. Nearly all scientific research programmes were shut down. The last substantial conference on LSD was in 1967 at Wesleyan University, and again it showcased interesting material.

One study gave a patient with breast cancer the chance to describe how LSD had helped in her final weeks. Music was played as the drug took hold, and she 'fused with the music and was transported on it. So completely was I one with the sound that when the particular melody or record stopped, however momentarily, I was alive to the pause, eagerly awaiting the next lap in the journey.'

As Huxley had found, her perception of time was radically altered:

'I was alone in a timeless world with no boundaries. There was no atmosphere; there was no colour, no imagery, but there may have been light. Suddenly, I recognised that I was a moment in time, created by those before me and in turn the creator of others. This was my moment, and my major function had been completed. By being born, I had given meaning to my parents' existence. I became poignantly aware that the core of life is love. At this moment I felt that I was reaching out to the world – to all people – but especially to those closest to me. I wept long for the wasted years, the search for identity in false places, the neglected opportunities, the emotional energy lost in basically meaningless pursuits.'

The patient had a pleasant olfactory or smell hallucination, of peaches, and she felt 'very close to a large group of people.' Her family noticed she had changed. 'I was radiant, they said. I seemed at peace, they said. I felt that way too. What has changed for me? I am living now, and being. I can take it as it comes.'

Some of her physical symptoms vanished and she felt more at peace with the fact of her impending death. LSD had made her less depressed and she 'returned to work and appeared in relatively good spirits' for five weeks. Her last weeks were far happier than she had ever imagined possible.

A second paper described how LSD helped a 40-year-old alcoholic who felt 'as if ten tons had fallen from my shoulders. I prayed to the Lord. Everything looked better all around me. The rose was beautiful. My children's faces cleared up. His wife reported there was 'peace and harmony in the home that had never existed before and that he had never been better.'

The ban on LSD research was in place when in May 1969, the Supreme Court declared the Marijuana Tax Act unconstitutional, and quashed Leary's 1965 conviction. Leary then ran for Governor of California against Ronald Reagan. John Lennon wrote a campaign song for Leary, the classic 'Come Together', which didn't have much effect on the voters. Reagan won – as he usually did, except when it came to the Oscars, defeating both Leary and incumbent Governor Edmund 'Pat' Brown whose son, Jerry Brown,went on to serve two terms as Governor in the 1970s and early 80s – and, at time of writing, has just been inaugurated to the office once again, at a very sprightly 72 years of age.

Seven months after his electoral defeat Leary was back in prison, where he was given psychological tests the Department of Corrections used to decide what kind of work new inmates were best suited to. As he had designed the tests himself, Leary knew how to play this game and provided answers which made him look very conventional, a green fingered-man who loved forestry and gardening. The trick worked and he was sent to work as a gardener in a low-security prison. He escaped in September 1970 and fled to Algeria where he tried to cosy up to Eldridge Cleaver and the remnants of the separatist Black Panthers 'government in exile.' Like the US government and his one-time Harvard colleagues, the Panthers do not seem to have been amongst Leary's fans, as Cleaver tried to hold him hostage, or so Leary claimed.

From Algeria, Leary fled to Switzerland, Vienna, Beirut and finally Kabul. The American authorities managed to lure him back to America in 1973. Leary now faced 95 years in prison. The authorities who arrested Leary were ironically just as responsible as he was for making LSD research impossible. The Cold War-era American National Security Establishment had high hopes for LSD too, but they were rather different from Leary's or Hoffman's. Rather than a tool of enlightenment or treatment for the dying, cold warriors believed that LSD might be a useful weapon.

From April 1953, the CIA tricked hundreds of its own employees, along with prostitutes, psychiatric patients, and members of the general public into taking LSD and other drugs to see if these could be turned into secret weapons. These 'experiments' were part of the notorious MK-ULTRA programme, an attempt to develop mind-control techniques. The military were convinced that American POWs had been subjected to brainwashing during the Korean War. This was a high-point of Cold War paranoia and received the Hollywood treatment in the original version of the film *The Manchurian Candidate*. A Korean War veteran brainwashed by the evil Commies is programmed to return to the USA as a sleeper agent. The film is gripping but the plot was a weird mix of paranoid fantasy and naivety.

The MK-ULTRA programme appears to have led to 'institutional psychosis' on the part of the CIA: it is said that during the MK-ULTRA years CIA agents learned to bring their own bottles to office parties and keep an eye on them just as young women are advised to keep an eye on their drinks for fear of spiking these days. But the CIA did not spike each others' drinks with 'date rape' tranquilisers: they were dosing each other with pure LSD.

The MK-ULTRA programme had a wonderfully named Operation – Midnight Climax – which involved CIA agents setting up brothels in San Francisco. Clients were filmed through one-way mirrors so agents could procure compromising photographs and record pillow talk from drug-loosened tongues. The human rights violations of MK-ULTRA were so outrageous that the CIA recruited and relied heavily upon a Federal Bureau of Narcotics agent, George White, who took great pleasure in dosing the unsuspecting, and was a sado-masochistic habitué of prostitutes himself. In a letter to his MK-ULTRA colleague, Sid Gottleib, White revelled in his role:

'I was a very minor missionary, actually a heretic, but I toiled whole-heartedly in the vineyards because it was fun, fun, fun. Where else could a red-blooded American boy lie, kill, cheat, steal, rape and pillage with the sanction and blessing of the All-Highest?' (Quoted in *The Strength of the Wolf*, Douglas Valentine, Verso, 2004, page 141.)

As Valentine notes, in his comprehensive study of *The Secret History of America's War on Drugs*: 'Where else indeed?'

Subjects in the 'Midnight Climax' operations reported few mystical experiences – they were in brothels, after all – but often said they would be able to withstand any form of interrogation, even physical torture, if they had taken LSD. This was just what the spies wanted to hear as they feared the Soviets had made phenomenal advances in paranormal research, and could, for example, communicate telepathically with dolphins armed with small nuclear devices. It would be amusing to argue that the Soviets and their North Korean allies had launched a phenomenally clever misinformation campaign, to convince their American opponents they had uncovered the secrets of the mind, a campaign that the CIA swallowed hook, line, and LSD-spiked drink. Amusing, but mistaken, as Russian intelligence proved no more realistic than their Western counterparts during the Cold War. Incredible as this official credulity – the belief that mind control of an almost magical extent was possible - now seems, it should be remembered that this research began shortly after the end of World War II, and the Nazis had experimented not just with mind control, but also the occult and demonology. At the time, truly anything seemed possible to the sworn Cold Warrior.

To combat such clear, present and deluded danger, the CIA recruited a Scottish psychiatrist, Donald Ewen Cameron, based in Canada. He hoped to treat schizophrenia by erasing existing memories and reprogramming the mind. He experimented not just with LSD but with electroconvulsive therapy, using thirty to forty times the normal therapeutic voltage. As no anaesthetics were administered, this amounted to torture. He put subjects into drug-induced comas for weeks, using insulin and powerful sedatives, and made them listen to tape loops of noise or simple repetitive statements. Most of his patients had come seeking treatment for relatively minor problems such as anxiety disorders and post-natal depression. Many left his 'treatment' permanently damaged, in some cases having lost the power of speech, unable to recognise their own parents, and even having forgotten their own names. Unbelievably, Cameron was the first chairman of the World Psychiatric Association.

When Leary got back to America in 1973, he was put in solitary confinement in Folsom Prison where he wrote his cosmic manifesto, *The Seven Tongues of God*, which claimed that the mind has seven circuits, producing seven levels of consciousness – the system was soon revised to include one more. Leary claimed that the first four of these were 'Terrestrial Circuits', while the second four circuits ('the Stellar Circuits' or 'Extra-Terrestrial Circuits'), were evolutionary by-products of the first four that would be triggered into activity by future human evolution. These transitions to the upper circuits would prepare the species for life in space – the fifth circuit, for example, would allow us to adjust to a zero-gravity environment.

As he grew more fixated on our extra-terrestrial future, Leary became a savage critic of the 'seductive dinosaur science' of ecology – there is, after all, no need to save the planet if we are shortly to shoot off to other worlds. Once the colonisation of space began, Leary claimed, only the most 'larval,' intellectually and philosophically backward humans, would choose to remain in 'the fouled nest' of Earth. Though his *Politics of Ecstasy* had noted that psychedelic visions often concerned subjects that preoccupied the drug user to begin with – religion in the case of theology students, for example – he does not seem to have noticed that his own obsession with colonising space reflected the widespread science fiction fantasies of the day.

In *Starseed* (1973) Leary travelled yet further towards the final frontier. The 'illuminati', he proposed, 5000 enlightened ones, could experience personal growth tripping round the galaxy while engaging in transcendental sexual acrobatics. Five thousand of Earth's most highly sexed and intelligent individuals would fly into space on Starseed 1 where they could 'orgy-porgy' in zero gravity while gazing at the stars. (The term 'orgy-porgy' is taken from Huxley's *Brave New World*, where the enslaved but happy citizens of the future's controlling regime indulge in regular feasts of soma, Huxley's ideal and yet-to-be-invented psychedelic tranquiliser, dancing and sex, chanting 'orgy-porgy' the whole time.)

In December 1974, The *New York Times* broke the MK-ULTRA story, leading to investigations by the U.S. Congress. In 1976, President Gerald Ford issued the first Executive Order on Intelligence Activities which banned 'experimentation with drugs on human subjects, except with the informed consent, in writing and witnessed by a disinterested party, of each such human subject'. But it was too late for the victims of MK-ULTRA, and the paper trail was rapidly incinerated. CIA Director Richard Helms ordered all MK-ULTRA files destroyed. Likewise, none of Cameron's personal records of his involvement with MK-ULTRA survive. His family destroyed them after his death.

In later years, Leary learned to keep his mouth shut about drugs, but continued to predict our imminent leap out into the waiting universe. He was an exhibitionist to the end and asked for his last minutes to be videotaped for eternity. As he lay dying, he said, 'Why not?' to his son Zachary and kept repeating the phrase in different intonations like an actor trying out different voices. His last word was 'beautiful.'

Seven grams of Leary's ashes were shot into space on a rocket carrying the remains of 24 other people including Gene Roddenberry, the creator of *Star Trek*. Leary had at last become starseed on the final frontier.

The last psychiatrist in Europe licensed to use LSD was genuinely interested in its therapeutic potential, rather than cosmic fantasies. Jan Bastiaans was a careful, rather dry man, quite unlike the theatrical Leary. Bastiaans was in his sixties when I met him at the University of Leiden in 1978, while I was making a film called *After the Hijack*. Three years earlier, a Dutch train had been hijacked by South Moluccan terrorists who wanted the Dutch to force the Indonesian government to hand back the South Moluccan Islands. The Dutch had been the former colonial rulers of Indonesia and even if they had obeyed the terrorists, there was no chance the Indonesians would have agreed to give up the islands. The first hijack ended in three deaths. My film examined what happened to the surviving hostages, after their release.

When a second train was hijacked in 1977, the Dutch government again had no idea how to handle the situation but it did not turn to Bastiaans. He had annoyed ministers by claiming that everyone who had been held on the trains would suffer from severe post-traumatic stress. Instead, the government called in a different psychiatrist to negotiate the release of the hostages. This psychiatrist was infuriated when the leading hijacker told him he, too, had read Freud and that there was no point in the shrink pretending to be a father figure. It is unwise to challenge psychiatrists on their own territory. The insulted Dutch shrink told the government the only solution was to bomb the train, so the air force was sent in. One man died; many were injured. The hijackings were deeply traumatic for Holland as a nation, and led some to question the limits of traditional Dutch liberalism, questions that have resurfaced in recent years as Islamism has flourished in the Netherlands.

Bastiaans was an orthodox Freudian and had studied survivors of the 1939–1945 war and the subsequent Dutch battle to keep Indonesia. Dutch solders often lived through hellish episodes in the jungle and as prisoners of war. He talked of patients who had seen beheadings and of a few who had decapitated their enemies themselves. In his doctoral thesis *The Psychosomatic Consequences of Oppression and Resistance* (1957), he described these barbarities. Soldiers and survivors often had delayed reactions to witnessing such horrors, especially those who were 'highly self-controlled personalities who tried hard to control, suppress or repress the painful traumatic consequences of the war'.

The link with Freud was clear. If someone could not face what had happened to him, what he had done or seen, he was bound to remain in an acute traumatic state, and powerless. The trick was to break through the trauma by enabling the patient to remember and articulate their pain, thus discovering its causes. In an orthodox Freudian manner, Bastiaans tried hypnosis, conventional analytic techniques and the more radical narco-analysis, in which he sedated patients into a hypnagogic state in the hope of uncovering repressed traumatic memories. It worked in some cases. If patients felt safe, 'an average number of eight sessions is usually sufficient to free the patient', Bastiaans said. But some patients needed between 800 and 1000 hours of traditional psychoanalysis and narcoanalysis to get better. Many would die before they were cured.

Bastiaans turned to LSD to speed up the process and, after five years, he concluded it could help three kinds of patient in particular; those who were rigid in their defence and coping mechanisms, those with survivor or concentration camp syndromes, and those who had not improved after many years of psychoanalysis. The best results were obtained with men he defined as 'inhibited fighters' who could not talk about their feelings. LSD liberated them as long as they were in a safe environment like his clinic. It usually did not need more than seven sessions with LSD to see the benefits.

Despite these impressive findings, many of Bastiaans' colleagues accused him of giving up the 'pure gold' of psychoanalysis for the silver of LSD psychotherapy. The criticisms upset Bastiaans. He told me he felt betrayed. After he retired, his work was not continued at Leiden University or his clinic in Oegstgeest. LSD research had come to a dead end, even though there was substantial evidence the drug had real, and manifold, therapeutic uses.

When one reviews the research of that era, it is not just the missed opportunities that stand out. Research on the motives behind habitual drug use was inconclusive and superficial. One of the leading psychiatrists to work with drug abusers in the 1970s, Sidney Cohen, argued there were five very different reasons for people trying drugs – and for people continuing to use them. There was by then an admittedly imperfect tradition of personality research in psychology, but it still seems rather naive for Cohen to have argued one could divide drug users into essentially five kinds of personality – the immature person, the depressed person, the anti-social person, the schizophrenic person and those who grow up in an environment where drugs are the norm. Cohen went on to give thoughtful portraits of each type, but this approach to the question of why people took drugs remained overly simplistic.

It should be said in Freud's favour that he never predicted how long it would take for the medications that could replace analysis to be perfected. His caution was wise. As the most complex structure in the known universe, the brain has so far evaded attempts at direct control – and psychiatric medications have proved, in some cases, to be far more addictive and dangerous in the long term than street drugs. Governments and medical establishments have certainly failed, to follow the central tenet of the Hipppocratic Oath: above all, do no harm. It is ironic, bitterly ironic as some medical historians see it, that the ban on LSD denied psychiatry a substance that can unquestionably be harmful but also seems to hold out the prospect of real healing in some cases. Such prohibitions, sadly, have always been motivated by political, rather than clinical, concerns.

Promotional poster for the film El Asesinato De Trotsky, 1972.

Chapter 14

The Russian Connection

When Lenin died, two ambitious men fought for control of the Russian Communist Party. The young Stalin (who had studied to be a priest) managed to outwit Leon Trotsky, forcing him into exile. After years in Turkey, France and Norway, Trotsky ended up in Mexico. This dislocation was to have major consequences, not just for the development of Trotskyism, but for cocaine research.

Stalin had no intention of allowing Trotsky to live and sent assassins after him. On May 24th 1940, Trotsky survived the first attempt on his life by a small team of Stalinist agents, but a second attempt, that August, saw Ramón Mercader kill him, famously, with a blow from an ice pick (declassified files have since shown Mercader was a Soviet Agent). By then Trotsky and his family had put down roots in Mexico. His great-granddaughter, Nora Volkow, was born in Mexico City. She is now the director of the American National Institute on Drug Abuse and one of the world's authorities on cocaine, neurotransmitters and the part they play in addiction and psychiatric illness.

We have seen how Otto Loewi surmised that messages in the brain depended on neurotransmitters like dopamine. New brain-imaging techniques show that cocaine addicts have fewer properly-functioning dopamine receptors than non-users, Volkow found. The results of this dopamine dysfunction are both peculiar and profound. An addict needs more extreme stimulation to experience pleasure. Normal stimuli – for example food, sex, a fine sunset – are simply too weak to impact upon an addict's brain. The addict's dopamine system needs the kick of cocaine to experience pleasure from anything, after years of abuse.

Freud wrote about how many neurotics cannot enjoy normal pleasures and so seek the outlandish. Addicts are, to an extent, similar to fetishists who can only be aroused by shoes, hats or the masochist's preferred form of pain. Addicts can only respond to something out of the ordinary – their drug of choice. Drug use has changed their biochemistry, and 'willpower' alone cannot undo this change, Volkow says. 'No one chooses to become addicted. They simply are cognitively unable to choose not to be addicted.' Much of that is due to the nature of their dopamine system.

Dopamine does not swish freely through the brain; there are specific dopamine receptors which receive and then transmit it from neuron to neuron. Cocaine works by binding to the so-called dopamine transporters – the proteins on nerve endings that suck up excess dopamine – and deactivating them. With these nerve endings out of action, dopamine builds up outside the neurons and this surplus dopamine increases the amount of the neurotransmitter that is available to the brain as a whole. The brain now works faster but it is, to use a crude metaphor, like an engine that's been over-oiled. Too much oil clogs the engine in the end.

In 1997 Volkow co-authored a paper which showed that cocaine blocked the 'dopamine transporter' system. She showed there was a correlation between the degree of blocking – the 'oil' in parts of the system where the brain would not have naturally produced it – and 'the magnitude of the self-reported high'. At least 47% of the transporter sites had to be blocked for subjects to experience cocaine's euphoriant effects.

In 2003 Volkow told the American Psychiatric Association: 'while this increase in dopamine is essential to create addiction, it does not actually explain addiction. If you give a drug of abuse to anyone, their dopamine levels increase. Yet the majority do not become addicted.'

Again we are faced with the complexity of the brain. The question is, why do increases in dopamine levels trigger craving for drugs in some people, but not in others? Part of the reason may lie in how vulnerable a person is to obsession and compulsion, Volkow claims. She then studied the frontal cortex, associated with higher thinking, an area few neuropsychologists had thought it to be involved in addiction. PET scan images of that area showed similar activity in both addicts and people with obsessive/compulsive disorder, however.

'It hit me completely,' Volkow said. 'These two diseases both have obsessive/compulsive behavior in common. One is an uncontrollable urge to take drugs, the other a compulsion about rituals.' Drugs could change brain chemistry in ways that triggered a compulsion to take more drugs. 'Drugs feel good, but that's the trivial explanation. What is the role of brain dopamine in the loss of control?' Volkow asks – and is still asking. It is a very hard question to answer definitively, given present limits on our understanding of the brain.

Until Hofmann synthesised LSD, the drugs that people used to experience euphoria were all based on natural substances – opium, hashish, the coca leaf and alcohol. The prohibition of LSD encouraged creative and subversive chemists to find new routes to chemical paradise – and oblivion. The greatest inventor of psychoactive compounds alive today, Alexander Shulgin, is the grandson of Ukrainian immigrants to the USA. At time of writing, he has recently suffered a major stroke, and an appeal has been put out on various drug-orientated websites for financial assistance to help with his recovery. No offence to the Shulgins, but there is a dark irony in the fact that one of the most prolific organic chemists in history, designer of hundreds of drugs, legal and illegal, finds himself with insufficient health insurance. As late-night talk show hosts are wont to say in the US: *only in America!*

Alexander Shulgin was fascinated by chemistry from an early age, and went to Harvard when only 16. In 1943, he dropped out of college and joined the Navy. In an odd echo of Fleischl, it was a thumb infection that first stimulated his interest in drugs. In 1944, a nurse gave Shulgin orange juice, shortly before an operation on his thumb. The orange juice, or perhaps fear of the operation, seem to have compelled Shulgin to auto-suggestion: the 19-year-old became convinced that the crystals at the bottom of the glass were 'knock-out drops'. In a perfect example of mind triumphing over matter, Shulgin fainted, as Freud had often done. When he recovered, Shulgin found out that the 'knock-out drops' were in fact nothing but sugar.

Shulgin received his Ph.D. in biochemistry at Berkeley in 1954, and went to work for Dow Chemicals. He made them a fortune by creating a substance very different from those now most associated with his name; it was no key to the doors of perception. In fact, his invention, Zectran, was the first biodegradable pesticide. As a reward for its commercial success, Dow gave Shulgin a free hand to pursue any research he chose, and this freedom changed Shulgin's career – and, in time, his world-view. He devoted himself to creating new psychoactive drugs and at first published his findings in conventional journals such as *Nature* and *The Journal of Organic Chemistry*. Shulgin wrote: 'I first explored mescaline in the late '50s. Three-hundred-fifty to 400 milligrams. I learned there was a great deal inside me.' He was overwhelmed by the realisation that everything he saw and thought:

> 'had been brought about by a fraction of a gram of a white solid, but that in no way whatsoever could it be argued that these memories had been contained within the white solid ... I understood that our entire universe is contained in the mind and the spirit. We may choose not to find access to it, we may even deny its existence, but it is indeed there inside us, and there are chemicals that can catalyze its availability.'

Shulgin felt he had to explore 'this remarkably rich and unexplored area'. He went about his exploration a little like a botanist looking for new specimens. His background as a commercial chemist made Shulgin methodical. He also had the knack of making useful friends. He met Bob Sager at a club of which Herbert Hoover, the legendary boss of the FBI, had been a member. Sager was head of the US Drug Enforcement Agency's Western Laboratories in San Francisco and the DEA needed information on the growing drug scene. Sager recruited Shulgin to give seminars to the DEA's agents, supplying them with samples and sometimes appearing as an expert witness on their behalf. In return, he was given a licence to develop, synthesise and test new psychedelic compounds on himself and small groups of friends.

Perhaps naively, Shulgin has claimed there was no link between the fact that he worked for the DEA and his being granted a Schedule 1 licence which allowed him to work with any illicit drug. Once he had the licence, he set up a laboratory in a small building behind his house.

The most controversial of Shulgin's 200-plus drug creations has been MDMA or ecstasy, which was hailed as a great mind-altering love drug: and then, typically, turned out to offer a flawed Nirvana. MDMA had been synthesised back in 1912 by Freud's old patrons, Merck of Darmstadt, but they couldn't see a market for it. The history of MDMA again shows the random nature of pharmaceutical history. Merck were looking for a drug that would suppress appetite. MDMA showed some promise in this respect – it is an amphetamine, and most amphetamines suppress appetite – but for unknown reasons, research seems to have been discontinued, and the drug was shelved. It seems likely that MDMA's unique euphoriant properties appeared bizarre and undesirable to early researchers, if the drug was tested on humans, and quietly abandoned. Or perhaps MDMA (ecstasy) just made no sense to a world that had yet to experience psychedelic rock and electronic dance music.

Shulgin tested his new compounds on himself first but he was wary and would begin with an 'allergy dose' of a compound's closest analogue, an inactive quantity, to test for allergic reactions. He would wait a day and ingest a larger amount. When a compound seemed interesting, his wife Ann would try it next. If she also thought it had possibilities, Shulgin would invite his 'research group' of six to eight close friends – two were psychologists, one was a fellow chemist – to try his new concoction. Ever cautious, Shulgin kept an anti-convulsant on hand in case someone had a bad reaction to the drug.

The research group created the Shulgin Rating Scale. Normal psychological tests are imperfect enough and the Shulgin Scale is no marvel of methodology. It asks subjects to record what they are taking, the dose and to describe what they experience. The experience can then be rated from Plus One to Plus Four.

For instance, when describing a compound he called 2CT–2 Shulgin reports: '... (with 22 mg) A slow onset. It took an hour for a plus one, and almost another two hours to get to a +++. Very vivid fantasy images, eyes closed, but no blurring of lines between 'reality' and fantasy. Some yellow-grey patterns à la psilocybin. Acute diarrhoea at about the fourth hour but no other obvious physical problems. Erotic lovely. Good material for unknown number of possible uses. Can explore for a long time. Better try 20 milligrams next time.' It does recall Freud saying that Cocaine made him feel State I or IIa.

The Scale differentiates four states:

PLUS ONE (+)
The drug is quite active. The chronology can be determined with some accuracy, but the nature of the drug's effects are not yet apparent.

PLUS TWO ++
The nature of the action of a drug is unmistakably apparent. But you still have some choice as to whether you will accept the adventure, or rather just continue with your ordinary day's plans if you are an experienced researcher.

PLUS THREE +++
One can no longer ignore its action. The subject is totally engaged in the experience, for better or worse.

PLUS FOUR (++++)
A rare and precious transcendental state which has been called a 'peak experience', a 'religious experience', 'divine transformation', a 'state of Samadhi' and many other names in other cultures. It is not connected to the +1, +2, and +3 of the measuring of a drug's intensity. It is a state of bliss, a participation mystique, a connectedness with both the interior and exterior universes, which has come about after the ingestion of a psychedelic drug, but which is not necessarily repeatable with a subsequent ingestion of that same drug. If a drug (or technique or process) were ever to be discovered which would consistently produce a plus four experience in all human beings, it is conceivable that it would signal the ultimate evolution. This would make Plus Four the peak of peak experiences, in other words.

Shulgin did not find his MDMA experience overly ecstatic,

however, and compared ecstasy to a 'low-calorie martini'. He was intrigued, though, by the way the drug made him feel intoxicated, disinhibited but also very clear-headed. 'It didn't have the other visual and auditory imaginative things that you often get from psychedelics,' he said. 'It opened up a person, both to other people and inner thoughts, but didn't necessarily color it with pretty colors and strange noises.' It might be well be of use in psychotherapy, Shulgin thought and introduced it to a therapist called Leo Zeff who started to use MDMA in small doses to help patients open up.

MDMA is only one of nearly 200 compounds Shulgin has invented. There seem to be an infinite number of slight chemical variations, which produce different experiences – pleasant or unpleasant, depending on the person, the substance, and the situation. Shulgin recorded many of them in the books *PiHKAL* (short for *Phenethylamines I Have Known and Loved*) and *TiHKAL*; *Tryptamines I have Known and Loved* (phenylthylamines and tryptamines being two chemical families particularly rich in psycho-activity), both co-written with his wife.

The first section of *PiHKAL, The Love Story*, describes how Shulgin and his wife Ann met, courted and shared many drug experiences. The second part, *The Chemical Story*, describes 179 phenethylamines. Each entry includes step-by-step instructions for synthesis, along with recommended doses and 'qualitative comments' such as those given as responses to the Shulgin Scale.

The following describes the effect of taking 60 milligrams of a substance called 3C-E and is obviously in the introspective tradition. Shulgin wrote: 'Visuals very strong, insistent. Body discomfort remained very heavy for first hour .... 2nd hour on, bright colors, distinct shapes – jewel-like – with eyes closed. Suddenly it became clearly not antierotic... Image of glass-walled apartment building in mid-desert. Exquisite sensitivity. Down by Midnight. Next morning, faint flickering lights on looking out windows.'

PiHKAL made Shulgin an underground celebrity. The Center for Cognitive Liberty and Ethics has an online *Ask Dr Shulgin* column that receives 200 questions a month. On independent drug-information Web sites such as www.erowid.com, you can find the *PiHKAL* and *TiHKAL* entries for dozens of drugs, not to mention lively debates on his work and inventions on drug forums. Shulgin has said that the pleasure of synthesising a new drug is like that of painting a fine picture or writing a good novel. Two years after *PiHKAL* was published, Shulgin's relationship with the DEA soured. They raided his lab and revoked his licence, after bringing him samples of drugs seized for forensic analysis; these drugs often turned out to be Shulgin's own designs, taken up and synthesised by underground chemists who were avid readers of Shulgin's books and recipes.

Since then, a chemical battle has waged. Shulgin serves up a new compound which cannot yet be declared illegal. To do that the authorities have first to buy and analyse it; only then can they decree he has brewed up another substance which has no medical use, *might be addictive* (my italics) and has to be placed on the list of Schedule I drugs. The second of these conditions is rather ambiguous, as addiction remains impossible to define – if one accepts, with Volkow, that addiction is in part a compulsion, then it could be said that some become addicted to cheeseburgers, soft drinks, and pornography. Shulgin has always, thus far, managed to outwit the law and lives as a free man on a ranch where he grows mescaline-containing cactic.

Plucky Shulgin against the Sheriff is a nice scenario but Shulgin's attitude to drug-related deaths seems very cavalier. He argues that a small percentage of users die from aspirin and, when asked if he could imagine a drug so addictive that it should be banned, he has said no. His only concession is that children should not be allowed to buy psychoactive drugs. He has worked independently for decades now, in the shadows of legality; one wonders if the DEA has decided not to prosecute Shulgin in part to avoid winning publicity for his work. In many ways, it seems a pity that Shulgin has worked in such relative isolation, as his ideas are not subjected to organised academic scrutiny.

America is a deeply puritanical country and official attitudes to drug research remain illogical – though mass-prescription of highly addictive painkillers, stimulants and anti-depressants show the War on Drugs started by President Nixon is neither consistent, nor, perhaps, intended to be. I have argued that the ban on LSD research put an end to important clinical studies. One group, however, eventually managed to get around the ban through the use of governmental contacts, helped by the fact that they are based at one of America's top medical universities, Johns Hopkins.

For some years Bill Richards and Roland Griffiths have been studying psychedelics, including psilocybin and mescaline, methodically. I talked to Griffiths, and he explained their latest research. It became clear that they have had to confirm some of the findings of earlier research because of the long period when work on LSD was banned.

Their experiments are simple in structure. Subjects are blindfolded and taken into what was called the 'psilocybin room', a comfortable living-room where they listen to classical music – mainly Bach masses – and are administered psilocybin. Many said that listening to Bach for six or more hours in the dark while being encouraged to introspect, was, in itself, a very powerful experience.

The results of the study were published in 2006. Richards and Griffiths noted that:

'When administered to volunteers under supportive conditions, psilocybin occasioned experiences similar to spontaneously occurring mystical experiences and were evaluated by volunteers as having substantial and sustained personal meaning and spiritual significance.'

They added:

'And, perhaps most significantly, those who have mystical experiences claim loss of a fear of death ... that they somehow feel part of something eternal. Not necessarily personal immortality – there's a paradox there – it's not denying death, but that somehow in spite of the reality of death, it's a good universe. Life makes sense. And there's every reason to live the rest of this lifetime as fully as possible. It's pretty inspiring.'

Subjects reached a mystical state which revealed 'a dimension of awesomeness, of profound humility, of the self being stripped bare . . . It's the sacred dimension of revelation, but it can be what Kierkegaard called 'fear and trembling' – incredibly profound and powerful.'

Two months later, 79% of the participants reported moderately to greatly increased life satisfaction and well-being. A follow-up study in 2008 suggested, as had been first argued in the 1960s, that LSD could lead to lasting changes. Griffiths told me he was struck by the fact that 'mystical experiences appear to have the ability to reorganise human behaviour and perception dramatically . . . all at once . . . And that's what conversion experiences are – experiences of great insight, or of religious meaning that push people to reorganise their priorities, their perceptions of the world drastically. And they change in ways that are most often good – altruistic, pro-social, and open to new experiences.'

There has also been less dramatic research on LSD, psilocybin and cluster headaches. Sewell, Halpern and Hope (2006) found that 22 out of 26 subjects who were given psilocybin said the drug stopped the onset of attacks and seven out of eight LSD users said that once they took the drug their headaches ceased. This finding is of particular importance, as cluster headaches are amongst the most painful of syndromes known to medicine, and highly resistant to conventional painkillers, including even opiates. Intriguingly, the most effective drugs in the treatment of migraine attacks – the triptans – are derived from the tryptamine structure, on which Shulgin did so much research. The samples in the cluster headache were small but the work was convincing enough to be published in a reputable journal, *Neurology*. These strands of evidence make it clear that LSD does have considerable therapeutic uses, and the suppression of research has come at a high price to medicine.

The situation with legal psychiatric medications is also problematic, but for very different reasons that highlight the difficulty of predicting how any substance will affect the brain. When I started to report on psychiatry 30 years ago, there was a major problem at Britain's most secretive asylum. It had been run since the 1950s by Dr Patrick McGrath. After I had made a film on Diana Irons, a teenage girl who had been sent to Broadmoor, I received permission from the Secretary of State for

Health to make a film about the hospital for ITV but McGrath was not having it. When I went to see him, he accused me of recording him secretly and had two nurses escort me out of 'his' hospital. ITV still wanted the film so we made it without any official help. I tracked down 33 ex-patients and produced *I was in Broadmoor*, a fierce critique of how the hospital operated.

Today, Broadmoor still houses many of the most difficult and dangerous patients in the UK, including the serial killer Peter Sutcliffe. One of the Kray twins spent years there. A less famous patient was Bill Collins who attacked his girlfriend when he was nineteen years old. He never denied hurting her or complained about being punished; the police found him weeping at her side. 'I was completely miserable,' he told me, 'but what I did was terrible.' He was sentenced to four years and sent to Wakefield Prison in 1962. He hoped prison would not mean the end of his education and started to study botany and biology. 'But I messed up,' Bill told me. He attacked a civilian instructor. A few weeks later he was bundled into a van, with no idea where he was being taken. He was terrified when the van pulled up at Broadmoor's gates.

The fact that Bill had been sentenced to only four years was soon forgotten and Bill was now detained at Her Majesty's interminable pleasure. When he got to Broadmoor 'the nurses asked me if I wanted to do it the hard way or the easy way. I asked if doing it the easy way would mean compromising my integrity. They replied: 'We know which way you want to do it.' He was put on high doses of anti-psychotics and tranquilisers to sedate him.

During one row nurses broke Bill's arm; he claims that ten years later they apologised and gave him half a bottle of whisky, a great treat in the hospital. By the early 1990s Bill did not think he would ever be allowed to leave Broadmoor, but in 2000, 38 years after he had received his four-year sentence, he was released to live in a secure unit near Newbury. Decades of psychiatric 'care' had taken their toll. Bill had no teeth and shambled like a very old man though he had just turned sixty. His speech was often hard to follow.

For many years, Bill's responsible medical officer was Dr Patrick McGrath.

'I often asked him to take me off my medication because it caused me so much pain and so many side-effects,' Bill said.

'Don't nag me, Bill,' Dr McGrath replied apparently. 'I'll take you off when you're ready.' It took more than 35 years for psychiatrists to decide Bill could do without the drugs. McGrath was dead by then and Bill had a new medical officer.

Eventually Bill was released from the secure unit and allowed to live in the community. His flat in Clapham, south London, was a splendid mess, of books, Victorian prints, files, general debris, two birdcages and a number of corsets. Bill had inherited some money and spent lavishly on corsets and also on the Queen Mother. While he was still in Broadmoor he started sending her flowers on her birthday and, when he got out, her equerry asked if the Queen Mother could do anything for him. So in June 2003, Bill hired top hat and tails, and attended the Derby as a guest of the Queen Mother. He felt it was a real triumph – rightly so.

Medication and his years in Broadmoor had made Bill a lesser man, he told me. He was no longer the person he had been or could have become. He was not unusual in feeling that the drugs that were supposed to help him had damaged him beyond repair.

There is, of course, a key difference between the drugs patients are prescribed and the drugs addicts use. In the first case, psychiatrists require patients to take the drugs; in the second case society tells users not to take them.

I have argued that cocaine was one of the first drugs to flip from miracle elixir to devil's brew and, then, that pharmaceutical companies were usually slow to accept data which showed new anti-psychotics and anti-depressants caused serious effects. Perhaps the most astonishing finding, though, concerned not drugs but placebos – treatments containing no active ingredient.

In May 2002 *The Washington Post* published an article *Against Depression, a Sugar Pill Is Hard to Beat* which attacked Big Pharma. 'A new analysis has found that in the majority of trials conducted by drug companies in recent decades, sugar pills have done as well as – or better than – anti-depressants. Companies have had to conduct numerous trials to get two that show a positive result, which is the Food and Drug Administration's minimum for approval.'

When the trials were completed and patients on placebos were told the truth about what they had been taking, they quickly deteriorated. 'People's belief in the power of anti-depressants may explain why they do well on placebos,' *The Washington Post* said.

In 2008 two psychologists used the Freedom of Information Act to obtain data from 47 studies used by the Federal Drugs Administration to approve the six anti-depressants prescribed most widely between 1987 and 1999. The 47 studies were not exactly a glowing endorsement. Anti-depressants worked 18% better than placebos, statistically significant, but hardly an overwhelmingly positive result.

Since the 1960s, pharmaceutical companies have often found that attack is the best form of defence when confronted with evidence that their products inflict serious side-effects. The makers of Prozac, Eli Lilly argued that the meta-study, which analysed 47 clinical trials, did not take into account the most recent research; GlaxoSmithKline warned one paper should not be circulated, as it might cause 'unnecessary alarm'. Alarm to whom? To poor patients and doctors, of course. Nothing was said about alarming the stock markets, institutions that are often gripped by fear and panic, rather like neurotics. Two British psychiatrists argued that the meta-analysis of 47 studies was tragically flawed. Its authors had the misfortune of coming from a psychology, rather than drug testing, background and had also been influenced by the 'down on anti-depressants' in the media. The pro-pharma shrink duo had flaws of their own; it turned out they had financial links to the pharmaceutical companies.

Problems with medications have not stopped pharmaceutical manufacturers exploring new markets, however. Until the 1980s, psychiatric orthodoxy claimed that children rarely suffered from psychiatric disorders. Children under sixteen did not suffer from schizophrenia, childhood depression was rare and so was child suicide. There was something naive about such views, but it had one huge benefit – children were hardly ever put on psychiatric medication. How blind those primitive shrinks were! Better research showed toddlers need their meds. So in recent years, fashionable drugs, such as Ritalin and the anti-depressant Paxil, have been prescribed to over 7 million children in America. These medications are said to cure children of attention deficit disorder and, in Paxil's case, of 'oppositional disorder'. The symptoms of this dubious 'disorder' are that children disobey their parents, teachers and doctors. Ritalin, methylphenidate, is an amphetamine analogue that functions much like speed, and is frequently abused, as Elizabeth Wurtzel describes memorably in her autobiographical account of addiction, *More, Now, Again*. Paxil, marketed in the UK as Seroxat, has been linked to suicide. This is one of the ironies of so-called 'anti-depressants' – they significantly increase the likelihood of suicide, according even to their own manufacturers, by a factor of 8.

In a 2009 issue of *Scientific American Mind*, Edmund S. Higgins estimates that 9% of boys and 4% of girls in the USA have been prescribed stimulants for attention deficit disorder. A number of researchers report predictable amphetamine side-effects amongst children prescribed Ritalin, Dextro-amphetamine or Adderall (a combination of dexamphetamine and amphetamine salts, which latter, in bootleg form, constitute the majority of street speed in the UK) such as hallucinations, difficulty sleeping, mood swings, stomach aches, diarrhoea, headaches and lack of appetite.

It might seem odd to give a stimulant like methylphenidate like Ritalin to children who are already hyperactive but there is evidence these drugs boost activity in the frontal cortex, which controls attention. Patients with attention deficit disorder have an underactive and sometimes smaller than average frontal lobe or cortex. (The two terms are often used synonymously.) The frontal cortex is that part of the brain often labelled as 'the executive' by Americans and is known to suppress emotions. From the late 1930s to the early 1960s, psychiatrists often performed lobotomies, cutting the links between the frontal lobe and the rest of the cortex. The operation was primitive, but lobotomised patients were rarely violent and certainly stopped smashing windows. Few psychiatrists claimed lobotomies were a cure, but many argued they were the best that could be done for desperately ill and otherwise untreatable patients. The operation is hardly ever performed now, partly because of ethical concerns and partly because high doses of medications produce similar results without doing such obvious and irreversible brain damage.

Good industries create new markets – and pharmaceutical companies have become expert at generating anxieties which then need to be eased by new-fangled medicines. This has led some psychiatrists to suggest that instead of disorders in need of treatments, we now have pharmaceutical companies inventing drugs that need to find a matching disorder, or, if necessary, invent one. In 2008 the Federal Drugs Administration allowed two new stimulants – Vyvanse (a form of dexamphetamine, lisdexamfetamine dimesylate) and Concerta (another brand of methylphenidate) – to be used to treat adults with attention deficit problems. Pharmaceutical companies have been suggesting for nearly ten years that even if we are 'sane', we need help with concentration.

Higgins pointed out some patients asked for magic bullets to boost their productivity. Prescriptions for methylphenidate and amphetamine rose by almost 12% a year between 2000 and 2005. Higgins asked the key question: do we know what the drugs are actually doing to the brain? He argued some studies since the 1970s have shown that normal children also become more attentive, and often calmer, after taking low-dose stimulants. One of the world's most respected neuropsychologists, Michael Gazzaniga has shown that students who take drugs like Ritalin score higher in IQ test scores. Despite such positive reports, traces of 'a sinister side to stimulants have also surfaced,' Higgins argued, citing Nora Volkow.

In 2007 Volkow studied how much seven- to ten-year-olds who took Ritalin grew over three years and compared their growth rates with those of children who did not take any stimulants. The medicated children were, on average, two centimetres shorter in height and 2.7 kilograms less in weight; they never caught up with children who did not take those medicines.

Human growth is controlled in part through the hypothalamus in the mid-brain and the pituitary gland at the base of the brain. Cocaine and Ritalin increase levels of dopamine in the hypothalamus and this excess dopamine may reach the pituitary. The mechanism by which

Ritalin stunts children's growth seems clear. It seems unlikely that drugs which have such a profound physical effect would do nothing else to the brain. After Volkow published her findings, the Food and Drug Administration (FDA) warned about other side-effects such as psychosis but the picture is more complex still. Most adults who have attention deficit disorder also have some other psychiatric diagnosis: they are depressed, suffer from an anxiety disorder or drug addiction. No one knows whether taking drugs like Ritalin in childhood might lead to such psychiatric conditions in adulthood.

It is not easy to study these issues in human beings. Logically, to address Higgins's questions, one would have to compare two groups of nine-year-olds. One would have been prescribed Ritalin or another attention-boosting medication, and a control group given a placebo. Somehow one would have to parcel out two exceptionally complex issues – what were the physical and psychological differences between these children when they were nine years old and what were their subsequent experiences over the next ten years? The researchers would then need to compare the two groups when the subjects were 19 years old and work out to what extent any differences between the two groups of 19-year-olds were due to consumption of Ritalin, allowing for all other conceivable variables (which could never be identified or controlled with certainty). In practical terms, such a study would be deemed unethical and could never be performed.

Animal studies are much more readily approved, and, of course, monkeys and rats can be 'sacrificed' so anatomists can examine their brains. Such studies suggest long-term use of Ritalin and cocaine may alter the very structure of the brain, especially in the frontal cortex, and produce long-term cognitive deficits. Addiction, Volkow has argued, comes about because of abnormalities in the dopamine system. Eric Nestler of the University of Texas Southwestern Medical Center offers some insight into how such abnormalities develop over time. He injected juvenile rats with a low dose of methylphenidate. When the rats became adult, those who had received methylphenidate were less responsive to 'normal' rewards such as sugar, sex, and novel environments. A study in Brazil found that rats who had taken methylphenidate when they were young were unusually anxious when they became adults.

But does this also happen in human children? Again it requires long- term and complex studies – and the pressure is always for rapid results.

For 30 years we have lived with battles between pharmaceutical companies, pressure groups and patients. These battles are not easy to solve but in the final chapter I return to one of the main themes of the book, a plea for more introspective research into the subjective effect of all drugs; in order to understand their effect, we need not only conventional trials, but first-person accounts of the actual experience of consuming the drug.

As it happens, 2012 will see the 100th anniversary of The Hague Convention on narcotics. The anniversary is unlikely to be celebrated, as the policies of the United Nations, the United States, the European Community and other bureaucracies have failed to control the international drugs trade. Indeed, many argue that these policies have succeeded only in providing a ready source of cash for organised crime.

A graphic anti-cocaine poster from the seemingly futile South American 'War on Drugs'.

Chapter 15

Market rules

CIUDAD JUÁREZ, Mexico

In the summer of 2009 Juan Antonio Román, deputy head of police, was riddled with fifty bullets as he got out of his pickup truck. The killers were taking no chances their target might survive. In 2009, according to *The Economist*, 2600 people were murdered in Ciudad Juárez in drug-related crimes and a further 3400 in Mexico as a whole. Drug cartels have been cocky enough to kill the governor of one state in Northern Mexico who dared speak out against them, as well as a number of celebrities. Mexico's drug lords are sending a blunt message to Mexico's President Felipe Calderón; he has no hope of stopping them supplying cocaine, marijuana and amphetamines to the United States.

The illegal drug business is now larger than the legitimate one. A site that analyses the international drug trade, Havocscope, estimates the world cocaine market is worth $70.45 billion a year while heroin and opium are worth $64.82 billion.

In Colombia drug barons have become so rich they can indulge in James Bond fantasies, investing in small, submarine-like boats which can carry 10 tons of drugs. The United States Navy, the Coast Guard, CIA and drug control agents from 12 other countries should be able to beat home-made subs into submission. Dream on. In 2006, these mini-subs smuggled between 500 and 700 tons of cocaine into the United States. That was a good year, however, as the Task Force managed to capture one sub in November 2006 and it now sits, as a trophy, in front of the Task Force command centre in Key West, Florida. The Task Force hasn't caught another mini-sub since.

Drug smuggling can be both high tech and homespun. When

23 year old Kayti Dryer walked off a flight from Jamaica to Manchester in 2009, she was carrying a golf bag; Kayti told the Manchester customs officers she'd taken the clubs on a golfing holiday to Montego Bay.

'What's your handicap?' asked a Customs agent, perhaps not thinking Kayti to be the most obvious or plausible of golfers.

'Handicap, what ... handicap?' Kayti said. She had no handicap, she wasn't disabled.

Customs realised that Kayti had no idea 'handicap' was a technical golf term. Officers seized her clubs and X-rayed them.

A hole in one for customs: inside the shafts of the clubs, they found £83,000 worth of cocaine. Petty cash by the standards of drug cartels, but still a decent catch.

Confusion rules when it comes to public policy. It has been estimated there are 17 million cocaine users in the world. In Britain in 2010, the House of Commons Public Accounts Committee said there were 330,000 heroin, cocaine and crack users who cost the UK £15 billion a year. One estimate claimed there were 1620 drug-related deaths in Britain in 2008–2009. The Committee thundered that the government's failure to evaluate the success of services to help addicts was 'unacceptable'.

One problem has been that research into what could help addicts does not produce clear results. Real life is not easy to study. Most research on personality and drug use still refers back to Eysenck's work in the 1950s. He suggested that drug use can modify personality. One might suppose there would be a relationship between a user's drug of choice and underlying personality traits – with the shy self-medicator reaching for drugs to help them become uninhibited, probably alcohol and/or stimulants, while the habitually anxious turn to sedatives and tranquilisers. But the theory has proved difficult to test because subjects have no consideration for researchers and use multiple drugs. One study of more than 1200 users found only 19% used a single substance – alcohol. The other 80% used many substances. Those like Hofmann and Freud who stay 'loyal' to one drug are rare.

This poly-drug use makes it even harder to develop effective policies and we face a combination of fear, ignorance and sheer confusion. Half of the British government's Advisory Committee on the Misuse of Drugs resigned between autumn 2009 and spring 2010 after Alan Johnson, the Home Secretary at the time, sacked Professor David Nutt, who chaired the Committee. Nutt had argued the unpardonable – that some Class A drugs should become Class B – and openly challenged the government's reversal of an earlier decision to re-classify cannabis from Class B to C. The re-classification of cannabis was pushed through Parliament against the Committee's advice, leading Nutt and many others to condemn it as a 'political decision' – middle-England voters are assumed to take a hardline view of all non-medicinal drug use. Certainly, it seems fair to say that in disregarding the advice of their scientific counsellors, the government were 'sending a message' that had nothing to do with science, and no one expects the statutory penalties for possession of a Class B drug, which can in theory include five years in prison, to be enforced. In practice, many caught with cannabis still face no greater sanction than a formal or informal caution – though police attitudes to the drug and its users vary widely by region. Penalties for possession of all drugs, indeed, often seem to be determined, like so much in British life, by a kind of 'postcode lottery'.

The remaining members of the Committee visited Holland. The Dutch may have liberal policies towards marijuana but they take a hard line on heroin and cocaine. If Kayti the non-golfer had landed in Amsterdam, more than her putter would have been probed. Since 2003 customs at Schipol airport have checked every orifice of every passenger arriving from drug-rich destinations like the Dutch Antilles and Suriname. The average number of mules per flight is fifty. One plane from Curaçao set a new record: 85 of its 200 passengers were smuggling drugs and they weren't just desperate students. One man arrested was the former Foreign Minister of a South American country.

The Dutch experience suggests that the average mule swallows about 1kg of cocaine, which has a street value of an estimated £120,000 in the UK.

Mules cost the European taxpayer dear, because they often need expensive medical treatment. French police found that 581 mules arrested at Paris airports between January 1999 and December 2002 had to be taken to accident and emergency departments because they collapsed or had seizures. They had swallowed condoms filled with drugs which often burst inside them. Five hundred and seventy-three mules had to be kept in hospital for an average of 5 days. Eight needed intensive treatment for poisoning and obstruction.

The situation was similar at Heathrow. Out of 572 mules arrested at the airport, 36 had to be rushed to Ashford Hospital for intensive care. The medical details are lurid. Often mules take drugs that make them constipated so they can hang on till they get to the first toilet beyond Customs. Seven mules nearly died of obstructions in their bowels. Hoarding faeces is a sign of financial greed, Freud claimed. He couldn't have dreamed of better proof. But the mules who are actually caught represent, as it were, the mere tip of the iceberg.

I can't help wondering what Karl Marx, having identified 'religion as the opium of the masses' would have made of the fact that two of the three main cocaine-producing areas in the world are now under Marxist control. Bolivia produced an estimated 113 tons of cocaine in 2008 and its Communist President, Evo Morales, is a former coca farmer, although he only backs the traditional chewing of the coca leaves, and opposes the extraction of cocaine (hence the slogan 'Coca is not cocaine.') In Peru, production topped 300 tons and the most fertile coca-growing areas are ruled by the Shining Path, an extreme Marxist movement which was almost wiped out in the 1990s. Thanks to drug profits, however, the Shining Path is back on the revolutionary road with the best weapons money can buy.

For users, drugs may be about getting the best high but, for the cartels, it's all about getting the best return. Like good capitalists such as pharmaceutical companies, they keep feeding new products onto the market. Illegal, semi-legal and legal highs are advertised with the same brio as the newest toothpaste. It is an irony that Chinese laboratories working out of a nominally Communist Republic are very much involved in manufacturing these substances.

Addiction has had a profound effect on crime and the prison population in Britain and, most dramatically, in America. The National Institute of Justice Arrestee Drug Abuse Monitoring Program provides a good snapshot of the situation. The Institute calculates the percentage of arrestees who test positive for drug use. The data are collected anonymously at the time of arrest in a number of American cities. No one is forced to take part.

The city whose criminals use drugs least seems to be Anchorage, Alaska. Even there, 42.5% of those arrested test positive, though this may be misleading, as possession of up to an ounce of cannabis for personal use is not an offence in Alaska, as deeply libertarian a state as it is conservative. The highest score for men was 78.7% in Philadelphia, Pennsylvania. In New York 82% of women arrested were on drugs and most were charged with prostitution, drug possession, or sales. Men and women arrested for car theft, robbery, and burglary also had high positive rates. Three quarters of those who tested positive for opiates also tested positive for another drug.

In 2008, a total of 1.5 million Americans were arrested for drug offences, most involving marijuana, and 500,000 of them were imprisoned. There are disturbing racial differences in patterns of drug arrests, prosecutions, sentencing and deaths. African-American drug users made up for 35% of drug arrests, 55% of convictions, and 74% of those sent to prison for drug possession. African-Americans were sent to state prisons for drug offenses a staggering 13 times more frequently than other ethnic groups.

In 2009, Senator Jim Webb of Virginia introduced bipartisan legislation to review USA incarceration policies. He had the support of both law enforcement and civil rights organisations and argued; 'The elephant in the bedroom in many discussions on the criminal justice system is the sharp increase in drug incarceration over the past three decades. In 1980, we had 41,000 drug offenders in prison; today we have more than 500,000, an increase of 1,200%.'

The British prison population has doubled in the last 15 years, and many of the 81,000 inmates in the UK suffer from mental illness. Penal experts claim that one third of Britain's prisoners have a serious psychiatric condition. The liberal policy of closing asylums has meant that many depressed and schizophrenic men and women live in the community with inadequate support and inevitably, some drift into crime. In prison they receive medication and many also use whatever 'recreational' drugs are on offer from fellow prisoners. Colin Moses, the Chairman of the Prison Officers Association, has said drugs in Britain's jails are reaching 'epidemic proportions' and added a lyrical touch. 'Sometimes it feels like it's snowing drugs because of the amount coming in over the walls.'

The failure of current policy is nicely illustrated by Huseyin Djemil, a long term addict who kicked the habit. Sixteen years after being released from prison, he was given the job of drugs strategy co-ordinator for London's seven prisons and in 2007 he was appointed head of drug treatment policy at the National Offender Management Service. He resigned weeks later, blaming the organisation's chaotic structure, and wrote a very critical 36-page pamphlet, which was published by the eminently respectable Centre for Policy Studies. He said:

'Drugs are widespread in British prisons, undermining any attempt to clean up prisoners from pre-existing addictions, greatly increasing the chances of recidivism and corrupting staff.'

Djemil attacked the then-Labour government for trying to manage the problem, rather than attempting to eradicate it. He argued that there are probably more drugs in prison now than ever before. If it were not tragic one could appreciate the irony. Some prisoners are going into Britain's jails clean, only to come out addicted.

A study at Cornton Vale, a women's prison in Stirling, found almost every single inmate had a drug problem. In most prisons over half the inmates use drugs, mainly cannabis, but often opiates as well. Experts can hardly stop pointing out the ironies. In an attempt at reform, many prisons announced they were setting up 'drug-free wings' where there would be constant searches to stamp out drugs. Neil McKeganey, professor of drug misuse research at the University of Glasgow, has found that the so-called 'drug-free wings' are now plagued by dealing.

Organised crime is targeting the prisons because the returns are so lucrative. The Serious and Organised Crime Agency estimates that about 30 major drug dealers control prison distribution networks across the UK. At Christmas 2007, the segregation cells of Whitemoor prison in Cambridgeshire were full, as prisoners sought refuge from the dealers they owed money to.

Djemil estimated the drugs trade in UK prisons is worth at least £59m, but admits the figure is probably much higher as prices in prison are steep. There are even cases where dealers have broken into prisons to do business, though there are less melodramatic methods of smuggling drugs inside. An inmate, for instance, can arrange for drugs to be thrown over the jail wall, where they are then 'fished up' by fellow prisoners while the guards are distracted.

In 2008 the Metropolitan Police quietly launched a specialist 'ghost', or undercover, squad to root out corrupt prison officers who were turning a blind eye to the trade. The Labour government, Djemil claimed, was very unwilling to share information and provide a clear picture of the problem. The use of mandatory drug testing, he argues, is probably encouraging greater use of Class A drugs in prison, in part because they are more rapidly eliminated from the system than cannabis, and thus less likely to be caught on a random screen. Again there is a paradox. An inmate who is a heroin addict can get on a detoxification programme that offers either methadone or its more expensive alternative, Subutex. The prisoner can then blame any positive result on the substitute drug. The Home Office, which ran Britain's prisons till May 2010, knew of this particular ploy for at least five years. In 2005 it published a little-noticed report, *Tackling Prison Drug Markets*, which stated: 'Prisoners have learnt a number of procedural and legal ways in which a positive test can be avoided, including refusing to do the test or ensuring they are being prescribed opiate-based medication through healthcare to cover illicit opiate use.'

The statistics underline how bad the situation has become. In 1997 just under 14,000 prisoners were on detoxification programmes. Today the number is over 51,000. According to the magazine *Druglink*, in some jails one in five prisoners now takes Subutex, because it is easy to smuggle in. Outside prison, the drug sells for £5 a tablet; inside, it goes for £40. If a prisoner does manage to leave jail 'clean', he may not manage to continue his abstinence once back in the community. Labour MP Paul Flynn recently told Parliament: 'The tragedy that continues these days is that people who go in as users and come out clean, who are put down as successes for the prison system, often die very quickly. Two of my constituents came out of prison drug-free: one lived a week, another lived a day.'

The internet has only made the problem more intractable – and some very dangerous substances are widely sold online. It takes three to five years for the Food and Drug Administration (FDA) to decide that a drug is safe (and they often seem to make mistakes) but dealers, of course, want to market any new drug as fast as possible. There is usually no data at all on the safety of the latest compound to hit the market, and when there is any such information, it tends to be anecdotal and unfit for the pages of a peer-reviewed journal. It is a little odd to find that *Mixmag*, a magazine about clubbing and electronic music, sometimes does produce accounts of introspective drug research. Its readers, however, are constant drug users, and share information concerning new compounds as they hit the scene.

One of the most worrying such recent drug fads has involved Mephedrone, 4-methylmethcathinone, a stimulant that has been described as similar to both MDMA and cocaine. *Mixmag* reported a survey of users. The methodology is not perfect, of course, as subjects who answer surveys are not necessarily typical. The results were nonetheless worrying, showing Mephedrone posed serious risks – indeed, it would appear to produce obvious toxic reactions more commonly than either MDMA or cocaine:

- 67% of users experienced excessive sweating
- 51% experienced headaches
- 43% experienced heart palpitations
- 27% experienced nausea
- 15% had blue or cold fingers

Anecdotal reports, *Mixmag* noted, were even more worrying. Some users had severe panic attacks, hallucinations and suffered from paranoia. This was not surprising, as Mephedrone was developed in backstreet sweatshop labs and has undergone no proper laboratory testing. No one knows what its medium-term or long-term effects might be.

Half the fifteen patients treated at Guy's Hospital in London after taking Mephedrone in 2009 were agitated and 20% had seizures. Nine out of another small sample of patients had a Glasgow Coma Scale score of 15, suggesting at least minor brain damage. There have been allegations that Mephedrone has caused fatalities, recalling the controversies surrounding deaths attributed to ecstasy in the early 1990s. After initial tabloid accusations, it has often been found that other substances were ingested alongside Mephedrone. In one famous case, deaths attributed to Mephedrone actually resulted from overdoses of the heroin-substitute *methadone*.

Some commentators argue that peer-to-peer web sites for drug users at least now offer good information about safety. Surfing the many drug sites has made me sceptical of this claim. While the semi-introspective reports posted owe much to Shulgin, many tend to focus on how the effects of drug A differ from, or complement, the effects of drug B rather than on any potential dangers. With thousands of reports out on the web, it's hard to generalise, but the following two accounts by users are interesting, intelligent and rather alarming.

One user bought 10 grams of Mephedrone from what he called a 'reputable online chemical supplier' but he was wary after a number of deaths in 2009 due to the mislabelling of a batch of the psychedelic Bromo-Dragonfly as 2C-B-Fly, a much milder compound. So, like Shulgin, he started with a low dose of 1 mg and gradually increased it to 25 mg taken in two doses.

The user's mood changed as soon as he took the drug. 'I felt an energetic lift, I was talkative and very clear headed... No significant physical effects were present. This experience gradually tailed off, with no ill comedown noted.' He then took a full dose and a week later 300 mgs in multiple doses, over the course of an evening at a party. He and his girlfriend felt slightly euphoric and very sociable. The report then charted minutely every dose taken and its effects.

'T+0:45 – I am feeling really good and I think the substance is nearing the peak. The party is unfolding in a beautiful urban back yard, surrounded by lush gardens and trees decorated with white mini-lights. Socialising is smooth and easy. I feel friendly, loving and outgoing, without feeling over-stimulated. My partner is not feeling as much as I am at this point.'

An hour and 15 minutes after taking the first dose, the user feels 'great. I feel lucid, socially competent, and very at ease. My mind is nicely tweaked, but my body feels mostly normal.' Unless the man was carrying a thermometer and an ECG machine with him at the party, he then just guessed 'heart rate is only slightly elevated, body temperature feels more or less normal.' Fifteen minutes later he notes, mock-poetically; 'Hark! Is that the first hint of drop-off I feel?' He takes another 100 mg and gives his partner the same. He does not feel very energetic but they dance. An hour later 'we're both feeling fantastic, very sociable, and agree this is one hell of a substance.'

Thirty minutes later, they go home where they take 3 ml of GHB, 0.25 mg of Xanax, 25 mg diphenhydramine (an anti-histamine with mild sedative and anti-psychotic effects) and 'some vapour hits of weed, hoping to bring on sleep quickly. We sit around and talk about the evening for an hour or so,' but they can't sleep because the man is having erotic fantasies. His partner suggests they have sex, but he is too exhausted to accept her offer. The couple take another 2 ml of GHB (a depressant) each, and he has 50 mg of dimenhydrinate, (the salt of diphenhydramine, slightly less potent a sedative). It does the trick as his sexual fantasies now give way to dreamy visions and he finally manages to fall asleep. 'I feel pretty tired the next day.'

The user concludes Mephedrone sits somewhere between Ritalin and Methylone and could be 'a light and effective medicine for use in relationship therapy, apparently with sex being a reasonable post-session prospect'.

'Recreationally, as a gentle social elixir it might just be about as good as it gets. I tend to get a bit too chatty on MDMA and Methylone,.. Most of all, I liked the fact that there was virtually no crash. I felt crappy the next day, but it just felt like a lack of sleep.'

He is already planning his next Mephedrone experience and will probably take the same total amount, 'but in repeated smaller doses, to get a more consistent effect over time; a sort of extended release plan if you wish (ask your doctor if Mephedrone ER® is right for you ... hehe).'

The end of the report is cavalier as he says 'remember folks ... there are no bad drugs, only bad usage patterns. Used cautiously and sensibly, I think Mephedrone is a very worthy substance.' The second user reports taking one tablet of Ambien, the brand name for the widely prescribed sedative Zolpidem, which can be bought on the web for as little as $2.49 a pill. Unlike Mephedrone, this drug has undergone extensive lab-testing. In 2007, the Food and Drugs Administration approved 13 generic versions of Zolpidem for prescription use in the US. It is available from several manufacturers in the UK, as a generic from Sandoz in South Africa, TEVA in Israel, as well as from other manufacturers such as Ratiopharm in Germany. Unlike the benzo-diazepine class of sedatives like valium/diazepam, ativan/ Lorazepam, Restoril/Temazepam that it was designed to replace, Zolpidem and the related substance Zopiclone – the 'Z drugs' – are widely unscheduled, and legal to possess without prescription. They were initially proposed, of course, as having limited abuse potential, but Zolpidem's sometimes bizarre effects have found a ready market amongst some aficionados of altered states.

The report does not make it clear whether the user/author was male or female, but Freud would have enjoyed the writing, which sparkles with imagination. The user encounters the goddess Lilith and finds his bed turned 'into a planet inhabited by ants to whom I was a god.'

Testifying to the drug's confusing nature, the user posted the unedited and incomprehensible entry from his journal that night:

My head is functioning a lttle below standard right now, /ex, /at thie time, I am wondering whu threr letters don't just fall off the top of the scree. Thimgd kaap changing and moniy, Anbieb is q sweetncqqr,,, i keep hearib cakcho nusixm,plus earklier 'i was suposed t o be a warlord for the dark anues if satan, thrb 'i was otummels diggigng htind. trippired otu likt shit., I saw the shadows cur ving around thr brightylyu lit sportdsaranea but ut was realls hjust a curtain and a gchair. Soneobejustrtold ne to get a cxhuairkrusty the clown comes onto tstage. the stage of my thughst this is a forgotteb bnothuingess befroe it ecvenbeca,e whole. Aduiss5+0n

User 2 edited this jumble into a coherent story afterwards and produced a witty account. 'At around 10 pm I swallowed two 10mg pills with a glass of water and went to my bed.' He lay down and swallowed two more pills with some milk and ate a few slices of turkey to kill the bitter taste.

A few seconds later he 'was hanging suspended from the edge of an infinitely tall cliff over a gigantic chasm of utter darkness. I was inside a huge sack woven from golden yarn. The sack was being pulled up the side of the cliff slowly by an unseen force, but since the cliff was infinitely tall I knew I would never reach the top'. He could see the cliff wall through the holes in the sack. 'I was not afraid of the height nor of possibly falling. It was a very pleasant feeling being suspended over nothingness inside a golden bag.'

But he was not alone because the goddess 'Lilith, was in the bag with me.' It is not easy to talk to a goddess and 'she communicated with me telepathically and I spoke to her with a series of guttural coughs.' Then he realised an entire community of bag-dwellers was 'dangling a few yards above me' but he could only see their silhouettes. He talked to them in Lilith's 'guttural cough language and they spoke to me by inhaling at different rhythms.' He hadn't lost all his sense of reality as he realised the bag was, in fact, his afghan which was pulled over his head.

He then went into his kitchen to get a soda. The room started spinning around and objects seemed to melt into each other. He saw rainbows everywhere and 'any lights (digital clock readouts, mainly, since it was night time) left brilliant tracers.' His ordinary kitchen top turned into a field where a hundred or so tiny men stood dressed in black clothes. They were frantically trying to get the kitchen top to balance itself as it was teetering over a giant drop like the van in the film *The Italian Job*. He tried to save them by pushing the counter but 'the little men started yelling at me and cursing me for interfering.' In the end the counter fell straight down to the floor. 'All the little men disappeared.' He then tangled with the shadow of a tall man in a large trench coat. Lilith suddenly appeared and the shadow was pulling her into the wall. 'I jumped at him to attack him and save Lilith but they vanished into the wall before I could grab them.' He saw Shadowman speed off into the night in an old car.

The user then went out to get cigarettes from his car and came back into his apartment only to find it had turned into an aquarium as 'electric blue manta rays were swimming around my feet.' He smoked a couple of cigarettes while the manta rays swam around. Then 'I saw some shadow children standing by a car and shined the flashlight at them. They disappeared into smoke.'

It seemed worth quoting this elaborate trip at length. As a fiction it is compelling, but as an introspective report it is badly flawed because it is clear the user polished and repolished it. The confusion shown so obviously in the journal entry made when he was actually feeling the effects of the drug may also explain why some people now opt for drugs which have a more focused effect – so called 'neuroenhancers' whose effects are not remotely spiritual or hallucinatory. Most are mild stimulants with effects similar to Ritalin.

The New York Review of Books (January 15th 2009) returned to the theme of drug companies and their corruption of doctors. Marcia Angell concluded no one knew how much money drug companies gave physicians and psychiatrists. She analysed the annual reports of the top nine American drug companies and estimated the money given to doctors 'comes to tens of billions of dollars a year. By such means the pharmaceutical industry has gained enormous control over how doctors evaluate and use its own products.' She added that the links between the companies and top medical schools affected 'the way medicine is practiced and even the definition of what constitutes a disease'.

The situation in Britain remains confused. In December 2010 the government launched yet another new drug strategy, 'Reducing demand, restricting supply, building recovery: supporting people to live a drug-free life'. Turning Point, a major charity, welcomed this more holistic approach which said recovery was a journey.

The trouble with journeys, however, is that they cost. On paper the new strategy sounds fine as it 'has recovery at its heart'. It puts more responsibility on individuals themselves to seek help and recognises the need for action on employment and housing. Then come the usual 'War on Drugs' blast as the strategy trumpets an 'uncompromising approach to crack down on those involved in the drug supply both at home and abroad'. Ironic proof of the fact that the government refuses to will the means to this end came over Christmas 2010 as a leaked email seemed to instruct Customs at Heathrow not to bother targeting potential drug smugglers because there was not enough money in the kitty to man the drug barricades properly. Despite the best intentions of the 2010 strategy, the Home Office and Department of Health have committed just £125m over the next financial year to the fight against drugs in England and Wales. We need more money and enhanced thinking. And to believe drug enthusiasts, the latter should not be hard to achieve.

In his book *The Neuro Revolution*, Zack Lynch suggests we are heading for what he calls 'the neuro-society.' Scientists will produce new neuroenhancers whose purpose is not to cure the sick but to improve the healthy. The aim of this form of drug use is neither enlightenment nor hedonism, but 'competitive advantage,' Lynch explains. He argues that we should stop being prissy about neuroenhancers, as they could be of great future significance in deciding which nations gain such a 'competitive advantage' in the medium-term. They are very popular in Asian countries, including those that generally take a hard line on 'recreational' drug use. Neuroenhancers do not induce euphoria, and could be seen as the perfect mid-point between 'recreational' and 'therapeutic' drug use. Lynch told *The New Yorker*, 'If you're a company that's got forty-seven offices worldwide, and all of a sudden your Singapore office is using cognitive enablers, and you're saying to Congress, "I'm moving all my financial operations to Singapore and Taiwan, because it's legal to use those there," you bet that Congress is going to say, Well, O.K. It will be a moot question then. It would be like saying, "No, you can't use a cell phone. It might increase productivity!"'

Lynch is not alone in advocating the use of cognitive enchancers. In 2002, researchers at Cambridge University gave 60 male volunteers standard cognitive tests. Half did the tests after taking modafinil which is better known by the brand-name 'Provigil' and was designed to treat narcolepsy, as an alternative to Ritalin and amphetamines. The second group in Cambridge received a placebo. The Provigil group performed better on several tests, including a visual recognition task and the 'digit span' test in which subjects are asked to repeat ever-longer strings of numbers forwards and then backwards. Writing in *Psychopharmacology*, the Cambridge group said the results suggested that 'modafinil offers significant potential as a cognitive enhancer.'

The Cambridge group then organised a survey and received 1427 responses – 62% of them from the USA. The survey – published in *Nature* – asked about Ritalin, Provigil and beta-blockers used to control high blood pressure. Sixty-two per cent of respondents had used Ritalin, 44% had used Provigil and 15% beta blockers. There was no embarrassment about 'going neuro'. A third of those who replied said they would give such drugs to their children to boost their performance at school if other pupils were also being given drugs.

Provigil has become a huge earner, with sales soaring from $196 million in 2002 to $968 million in 2008. Its manufacturer Cephalon won approval from the Food and Drug Administration to market the drug in 1998, but only for one diagnosis: 'excessive daytime sleepiness' caused by narcolepsy. By 2004, Cephalon managed to get the drug also approved for sleep apnoea, disrupted breathing while asleep. The drug also helps with 'shift-work sleep disorder'.

Cephalon insists it does not condone the 'off-label' use of Provigil. Nevertheless, in 2002, the company sent out marketing materials suggesting the drug as a remedy for tiredness and decreased activity, neither of which are actual illnesses. Six years later, after being reprimanded by the Food and Drug Administration, Cephalon had to pay $425 million in damages. Nevertheless. Cephalon plans to introduce the also cutely-named Nuvigil, a longer-lasting version of Provigil. Nuvigil will remedy excessive sleepiness associated with schizophrenia, bipolar depression, traumatic injury, and jet lag. So it's a proper drug for proper diseases. Cephalon added, though, it might just be that 'as part of the preparation for some of these other diseases, we're looking to see if there's improvement in cognition.' (Candace Steele, spokesperson for Cephalon).

The indefatigable Nora Volkow again was critical; she reported on ten men who took either Provigil or a placebo. With Provigil dopamine levels in the brain increased just as with cocaine. 'Because drugs that increase dopamine have the potential for abuse,' Volkow's report concluded, 'these results suggest that risk for addiction in vulnerable persons merits heightened awareness.' Her anxiety was echoed on the website Erowid by a former biochemistry student who said that he had succeeded in kicking cocaine and opiates but couldn't stop using Provigil. Whenever he ran out of the drug, 'I start to freak out. After 4–5 days without it, the head fog starts to come back.' Many other such reports have been filed online.

Some scientists still enthuse about neuro-boosters, however, just as Freud promoted cocaine, in part for similar reasons. A group recently declared in *Nature* in 'Towards Responsible Use of Cognitive Enhancing Drugs by the Healthy', that smart pills had their place. 'Like all new technologies, cognitive enhancement can be used well or poorly,' the article said. 'We should welcome new methods of improving our brain function . . . Safe and effective cognitive enhancers will benefit both the individual and society.' Even the usually staid British Medical Association said that 'universal access to enhancing interventions would bring up the base-line level of cognitive ability, which is generally seen to be a good thing.' Both critics and advocates of the widespread use of neuroenhancers have referred to their effects as 'cosmetic neurology'. It's a sloppy phrase and it does not do justice to the complexity of the issue. Altering the cognitive capacity of the brain, even if that is possible, has far greater implications than any mere cosmetic procedure.

The mind-expanding Sixties are gone, however. Neuroenhancers don't open the doors of perception, free us from the chains Karl Marx urged us to escape, dissolve the limits of our daily selves or let us find the shadow of divinity in our souls. They are about managing to focus for a few extra hours to finish writing a sales report or study for finals. The neuroenhancers are, in fact, capitalism enhancers. Marx would have had something ironic to say about chemicals that chain the alienated worker to their computer and make them a more productive drone. Though Freud praised cocaine and tobacco for helping him concentrate, he might also have been appalled by the cult of Provigil. Being a bit sharper at IT was not what he had in mind when he memorably said that analysis should make people free 'to love and to work'.

This account of Freud's work and its legacy in terms of drugs pushes me towards two conclusions – one about the nature of research, the second about the nature of drug policy. Freud, James and others were interested in cocaine, mescaline and nitrous oxide because they hoped to learn more about the brain. We do know more about the brain than ever before, but perhaps rather less than we might have expected 160 years after Brücke and Helmholtz issued their rousing Physicalist declaration.

There are many reasons for this relative failure. The sheer complexity of the brain is one. Where drugs are concerned, pharmacological studies are too often influenced by financial considerations to be wholly reliable, while research into 'recreational' substances has, for the most part, been very haphazard. Hofmann was unusual in studying LSD for 50 years, for example. Most of those involved in analysing their own responses to drugs moved on soon to other fields. Freud stopped writing about cocaine; Havelock Ellis put far more energy into his studies of sexual behaviour than into mescaline; Huxley went back to writing novels and polemics.

Additionally, the emphasis in university brain research in America and Britain at least has been much more focused on what one might call 'deserving diseases' such as stroke, Parkinson's and autism. There is less sympathy for drug addicts than victims of such illnesses, and a feeling that they already cost the community too much.

New sophisticated brain-imaging techniques may show how the brain responds to new stimuli and to drugs, but there are many individual differences, which is hardly surprising given the complexity of the cortex. The complexity is physical, chemical and philosophical. The mind/body problem hasn't been solved, which is also not surprising as it has defeated great philosophers for at least 400 years. The problem was never one of those problems that would dissolve if expressed properly. Wittgenstein argued that if you asked the right questions in the right language, issues that had plagued philosophers for centuries could melt away. The mind-body problem, however, is stubbornly practical and real. Seeing which neurons fire in given areas of my cortex when I see a green triangle doesn't reveal how matter becomes mind, how the pattern of neurons firing becomes the thought, for example, that I like green triangles and they remind me I had to play the triangle in the school band because I always messed up the scales on the violin. Two different languages are at work – the language of physics, chemistry and biology on the one hand and the language of subjectivity and introspection on the other. The person who works out how to convert one into the other will deserve more than just one Nobel Prize, and it may be that such a conversion can only ever be approximate.

Nevertheless, more and better introspective research would represent a modest step forwards. That would require a kick in the cortex or, to put it more formally, a change of attitude to what is considered legitimate research amongst psychologists. Jack and Roepstorff argue 'the growth of cognitive science has made it clear we need introspection to tackle core theoretical issues like consciousness and subjective states.' Academic psychologists 'resist' introspection even if that resistance is illogical. Psychologists know that subjects of cognitive experiments 'are almost invariably conscious', yet they choose to ignore that consciousness. Sadly, decades as a psychologist has taught me that the discipline is, all too often, a stranger to logic. Jack and Roepstorff are right to say, 'experience is still regarded as a problem, rather than a resource ready to be tapped.' This rejection of subjectivity limits psychology. That will remain the case, as long as many psychologists care more about their discipline being accepted as a 'science' than how useful its discoveries actually are.

Jack and Roepstorff concede, though, that they are not going to change psychology quickly. Let psychologists carry on with their objective experiments, they suggest, but add a new emphasis. Let subjects do the traditional objective measurable task – do they respond to stimuli more quickly when they have taken a given compound? But then interview the subject and ask the questions one would ask in an introspective study:

What was it like for you?

What did it make you remember?

What do you think was going on in your body?

'Such retrospective reports will considerably enrich experimenters' understanding of 'what it is like' to do the task, potentially revealing unexpected and important experiential phenomena,' Jack and Roepstorff argue. They also suggest that experiments that involve brain-imaging should have three components:

- The traditional objective measurement of behaviour.
- The traditional recordings of brain activity, improved by the latest technological advances, including, now, the latest brain-imaging techniques.
- Introspective evidence, which they would hope to relate to both of the above.

Jack and Roepstorff call these approaches 'different layers of description' and 'cannot see any logic to the current practice of ignoring one of these sources of evidence, the introspective report. They quote the biologist Seymour Kety who stated, 'Nature is an elusive quarry, and it is foolhardy to pursue her with one eye closed and one foot hobbled.' In a paper on the future of experimental psychology, Alan Costall (2010) argued that science is 'a human project' and that 'many of the major figures in recent evolutionary psychology are deeply confused about the place of subjectivity in objective experimental research.'

It seems a sensible and modest proposal – but would require psychologists to become more open-minded. They could start by reading John B. Watson, the founder of behaviourism, generally seen as a key early proponent of 'hard empiricism' in psychology. Far from being dogmatic, Watson often talked to his experimental subjects in depth, which was natural, as many of them were colleagues at Johns Hopkins. (Watson and Karl Lashley, a fellow psychologist, enjoyed themselves one summer studying how drinking bourbon affected their skills at archery and typing. The experiment allowed them to obtain some bourbon legally during Prohibition and, of course, to claim the cost of the booze as vital research expenses.) As psychology has mushroomed as an academic discipline, more and more experiments have been performed on a sample of first-year students, often by their own teachers – and psychologists talk to such subjects far less than they would those drawn from their peer group.

It's not just a question of methodology but one of social standing. When Freud used Herzig as a subject, and, indeed, when Havelock Ellis gave mescaline to his artist friends, there was equality between the researchers and their subjects, making the former more inclined to take their participants seriously.

As well as fighting for more rounded research, history suggests we need a more rational approach to drug policy in all areas. My proposals in this regard echo to some extent those of David Healy, the author of *The Creation of Psychopharmacology*. Despite the moral panics and endless tabloid horror stories, governments have failed to control the drugs trade. Some argue that all drugs should be legalised. Alcohol and tobacco are deeply harmful, after all, but remain legal. There are obvious dangers in legalising all drugs, however.

One alternative approach would be to make all currently illegal drugs available from chemists – and only from chemists. They could be bought without prescription but only by individuals who had registered as drug users (a register that would need to be zealously protected from prying eyes). One advantage of such a system would be that people would know what they were buying, as chemists would not be allowed to sell adulterated drugs. When Freud ordered his gram of cocaine from Merck he did not have to worry about its purity.

Any person who registered as a drug user would have to be seen first either by a doctor or a qualified drug worker. They would agree what would, in effect, be the user's drug ration. If we are in a *war on drugs*, after all, rationing makes sense. One might be able to buy, for example, a small quantity of cocaine four times a month and never more than once a week. This would be similar in many ways to the policy that the British government operated for over 50 years after the Rolleston report. Heroin addicts were treated with prescription heroin. The system began to break down in the 1970s but when I made *Kicking the Habit* I interviewed a few – I stress a few – addicts who managed to hold down jobs and have a relatively normal family life. It is hard to know how much the kind of system I am suggesting would cost to create but it is not likely to be more than the £15 billion the Public Accounts Committee calculated the drug business costs Britain.

Such a policy would not eliminate the illegal drugs trade but it would reduce it significantly. A modified version of this might also work in prisons where, as we have seen, chaos currently rules. Of course, any such system would inevitably be abused by some who would sell on their ration of drugs to others but this could be managed, at least to some extent, by retaining the criminal penalties for unlicensed drug sales, and making users undergo regular urinalysis, to ensure that they only consume their designated drug ration. A small fee – much lower than black market rates – paid by recreational drug users could then be hypothecated for use in combating the problems caused by drug use. Such an approach would do much to rob illicit drug use of its glamour, and, combined with a reasoned medical approach to chronic addiction, would seem to offer a real hope of reducing drug-related violence. The tide in many countries has turned against the model of a *War on Drugs*, with effective decriminalisation of possession for personal use in Portugal having proved relatively successful. Portugal has one of the lowest rates of violent crime in Europe. A truce in the *War on Drugs* would be imperfect – but surely, nonetheless, an improvement on the present situation.

It is time now to return to Freud and Hofmann. Hofmann continued to believe in the therapeutic benefits of LSD until his death at the age of 102. LSD and the other psychoactive drugs 'changed my life, insofar as they provided me with a new concept about what reality is,' he said, adding:

'Before, I had believed there was only one reality: the reality of everyday life. Under LSD, however, I entered into realities which were as real and even more real than the one of everyday ... I became aware of the wonder of creation, the magnificence of nature and of the plant and animal kingdom. I became very sensitive to what will happen to all this and all of us.'

After many many 'acid trips', Hofmann finally gave up psychedelics. "I know LSD; I don't need to take it anymore," he said. He had learned, he believed, all he could from the drug.

If Freud had taken mescaline, rather than cocaine, or if some time traveller had offered him LSD, would he have developed psychoanalysis in a different way? The evidence suggests he might well have done. LSD seems to deal with one of the great problems analysts work through with their clients – resistance. We don't understand why LSD opens up the repressed. but the evidence from Bastiaans and others makes it clear that it often does so. Of course, it is possible that Freud on acid would have made the opposite decision to the historical Freud on coke, and devoted himself to metaphysics and philosophy rather than the subconscious. Perhaps an acid-inspired Freud would even have undergone a conversion experience, turned his back on science and his atheism, and become a rabbi.

Less whimsically, it is a pity that Hofmann seems to have known nothing about Freud's work on cocaine and did not travel to London when he first discovered LSD. The young chemist and the old analyst would have had a great deal to say to one another, and might, between them, have opened doors to yet new realms of perception.

References

Freud's work and the commentaries on Freud's work are very extensive so this general bibliography of works by or about Freud is divided into four sections:

1. Works by Sigmund Freud

All references are to the Standard Edition, edited by James Strachey with the help of Anna Freud. It was published by The Hogarth Press of London which was run by Leonard and Virginia Woolf. It is abbreviated to SE and the figure that follows refers to the volume. The dates of the works are those of the first publication in German.

1895. *Project for a Scientific Psychology.* SE 1.

1895. *Studies in Hysteria.* SE 2.

1899. *The Interpretation of Dreams.* SE 4–5.

1903. *Jokes and their Relation to the Unconscious.* SE 8.

1909. *Little Hans: Analysis of a phobia in a five-year-old boy.* SE 10, pp. 1–149.

1913. *Totem and Taboo.* SE 13: pp. 1–161.

1914. *The Moses of Michelangelo,* originally published in *Imago.* SE 13, pp. 211–238.

1920. *Beyond the Pleasure Principle.* SE 18, pp. 7–64.

1923. *The Ego and the Id.* SE 19, pp. 3–66.

1925. An *Autobiographical Study.* SE 20, pp. 3–70.

1925. *Resistances to Psycho-Analysis.* SE, 19.

1926. *On Dostoevsky.* SE 20.

1927. *The Future of an Illusion.* SE 21, pp. 3–56.

1932. *Why War?* Pamphlet for the League of Nations. SE 22, pp. 197–215.

1937. *Analysis Terminable and Interminable.* SE 23, pp. 209–253.

1937. Translation of Marie Bonaparte's *Topsy.* Albert de Lange: Brussells.

1938. *Moses and Monotheism.* SE 23, pp. 3–137.

1940. *An Outline of Psychoanalysis.* SE 23, pp. 141–207.

Freud excluded his work on cocaine from the Standard Edition but a useful compendium can be found in: Byck, Robert. (Ed.) (1975) *The Cocaine Papers*. New York, New American Library (Meridian).

This reproduces all Freud's writings on cocaine and some commentaries including:

Freud, Sigmund. (1974) *Über coca*. Originally published in German, 1884.
Freud, Sigmund. (1974) *Addenda to Über coca*. Originally published in German, 1885.
Freud, Sigmund. (1974) *Craving for and fear of cocaine*. Originally published in German, 1887.

2. Freud's Letters

Freud, Sigmund. (1961) *Letters of Sigmund Freud 1873–1939* (Freud, Ernst Ed.) London: Hogarth.
Freud, Sigmund. (1960) *Letters*. New York: Basic Books.
Freud, Sigmund. (1989) *Letters of Sigmund Freud and Eduard Silberstein: 1871–1881*. Cambridge, MA: Harvard University Press.
Freud, Sigmund. *Letters (1914–1938)* MS collection in John Rylands Library University of Manchester. The collection includes letters from his nephew Samuel.
Freud, Sigmund. (1985) *The complete letters of Sigmund Freud to Wilhelm Fliess, 1887–1904* (Masson, Jeffrey M. Ed. and Trans.). Cambridge, MA: Harvard University Press.
Freud, Sigmund. (1998) *Briefbraute*. Frankfurt: Fischer.

3. Works by relatives and friends

Bernays, Edward. (1923) *Crystallizing Public Opinion*. Papers of Edward Bernays held in the Library of Congress.
Bernays, Edward. (2004) *Propaganda*. Brooklyn, N.Y.: Ig Publishing.
Bernays-Freud, Anna. (1940) My brother Sigmund Freud. *American Mercury*, 51(203), pp. 335–342.
Bernays-Freud, Anna. (2005) *Eine Wienerin in New York*. Berlin: Aufbau-Verlag.
Bernays-Heller, Judith. (1973) 'Freud's mother and father' in *Freud as we knew him* (Ruitenbeck, Hendrick M. Ed.). Detroit: Wayne State University Press.
Berthelsen, Detlef. (1991) *La Famille Freud au jour le jour; souvenirs de Paula Fichtl*. Paris: Presses Universitaires de France.
Freud, Martin. (1957) *Glory reflected: Sigmund Freud—man and father*. London: Angus & Robertson.
Zweig, Stefan. (1931) *Mental Healers*. London: Cassell and Co.

4. Biographies and Aspects of Freud's work

Baur, Eva G. (2005) *Freud's Wien: eine Spurensuche.* München: Verlag C.H. Beck.

Bertin, Celia. (1987) *Marie Bonaparte: a life.* New Haven: Yale University press.

Farrell, Brian A. (1981) *The Standing of Psychoanalysis.* Oxford: Oxford University Press.

Ferris, Paul. (1997) *Dr Freud: a life.* London: Sinclair-Stevenson.

Forrester, John. (1997) *Dispatches from the Freud Wars: psychoanalysis and its passions.* London: Harvard University Press.

Gay, Peter. (1988) *Freud: A Life for Our Time.* London: Dent.

Grosskurth, Phyllis. (1982) The Shrink Princess. *New York Review of Books*, December 16th 1982, 29(20).

Hayman, Ronald. (1999) *A Life of Jung.* London: Bloomsbury.

Hogenson, George B. (1994) *Jung's Struggle with Freud: a metabiological study.* Brooklyn, NY: Chiron Publications.

Jones, Ernest R. (1953–1957) *Sigmund Freud.* (3 Vols) New York: Basic Books.

Malcolm, Janet. (1985) *In the Freud Archives.* New York: Knopf.

Masson, Jeffrey M. (1984) *The Assault on Truth: Freud's suppression of the seduction theory.* New York: Farrar, Straus and Giroux.

Rand, Nicholas & Torok, Maria. (1997) *Questions for Freud: the secret history of psychoanalysis.* London: Harvard University Press.

Sulloway, Frank J. (1979) *Freud, Biologist of the Mind: beyond the psychoanalytic legend.* New York: Basic Books.

Wollheim, Richard. (1971) *Freud.* London: Fontana/Collins.

Wollheim, Richard. (Ed.) (1974) *Freud: A Collection of Critical Essays.* Garden City, N.Y.: Anchor Books.

Wollheim, Richard & Hopkins, James. (Eds.) (1982) *Philosophical Essays on Freud.* Cambridge: Cambridge University Press.

Wortis, Joseph. (1954) *Fragments of an analysis with Freud.* New York: Simon & Schuster.

Young-Bruehl, Elisabeth. (2008) *Anna Freud: a biography.* (2nd ed.) London: Yale University Press.

Chapter References

Introduction

Burroughs, William S. (2010) *The Naked Lunch: the restored text.* London: Fourth Estate.

Burroughs, William S. Jr. (1970) *Speed.* London: Olympia Press Ltd.

Burroughs, William S. Jr. (1973) *Kentucky Ham.* New York: E.P. Dutton.

Kicking the Habit. Film for the ITV Network first screened July 9th 1985.

Goethe, Johann Wolfgang von. (1999) *Faust: the first part of the tragedy with unpublished scenarios for the Walpurgis Night and the Urfaust.* (Trans.Williams, John R.) Ware, Herts.: Wordsworth Editions Limited.

Chapter 1

Freud's early papers on physiology and eels are:

Freud, Sigmund. (1877a) Beobachtungen über Gestaltung und feineren Bau der als Hoden beschriebenen Lappenorgane des Aals. [Observations on the Formation and More Delicate Structure of Lobe-Shaped Organs of the Eel Described as Testicles.] *Sitzungsberichte der Kaiserliche Akademie der Wissenschaften* (Wien), 75: pp. 419–431.

Freud, Sigmund. (1877b) Uber den Ursprung der Hinteren Nervenwurzeln im Ruckenmark von Amnocoetes (Petromyzon Planeri). [On the Origin of the Posterior Nerve Roots in the Spinal Cord of Amnocoetes (Petrmyzon Planeri).] *Sitzungsberichte der Kaiserliche Akademie der Wissenschaften* (Wien), 75, pp. 15–30.

Freud, Sigmund. (1878) ber Spinalganglien und Rückenmark des Petromyzon. [On the Spinal Ganglia and Spinal Cord of the Petromyzon.] *Sitzungsberichte der Kaiserliche Akademie der Wissenschaften* (Wien), 78, pp. 81–167.

Freud, Sigmund. (1884) A new histological method for the study of nerve-tracts in the brain and spinal chord. *Brain: A Journal of Neurology*, 7, pp. 86–88.

Other references:

On Behaviourism and its virtues and vices there is a long debate. For two works that catch the flavour of the passions aroused, see the positive:

Broadbent, Donald. (1961) *Behaviour.* Oxford: Oxford University Press.

And the negative:

Jordan, Nehemiah. (1968) *Themes in Speculative Psychology.* London: Tavistock.

On Clinton and inhaling substances and exhaling falsehoods see:

Hitchens, Christopher. (2000) *No One Left to Lie to: the triangulations of William Jefferson Clinton.* London: Verso.

On the Club des Haschischins see:

Théophile Gautier, Pierre J. (1846) Le club des Haschischins. *Revue des Deux Mondes*, February 1st 1846.

On Humphry Davy see:

Thorpe, Thomas E. (2007) *Humphry Davy, poet and philosopher.* Stroud: Nonsuch.

On Freud and Jung see:

Hogenson, George B. (1994) *Jung's Struggle with Freud: a metabiological study.* Op cit.

On Melitta Schmideberg see:

Schmideberg, Melitta. (1948) *Children in Need.* London: Published for Psychological & Social Series by G. Allen & Unwin.

In 1957 she started The International Journal of Offender Therapy and Comparative Criminology.

On Alexander Shulgin see:

Shulgin, Alexander & Shulgin, Ann. (1991) *Pihkal: a chemical love story.* Berkeley, CA.: Transform Press.

On John B. Watson see:

Cohen, David. (1979) *J.B. Watson, the founder of Behaviourism: a biography.* London: Routledge & Kegan Paul.

Other references:

Benaim, Valerie & Azeroual, Yves. (2010) *Nicolas Sarkozy and Carla Bruni: the true story.* London: Cutting Edge Press.
Bloom, Harold. (1991) The Art of Criticism No. 1. (Interviewed by Antonio Weiss). *Paris Review*, Spring 1991: No. 118.
Boxer, Sarah. (1997) Flogging Freud. *New York Times*: August 10, 1997.
Clapton, Eric with Sykes, Christopher S. (2008) *Eric Clapton: the autobiography.* London: Arrow.
Cohen, David. (1977) *Psychologists on Psychology.* London: Routledge & Kegan Paul.
Cohen, David. (2004) *Diana: Death of a Goddess.* London: Century.
Cohen, David. (2010) *The Escape of Sigmund Freud.* London: JR Books.
Edmonds, David & Eidinow, John. (2001) *Wittgenstein's Poker.* London: Faber & Faber.
Eysenck, Hans J. (1985) *The Decline and Fall of the Freudian Empire.* Harmondsworth: Viking.
Farrell, Brian A. (1981) *The Standing of Psychoanalysis.* Op cit.
Frankl, Viktor E. (2006) *Man's search for meaning: an introduction to logotherapy.* Boston: Beacon Press
Gore, Al & Gore, Tipper. (2002) *Joined at the Heart: the transformation of the American family.* New York: Henry Holt
Granahan, Tom. (2007) High Finance. *Investment Dealer's Digest*, December 21st, 2007.
James, William. (1950) *The Principles of Psychology.* New York: Dover.

Laing, Ronald D. (1960) *The Divided Self: an existential study in sanity and madness*. London: Tavistock.

Menninger, Karl. (1973) *Sparks*. New York: Thomas Y. Crowell

Miller, Neal E. & Dollard, John. (2000) *Social Learning and Imitation*. London: Routledge.

Obama, Barack. (2008) *Dreams From My Father: a story of race and inheritance*. Edinburgh: Canongate.

Reich, Wilhelm. (1970) *The Mass Psychology of Fascism*. New York: Farrar Strauss and Giroux.

Skinner, Burrhus F. (1976) *Particulars of my Life*. London: Cape.

Wittgenstein, Ludwig. (1970) *Lectures and conversations on aesthetics, psychology and religious belief*. Oxford: Blackwell.

Chapter 2

On Jones himself see:

Maddox, Brenda. (2006) *Freud's Wizard: the enigma of Ernest Jones*. London: John Murray.

On William Gladstone's nocturnal habits see:

Magnus, Philip. (2001) Gladstone: a biography. London: Penguin

The famous quote 'humankind cannot bear too much reality' comes from Burnt Norton, one of the Four Quartets published by Faber and Faber where Eliot was a director. One of the less known facts about Eliot is that he met, encouraged and published the science fiction author Brian Aldiss, who told the current author that his science fiction was very influenced by Freud.

Eliot, Thomas S. (1943) Four Quartets. London; Faber and Faber.

Other references:

Bell, Sanford J. (1902) 'A Preliminary Study of the Emotion of Love between the sexes'. *American Journal of Psychology*, 13(3), pp. 325–54.

Bernard Shaw, George. (2003) *Pygmalion*. Harmondsworth: Penguin.
First produced in 1912, this was the play in which Alfred Doolittle first dazzled the middle class with his radical morality. The author had the honour of interviewing Stanley Holloway who played the part in My Fair Lady.

Broderau J, (1906) *Opium Morphine and Cocaine*; Cours de medicine legale a la Faculte de Medecine Paris.

Doyle, Arthur Conan. (1890) *The Sign of Four*. London: Spencer Blackett.

Eastman, Max. (1942) *Heroes I have known: twelve who lived great lives*. New York: Simon and Schuster.

Einstein, Albert & Freud, Sigmund. (1932) *Why War?* Op cit.

Ellis, Havelock. (2006) *Studies in the Psychology of Sex.* (6 vols) Charlston, SC.: Bibliobazaar.

Eyguesier, Pierre. (1983) *Comment Freud devint drogman: études sur la coca et la cocaïne la Belle époque* (Bibliothèque des Analytica) Paris: Seuil.

Jastrow, Joseph. (1932) *The House that Freud Built.* London, Rider.

Jones, Ernest R. (1931) *The Elements of Figure Skating.* London: Methuen.

Jones, Ernest R. (1953–1957) *Sigmund Freud.* (3 Vols). Op cit.

Lewis, David. (2003) *The Man who Invented Hitler.* London: Headline.

Malcolm, Janet. (1985) *In the Freud Archives.* Op cit.

Masson, Jeffrey M. (1984) *The Assault on Truth: Freud's suppression of the seduction theory.* Op cit.

The letter where Freud admits to what we would now call an inappropriate dream about his daughter Mathilde was written to Fliess in May 1897 and can be found in: Masson, Jeffrey M. (1984) *The letters of Freud and Fliess.* Op cit.

Schnitzler, Arthur. (2007) *La Ronde.* (Trans. Unwin, Stephen & Zombory-Moldovan, Peter.) London: Nick Hern Books.

Schur, Max. (1972) *Freud, Living and Dying.* London: Hogarth Press.

Sophocles. (1939). *Oedipus Rex. In The Oedipus Cycle: an English version.* (Trans. Fitts, Dudley & Fitzgerald, Robert). New York: Harcourt, Brace & World.

Swales, P.J. (1981, April 27). *Freud, Faust, and cocaine: New light on the origins of psychoanalysis.* Unpublished lecture, New York University.

Thornton, Esther. (1983) *Freud and Cocaine: the Freudian fallacy.* London: Blond and Briggs.

Thurber, James G. (1939) *Let Your Mind Alone!* New York: Grosset & Dunlap.

Thurber, James G. & White, Elwyn B. (1952) *Is Sex Necessary? Or, why you feel the way you do.* New York: Harper.

Von Scheidt, Jürgen. (1973) *Freud und das Kokain: die Selbstversuche Freuds als Anstoss zur 'Traumdeutung'.* München: Kindler.

Zweig, Stefan. (1931) *Mental Healers.* Op cit.

Chapter 3

On Freud's childhood see:

Gicklhorn, Renée. (1969). The Freiburg period of the Freud family. *Journal of History of Medicine and Allied Sciences*, 24(1), pp. 37–43.

And:

Sajner, Josef. (1968). Sigmund Freud's Beziehungen zu seinem Geburtsort Freiburg (Pribor) und zu Maehren. *Clio Medica*, 3, 167–180.

Other references:

Krüll, Marianne. (1979). *Freud und sein Vater: Die Entstehung der Psychoanalyse und Freuds ungelöste Vaterbindung*. München: Beck.
Krüll, Marianne. (1986). *Freud and His Father*. (Trans. Pomerans, Arnold J.). New York: W.W. Norton.)
Rand, Nicholas & Torok, Maria. (1997) *Questions for Freud: the secret history of psychoanalysis*. Op cit
Vitz, Paul. (1993) *Sigmund Freud's Christian Unconscious*. Grand Rapids: William Eerdmans.

The letter in which Freud compares missing Anna to missing smoking a cigar was written to Lou Andreas Salome in 1922 and is quoted in: Young-Bruehl, Elisabeth. (2008) *Anna Freud: a biography*. Op cit.

Chapter 4

For a good history of Coca-Cola see:

Pendergrast, Mark. (2000) *For God, country and Coca-Cola: the history of the world's most popular soft drink*. London: Orion Business.

On Cortés see:

Diáz del Castillo, Bernal. (1963) *The conquest of the New Spain*. (Trans. Cohen, John M.) Harmondsworth: Penguin.
Vailliant, George C. (1944) *Aztecs of Mexico: origin, rise and fall of the Aztec nation*. Garden City, N.Y.: Doubleday.

On Humphry Davy see:

Thorpe, Thomas E. (2007) *Humphry Davy, poet and philosopher*. Op cit.

On Mantegazza see:

Mantegazza, Paolo. (1858) *On the hygienic and medicinal properties of coca and on nervine nourishment in general* in Andrews, George & Solomon, David (1975) *The coca leaf and cocaine papers*. New York: Harcourt Brace Jovanovich.

On Paracelsus do not be put off by the fact Prince Charles is a fan. The best biography is:

Ball, Philip. (2007) *The Devil's Doctor: Paracelsus and the World of Renaissance Magic and Science*. London: Arrow.

On Von Tschudi and Niemann see:

Karch, Steven B. (1998) *A brief history of cocaine*. Boca Raton: CRC Press.

Other references:

Aschenbrandt, Theodore. (1883) On the Workings of Cocaine. *Deutsche Medicine Wochenschrift*, 12th December.

Baudelaire, Charles. (1971) *Artificial Paradise: on hashish and wine as a means of expanding individuality*. (Trans. Fox, Ellen.) New York: Herder and Herder.

Christison, Robert. (1876) Observations on the Effects of Cuca, or Coca, the Leaves of Erythroxylon Coca. *British Medical Journal*, 1(800), p. 527.

Gautier, J. in: Eyguesier, Pierre. (1983) *Comment Freud devint drogman: études sur la coca et la cocaïne la Belle époque*. Op cit.

Gautier, Théophile. (1846) *Le Club des Haschischins*. Op cit.

Hayter, Alethea. (1968) *Opium and the Romantic Imagination*. London: Faber and Faber.

James, William, 'Subjective Effects of Nitrous Oxide' quoted in Le Doux, Joseph E. (1996) *The Emotional Brain: the Mysterious Underpinnings of Emotional Life*. New York: Simon and Schuster.

James, William. (1983) *The Varieties of Religious Experience: a study in human nature*. (Ed. Marty, Martin E.) Harmondsworth: Penguin.

Maisch, John M. (1861) On Coca Leaves, *Medical and Surgical Reporter* (Philadelphia), 6(18), p. 399.

Merck, E. (1975). *Cocaine and its salts*. In Byck, Robert (Ed.) (1975) *The Cocaine Papers*. New York: New American Library (Meridian).

De Quincey, Thomas. (2008) *Confessions of an English Opium Eater*. (Ed. Lindop, Grevel) Oxford: Oxford University Press.

Chapter 5

On Martha Bernays see:

Behling, Katja. (2005) *Martha Freud: a biography*. Cambridge: Polity.

On Josef Breuer see:

Oberndorf, Clarence P. (1953) Autobiography of Josef Breuer (1842–1925). *International Journal of Psycho-Analysis*, 34, pp. 64–67.

On Fleischl see:

Medwed, Hans-Peter. (1997) *Ernst Fleischl von Marxow (1846–1891): Leben und Werk*. Tübingen: MVK Medien Verlag Köhler.

On Freud's habit of borrowing money, see his letters to Martha June 6th 1885, Feb 10th 1886, May 13th 1886 – and the theme reappears in a slightly different form in a letter Freud wrote from London in 1938 to his lawyer, Dr Indra. The Nazis wanted to seize one of his foreign bank accounts in Dutch guilders and Freud asked Indra to protest he had been promised he could use the money to start a new life in Britain. Anton Sauerwald, the Nazi who helped Freud get out of Austria, tried to persuade the Gestapo not to insist on getting the Dutch monies. Freud sometimes used the Yiddish term 'schnorrer' to carp about certain individuals who sponged off others, but in his youth he was a bit of a 'schnorrer' himself.

On Hansen see:

Gauld, Alan. (1992) *A History of Hypnotism*. Cambridge: Cambridge University Press.

On Anna O. there is an extensive bibliography including:

Borch-Jacobsen, Mikkel. (1996) *Rembering Anna O.: a century of mystification*. (Trans. Olseon, Kirby) New York: Routledge.

Jones, Ernest on Anna O. in Jones, Ernest R. (1953–1957) *Sigmund Freud*. Op cit, Vol. 1.

Skucs, Richard A. (2006) *Sigmund Freud and the History of Anna O.: reopening a Closed Case*. Basingstoke: Palgrave Macmillan.

Other references:

Bernays-Freud, Anna. (2005) *Eine Wienerin in New York*. Op cit.

Breslau N. Lucia V.C. and Alvarado M.P.H. (2006) Intelligence and Other Predisposing Factors in Exposure to Trauma and Posttraumatic Stress Disorder, *Arch Gen Psychiatry*. 2006; 63:1238–1245.

Darwin, Charles. (1985) *The correspondence of Charles Darwin*. (Vol. 2) (Burkhardt, Frederick & Smith, Sydney Eds.) Cambridge: Cambridge University Press.

Freud, Sigmund 1880) in *Brain*. Op cit.

Freud, Sigmund and Silberstein, Eduard. (1989). *Letters of Sigmund Freud and Eduard Silberstein: 1871–1881*. Op cit.

The letter Freud wrote to Stefan Zweig about Anna O came 50 years after the events. It was dated September 30th 1934 and is to be found in Freud's Letters (1961) Op cit.

Freud, Sigmund (1998) *Briefbraute*. Op cit.

Freud on Brücke in: Freud, Sigmund. (1925) *An Autobiographical Study*. Op cit.

Knopmacher, Hugo: papers in the Freud Collection held at the Library of Congress.

Knopfmacher, Hugo. (1979). Sigmund Freud in high school. *American Imago*, 36, 287–300.

Loas, G., Atger, F., Perdereau, F., Verrier, A., Guelfi, J.D., Halfon, O., Lang, F., Bizouard, P., Venisse, J.L., Perez-Diaz, F., Corcos, M., Flament, M., Jeammet, P.,

2002. Comorbidity of dependent personality disorder and separation anxiety disorder in addictive disorders and in healthy subjects. *Psychopathology* 35, 249– 253.

Chapter 6

On Freud's bowels, the most interesting remarks about his Konrad are quoted in: Freud, Sigmund to Jung, Carl J. October 4th 1909 in McGuire, William. (1974) *The Freud/Jung Letters: The Correspondence Between Sigmund Freud and C.G. Jung.* Princeton: Princeton University Press.

Von Anrep, Vassily. (1880) On the physiological action of cocaine *Pfluges Archives ges. Physiology* 21, pp. 38–77.

Palmer, E.R. (1880) Erythroxylon coca as an antidote to the opium habit. *Therapeutic Gazette.* 1, pp. 163–164.

The letter in which Freud warned Martha Woe to you my Princess' was dated June 2nd 1884 in: Freud, Sigmund. (1998) *Briefbraute.* Op cit.

For the dealings between Merck and Fleischl see:

Hirschmüller, Albrecht. (1995) E. Merck und das Kokain: zu Sigmund Freuds Kokainstudien und ihren Beziehungen zu der Darmstädter Firma. *Gesnerus.* 52(1-2), pp. 116-32.

Other references:

Festinger, Leon; Riecken, Henry & Schachter, Stanley. (1964) *When Prophecy Fails.* New York: Harper & Row.

Fleischl to Eitelberger & Brücke to Du Bois quoted in: Medwed, Hans-Peter. (1997) *Ernst Fleischl von Marxow (1846–1891): Leben und Werk.* Op cit.

Freud, Sigmund. *Ein Fall von hirnblutung mit indirekten basalen herdsymptomen bei skorbut.* Vienna, 1884.

Freud, Sigmund. (1884) *Über Coca.* Op cit.

Freud, Sigmund letter to Martha of Oct. 5th 1885 in Freud, Sigmund. (1998) *Briefbraute.* Op cit.

Freud, Sigmund letters to Martha of Oct. 13th and 28th 1885 in Freud, Sigmund. (1998) *Briefbraute.* Op cit.

Freud, Sigmund letter to Martha of 9th May 1884 in Freud, Sigmund. (1998) *Briefbraute.* Op cit.

Hirschmüller, Albrecht. (1995) Op cit .

Israëls, Han. (2006) *Der Wiener Quacksalber : kritische Betrachtungen über Sigmund Freud und die Psychoanalyse.* Jena: Verlag Dr. Bussert & Stadeler (translated as Freud and his Lies).

Masson, Jeffrey M. (1984) *The assault on truth: Freud's suppression of the seduction theory.* Op cit.

Chapter 7

On Hortense Becker and Ernst Freud see:

Becker, Hortense. (1974) Op cit.

On Charcot see:

Goetz, Chistopher; Bonduelle, Michel & Gelfand, Toby. (1995). *Charcot: Constructing Neurology*. Oxford: Oxford University Press.

See also:

Freud, Sigmund. (1886). Report of my studies in Paris and Berlin. *Standard Edition*, 1, 3–17.

On Alphonse Daudet, the French writer see:

Dufiuf, Anne-Simone. (2005) *Alphonse Daudet*. Rennes: Éditions Ouest France.

On William Halsted, the 'father of American surgery' see:

Nuland, Sherwin B. (1988). *Doctors: the Biography of Medicine*. New York: Knopf.

On Josef Herzig see:

Oberhummer, Wilfrid. (1969) 'Herzig, Josef', in *Neue Deutsche Biographie*, Vol. 8. Berlin: Duncker & Humblot.

On Koller, the best sources are his daughter Hortense:

Becker, Hortense. (1974) 'Coca Koller.' In Byck, Robert (Ed.), *Cocaine papers by Sigmund Freud*. Op cit.

And:

Koller, Karl. (1884) Vorlaufige Mittheilung über locale Anasthesirung am Auge. *Klinische Monatblatt Augenheilkunde*, 22, pp. 60–3.

See also:

Galbis-Reig, David. (2002) *Sigmund Freud and Carl Koller: the controversy surrounding the discovery of local anesthesia*. In: Diz J.C., Franco A., Bacon D.R., Rupreht J., and Alvarez J., (Eds.) *The History of Anesthesia: Proceedings from the Fifth International Symposium on the History of Anesthesia, Santiago de Compostela, Spain, 19–23 September, 2001.* International Congress Series, No. 1242. London: Elsevier Science, pp. 571–575.

Goldberg, Morton F. (1984) Cocaine: the first local anesthetic and the 'third scourge of humanity:' a centennial melodrama. *Archives of Ophthalmology*, 102 (10), pp. 1443–1447.

Noyes, Henry D. (1884) The Ophthalmological Conference in Heidelberg. *New York Medical Record*, 26, pp. 417–8.

Archer W.H., (1940) The History of Anesthesia, in Anderson, George M. (Ed.) (1940) *Proceedings Dental Centenary Celebration: 1840–1940*, Maryland State Dental Association.

Kolbasenko, I.S., (1888) Cocaine in Teeth Extraction. *Russkaia Meditzina* (St Petersburg), 39, p. 623.

On Zinner and the duel see:

Becker, Hortense. (1974) '*Coca Koller.*' Op cit.

Other references:

Daudet, Alphonse. (2002) *In the Land of Pain* (Trans. Barnes, Julian). London: Jonathan Cape.

Daudet, Alphonse. (2005) *Lettres de mon Moulin*. Paris: Distribooks.

Daudet, Alphonse. (2007) *Tartarin de Tarascon*. Whitefish, MT: Kessinger.

Freud, Sigmund. *Nachtrage der coca*. In: Byck, Robert. (Ed.) (1975) *The Cocaine Papers*. Op cit.

Freud's letters to Martha of March 10th 1885 and also letters of March 16th, March 21st and May 12th in *Briefbraute*. Op cit.

Freud, Sigmund letter to Martha August 28th 1885 in *Briefbraute*. Op cit.

Freud, Sigmund letter to Martha November 24th 1885 in *Briefbraute*. Op cit.

Freud, Sigmund letter to Martha March 19th 1886 in *Briefbraute*. Op cit.

Freud, Sigmund to letter to Carl Koller September 28th 1886 in Becker H. (1974). Op cit.

Freud, Sigmund. (1893) *Obituary of Charcot* in Freud's Standard Edition vol. 3. Op cit.

Freud, Sigmund. (1925) *A Study in Autobiography*. Op cit.

For details of Fleischl's death including comments by Exner see:

Medwed, Hans-Peter. (1997) *Ernst Fleischl von Marxow (1846–1891): Leben und Werk*. Op Cit.

Hammond, William A. (1886) Cocaine and the so-called cocaine habit. *New York Medical Journal*, 44, pp. 637- 639.

On arguments for and against cocaine see:

Halsted, William S. (1885) Practical comments of the Use and Abuse of Cocaine. *The New York Medical Journal*, 42, pp. 294–5.

293

Chapter 8

On John Beard see:

Beard, John. (1902) Embryological aspects and etiology of carcinoma. *The Lancet* 159(4112), pp. 1758–61.
Beard, John. (1911) *The Enzyme Treatment of Cancer.* London: Chatto and Windus.

On Emma Eckstein see:

Masson, Jeffrey M. (1984) *The assault on truth: Freud's suppression of the seduction theory.* Op cit. & his interview with Robyn Williams 'the story of Emma Eckstein's surgery' on ABC Radio National (second broadcast June 3rd 2006).
Freud, Sigmund to Fliess, Wilhelm: letters of March 8th 1895, March 20th 1895 and April 24th 1895, June 12th 1895, August 26th 1895 in Masson, Jeffrey M. (1984) *The assault on truth: Freud's suppression of the seduction theory.* Op cit.

On Fliess see:

Swales, P.J. (in press). *Wilhelm Fliess: Freud's other.* New York: Random House.
Freud, Sigmund to Fliess, Wilhelm in Masson, Jeffrey M. (1984) *The assault on truth: Freud's suppression of the seduction theory.* Op cit. p. 268.

On John Noland Mackenzie see:

Mackenzie, John Noland. (1906) The teaching of Laryngology in Johns Hopkins University. *The Laryngoscope,* 16(11), p 906–909.

Other references:

Martindale, William. (1886) *Coca and Cocaine.* London: H.K. Lewis.
Freud, Sigmund. (1895) The Case of the Smell of Burnt Pudding in *Studies in Hysteria.* Op cit.
Freud S. (1895) *A Project for A Scientific Psychology.* Op cit.
Freud, Sigmund to Fliess, Wilhelm: letter of 22 December 1897 in Masson, Jeffrey M. (1984) *The assault on truth: Freud's suppression of the seduction theory.* Op cit.
Sulloway, Frank J. (1979) *Freud: biologist of the Mind.* Op cit.

Chapter 9

On Irma's dream see

Erikson, Eric. (1954) The dream specimen of psychoanalysis. *Journal of the American Psychoanalytic Association*, 2, pp. 5–56.

Freud, Sigmund. (1899) the dream of being dissected is in *The Interpretation of Dreams* (1899). Op cit.

Other references:

Nordenskjold. (1904) *The Antarctic*; now available from Whitefish M.T.; Kessinger Publishing.

Velikovsky, Immanuel. (1941) The dreams Freud dreamed. *Psychoanalytic Review*, 28, pp. 487–511.

Von Scheidt, Jürgen. (1973) *Freud und das Kokain: die Selbstversuche Freuds als Anstoss zur 'Traumdeutung'*. Op cit.

Zizek, Slavoj. (2006) Is psychoanalysis really outmoded? A propos to the 150th anniversary of Freud's birth, *Journal of European Psychoanalysis*, 2(23).

Chapter 10

On Havelock Ellis see:

Ellis, Havelock. (2008) *My Life: autobiography of Havelock Ellis*. Whitefish M.T.: Kessinger Publishing.

Other references:

Ellis, Havelock. (1897) A note on the phenomena of mescal intoxication. *The Lancet*, 149(3849), pp. 1540–2.

Ellis, Havelock. (1898) Mescal: a new artificial paradise. *The Contemporary Review*, January 1898.

Meyers, Annie C. (1902) *Eight years in Cocaine Hell*. Chicago: Press of the St Luke Society.

Wells, Herbert G. (1899) *When the Sleeper Awakes*. Leipzig: Bernhard Tauchnitz.

Chapter 11

On the anti tobacco movement at the turn of the century see:

Snowdon, Christopher. (2009) *Velvet glove, iron fist: a history of anti-smoking*. Middleton Quernhow: Little Dice.

On both Otto Gross and Wilhelm Stekel see:

Brome, Vincent. (1984) *Freud and his Disciples: the struggle for supremacy*. London: Caliban Publications.

On Karl Kraus see:

Timms, Edward. (1986) *Karl Kraus, apocalyptic satirist: the post-war crisis and the rise of the Swastika*. New Haven: Yale University Press.

On Otto Loewi see:

Raju, Tonse N.K. (1999) 'The Nobel chronicles. 1936: Henry Hallett Dale (1875–1968) and Otto Loewi (1873–1961).' *The Lancet*, 353(9150), 30th January 1999, p. 416.

On Wilhelm Reich see:

Sharaf, Myron. (1984) *Fury on earth: a biography of Wilhelm Reich*. London: Hutchinson Press.

Other references:

Bhargava A.P. (1916) *Cocaine, and its demoralising effects*. Allahabad: Oriental Press.
Christie, Agatha. (1926) *The Murder of Roger Ackroyd*. London: W. Collins, Sons & Co.
Christie, Agatha. (1947) Hell, in *The Labours of Hercules*. London: W. Collins, Sons & Co.
Sayers, Dorothy L. (1995) *Murder Must Advertise*. New York: Harper Torch. Original edition 1933.
Cohen, David. (1979) *J.B. Watson, the founder of behaviourism: a biography*. Op cit.
Dostoevsky, Fyodor. (1966) *The Gambler, Bobok, and A Nasty Story*. Harmondsworth: Penguin.
Elkin, Evan J. (1994) Freud's Passion. *Cigar Aficionado*, Winter 1994.
Freud, Martin. (1957) *Glory Reflected*. Op cit.
Holroyd, Michael. (1989) *Bernard Shaw: Vol. 2, 1898–1918: The pursuit of power*. Harmondsworth: Penguin.
Rolleston, Humphrey. (1926) *Report of the Departmental Committee on Morphine and Heroin Addiction*. London: HMSO.

Chapter 12

On Marie Bonaparte see:

Bertin, Celia. (1987) *Marie Bonaparte*. Yale University press: New Haven.

REFERENCES

On Paul Fichtl and Freud in London see:

Berthelsen Detlef. (1991) *La Famille Freud au jour le jour; souvenirs de Paula Fichtl.* Op cit.

On Robert Fliess see:

Fliess, Elenore. (1982). Robert Fliess: A Personality Profile. *American Imago,* 39: pp. 195–218.

On Matthias Göring and the bizarre tale of Nazism's fascination with therapy see:

Cocks, Geoffrey. (1987) *Psychotherapy in the Third Reich.* (2nd ed,) Oxford: Oxford University Press.

On Albert Hofmann and Bicycle Day see:

Hofmann, Albert. (1980) *LSD: My Problem Child.* New York: McGraw Hill.

On Jung see:

Léon, M. (1946) *The Case of Dr Carl Gustav Jung: Pseudo-scientist Nazi Auxiliary.* Report to U.S. Department of State and Nuremberg Tribunal.

On Carl Rogers see:

Cohen, David. (1997) *Carl Rogers: a critical biography.* London: Constable.

Other references:

Freud Sigmund to Freud Alexander, letter dated April 19th 1938 re cigars.
Freud Sigmund, letter to a would-be patient, letter dated May 15th 1933.
Jones, Ernest R. (1940) Funeral Oration. *American Imago,* 1B, pp. 1–3.
Glover, Edward. (1939) Sigmund Freud (May 6, 1856 – September 23 1939): A broadcast tribute. *The Listener,* 28th September 1939.
Busch, Anthony K. & Johnson Warren C. (1950) L.S.D. 25 as an aid in psychotherapy: preliminary report of a new drug. *Diseases of the Nervous System,* 11(8), pp. 2–4.
Huxley, Aldous. (1932) *Brave New World.* London: Chatto & Windus.
Huxley, Aldous. (1954) *The Doors of Perception.* London: Chatto & Windus.
Wells, Herbert G. (1996) The Door in the Wall; Fairfield: 1st World Publishing. Originally published 1906.
Healy, David. (2002) *The Creation of Psychopharmacology.* Cambridge, MA: Harvard University Press.

Kuhn, R. on Tricyclics quoted in: Fangmann, Peter; Assion, Hans-Jörg; Juckel, Georg; González, Cecilio ¡lamo; López-Muñoz, Francisco. (2008) Half a Century of Antidepressant Drugs: On the Clinical Introduction of Monoamine Oxidase Inhibitors, Tricyclics, and Tetracyclics. Part II: Tricyclics and Tetracyclics. *Journal of Clinical Psychopharmacology*, 28(1), pp 1–4.

Heffer, Simon. (1998) *Like the Roman: the life and times of Enoch Powell*. London: Weidenfield.

Chapter 13

On Bastiaans see:

Cohen, David. (1991) A war of nerves. *New Scientist*, 1759: 9th March 1991.

On Timothy Leary see:

Allegro, John M. (2009) *The Sacred Mushroom and the Cross: A Study of the Nature and Origins of Christianity Within the Fertility Cults of the Ancient Near East*. 40th anniversary edition with an afterword by Carl A.P. Ruck. [S.I.]: Gnostic Media Research & Publishing.

On the MK–ULTRA story see:

Thomas Gordon. (1988) *Journey into madness: medical torture and the mind controllers*. London: Bantam.

On Wasson R. see:

Wasson, Robert G. (1957). Seeking the Magic Mushroom. *Life Magazine*, May 13th 1957.

Other references:

Bastiaans J. (1957) *The psychosomatic consequences of oppression and resistance*. Unpublished Ph.D thesis, University of Amsterdam.

Cohen, Sidney. (1976) *The Drug Dilemma*. London: McGraw Hill.

Dyck, Erika. (2006) 'Hitting Highs at Rock Bottom': LSD Treatment for Alcoholism, 1950–1970. *Social History of Medicine*, 19(2), pp. 313–329.

Hofmann, Albert. (1980) *LSD: My Problem Child*. Op cit.

Leary, Timothy. (1964) The Religious Experience: its production and interpretation. *The Psychedelic Review*, 1(3), pp. 324–346.

Leary, Timothy. (1973) *Starseed*. San Francisco: Level Press.

Newberg A., d'Aquili E. and Rause V. (2002) *Why God won't go away*. New York; Ballantine.

Stanley, Owsley. (2006) Comment on Timothy Leary posted on internet bulletin board. Available at: http://forum.lowcarber.org/showpost.php?p=6064486&postcount=1637

Chapter 14

On Bill Collins see:

Cohen, David and Goodchild, Sophie. (2007) Free after 36 years: the man who was left to rot in Broadmoor. *The Independent on Sunday*, 7th January 2007.

On oppositional disorder see:

Higgins, Edmund S. (2009) Do ADHD Drugs Take a Toll on the Brain? *Scientific American Mind*. July 22.

On Patrick McGrath see:

Cohen, David. (1981) *Broadmoor*. London: Psychology News Press.

And:

I Was in Broadmoor. Documentary first broadcast on the ITV network in June 1981.

On Shulgin see:

Shulgin, Alexander and Shulgin, Ann. (1991) *Pihkal: a chemical love story*. Op cit.

Other references:

Dyck, Erika. (2005) Flashback: psychiatric experimentation with LSD in historical perspective. *Canadian Journal of Psychiatry* 50(7), pp. 381–388.

Gazzaniga, Michael S. (2005) Smarter on Drugs. *Scientific American Mind*, September 21.

Griffiths, Roland; Richards, William A.; Johnson, Marshall W.; McCann, Una & Jesse, Robert L. (2008) Mystical-type experiences occasioned by psilocybin mediate the attribution of personal meaning and spiritual significance 14 months later. *Journal of Psychopharmacology*, 22(6), pp. 621–632.

Griffiths, Roland; Richards, William A.; McCann Una & Jesse Robert L. (2006) Psilocybin can occasion mystical-type experiences having substantial and sustained personal meaning and spiritual significance. *Psychopharmacology* (Berlin), 187(3), pp. 268–83; discussion pp. 284–292.

Johnson Marshall W.; Richards, William A. & Griffiths, Roland. (2008) Human hallucinogen research: guidelines for safety. *Journal of Psychopharmacology*, 22(6), pp. 603–620.

Kirsch, Irving; Deacon, Brett J.; Huedo-Medina, Tania B.; Scoboria, Alan; Moore, Thomas J. & Johnson, Blair T. (2008) Initial Severity and Antidepressant Benefits: A Meta-Analysis of Data Submitted to the Food and Drug Administration. *PLoS Medicine*, 5(2), e45.

Nestler, Eric J. (2008) Research Highlights. *Nature* 451(7182), p. 1033 (28 February 2008).

Vedantam, Shankar. (2002) Against Depression a sugar pill is hard to beat: Placebos Improve Mood, Change Brain Chemistry in Majority of Trials of Antidepressants. *Washington Post*, May 2, 2002, p. A01.

Volkow, Nora D.; Fowler, Joanna S. & Wang, Gene-Jack. (2002) Role of dopamine in drug reinforcement and addiction in humans: results from imaging studies. *Behavioural Pharmacology*. 13(5/6), pp. 355–366.

Volkow, Nora D. Quoted in Rosack, Jim. (2003) Volkow to Head Federal Addiction Research Agency. *Psychiatric News*, 38(6), p. 12.

Swanson, James M.; Elliott, Glen R.; Greenhill, Laurence L.; Wigal, Timothy; Arnold, L. Eugene; Vitiello, Benedetto; Hechtman, Lily; Epstein, Jeffery N.; Pelham, William E.; Abikoff, Howard B.; Newcorn, Jeffrey H.; Molina, Brooke S.G.; Hinshaw, Stephen P.; Wells, Karen C.; Hoza, Betsy; Jensen, Peter S.; Gibbons, Robert D.; Hur, Kwan; Stehli, Annamarie; Davies, Mark; March, John S.; Conners, C. Keith; Caron, Mark & Volkow Nora D. (2007) Effects of stimulant medication on growth rates across 3 years in the MTA follow-up. *Journal of the American Academy of Child and Adolescent Psychiatry*, 46(8), pp. 1015–27.

Wurtzel, Elizabeth. (2002) *More, Now, Again: a memoir*. London: Virago.

Chapter 15

On the saga concerning David Nutt see:

Aitkenhead, Decca. (2010) David Nutt: 'The government cannot think logically about drugs'. *The Guardian*, Monday 6th December 2010.

Cohen, Sidney. (1976) *The drugs dilemma*. Op cit.

On Watson, Lashley and shooting arrows while drunk see:

Cohen, David. (1979) *J.B. Watson, the founder of Behaviourism: a biography*. Op cit.

Other references:

Costall A. (2010) Looking ahead, the future of experimental psychology. *The Psychologist*, 23, p 1022–1023.

Greeley, Henry A.; Sahakian, Barbara; Harris, John; Kessler, Ronald C.; Gazzaniga, Michael; Campbell, Philip & Farah, Martha J. (2008) Towards responsible use of cognitive-enhancing drugs by the healthy. *Nature*, 456(7223), pp. 702–705 (11 December 2008).

Healy, David. (2002) *The Creation of Psychopharmacology*. Op cit.

Hofmann, Albert. (1980) *LSD: My Problem Child*. Op cit.

House of Commons Public Affairs Committee. (2009) *Report of the Seventh Session*. London: HMSO

Jones, Roy; Morris, Kelly & Nutt, David. (2008) *Cognition Enhancers*. In: Nutt, David; Robbins, Trevor W.; Stimson, Gerald V.; Ince, Martin & Jackson, Andrew (Eds.) (2008) *Drugs and the Future: brain, science, addiction and society*. London: Academic Press.

Jack, Anthony and Roepstorff, Andreas (Eds.) (2003) *Trusting the Subject? The use of introspective evidence in cognitive science*. Exeter: Imprint Academic.

Lynch, Zack. (2009) *The Neuro Revolution: How Brain Science Is Changing Our World*. New York: St Martin's Press.

Volkow, Nora D; Swanson, James M. (2008) The action of enhancers can lead to addiction. *Nature*, 451(7178), p. 520.

Index

Picture credits

The colour plates include material from two magazines I used to write for in the 1970s, *Lords* and the *French Psychologie*. Both are now defunct, Tony Jadunath was in Broadmoor and I commissioned pictures from him in the 1980s. I have been unable to trace him and hope he is well. All other pictures either appear to be in the public domain or I have commented on them under the normal terms of fair dealing.